T0388398

European Integration and Disintegration

European integration is an ambitious goal that attempts to reconcile grandiose visions for the future of Europe with complicated national attitudes toward unity. The added complexity of political crises, which have characterized the European project from its outset, makes the success of the European Union far from guaranteed. Today, European unity is once again at an existential crossroad, with internal and external challenges threatening its integration. This volume uniquely brings together the novel perspectives of Europe's emergent generation of thinkers to analyze through interdisciplinary lenses these various disintegrative pressures. Students and scholars of Europe as well as those interested in the future of European cohesion will enjoy this volume, both for the interdisciplinary analysis it brings forth and for the window it provides into the thinking of Europe's next generation of leaders.

Nick Cohen is a historical researcher, currently at Schmidt Futures. He is also an advisor to the Wilson Center's Cold War Archives Research Institute. A former Schepp Scholar, he holds an MA from Columbia University, where he studied transatlantic diplomatic history, and a BA from Carleton College in International Relations.

Ayana Dootalieva is a lawyer at the Brussels Bar where she practices European and Belgian public and environmental law. She is trained in law and social sciences and holds degrees from Ghent University (Belgium) and Columbia University (NY, USA). Ayana is interested in the interplay between law, governance, and policy.

Routledge Studies in Modern European History

For more information about this series, please visit: https://www.routledge.com/Routledge-Studies-in-Modern-European-History/book-series/SE0246

European Integration and Disintegration

Essays from the Next Generation of
Europe's Thinkers

Edited by
Nick Cohen and Ayana Dootalieva

Routledge
Taylor & Francis Group

LONDON AND NEW YORK

First published 2022
by Routledge
4 Park Square, Milton Park, Abingdon, Oxon OX14 4RN

and by Routledge
605 Third Avenue, New York, NY 10158

Routledge is an imprint of the Taylor & Francis Group, an informa business

British Library Cataloguing-in-Publication Data
A catalogue record for this book is available from the British Library

Library of Congress Cataloging-in-Publication Data
Names: Cohen, Nick, 1996- editor, writer of introduction. |
Dootalieva,
Ayana, 1994- editor, writer of introduction.
Title: European integration and disintegration: essays from the next generation of Europe's thinkers / edited by Nick Cohen and Ayana Dootalieva.
Description: New York: Routledge, 2022. | Series: Routledge studies in modern European history | Includes bibliographical references and index.|
Identifiers: LCCN 2021059818 (print) | LCCN 2021059819 (ebook) |
Classification: LCC D2024.E975 2022 (print) | LCC D2024 (ebook) | DDC 940.56—dc23/eng/20220105
LC record available at https://lccn.loc.gov/2021059818
LC ebook record available at https://lccn.loc.gov/2021059819

ISBN: 978-1-032-00978-0 (hbk)
ISBN: 978-1-032-02204-8 (pbk)
ISBN: 978-1-003-18234-4 (ebk)

DOI: 10.4324/9781003182344

Typeset in Times New Roman
by codeMantra

Printed in the United Kingdom
by Henry Ling Limited

Contents

vi *Contents*

Illustrations

Acknowledgments

We owe a great deal of gratitude to many individuals who have helped us in producing this volume, whether directly or indirectly. To everyone who has supported us in thinking this collection through, thank you. We also wish to thank the European Institute at Columbia University – we, the editors and authors, first met through the European Institute's capstone seminar, without which this volume would not have come together. In particular, we would like to thank Tsveta Petrova, whose early guidance in those seminars is present throughout the pages of this volume. To all of our advisors and mentors at Columbia University, we owe a collective thank you for your intellectual guidance as we each thought through the future of the European Union. We also wish to acknowledge Andrea Szabó and the Heinrich Böll Stiftung for granting us permission to reproduce their images in this volume. To Clara Levrero, who expertly provided much-needed assistance in the final moments of this project, a huge thank you! And last, but certainly not least, we would like to thank our editor, Rob Langham, and his exceptional assistant, Zoe Thomson, who believed in this volume from the outset and who have expertly shepherded it to its current version.

Contributors

Ali Cain graduated from Columbia University's European History, Politics and Society Program in May 2021. Her research interests include far-right populism, refugee policy, and human rights. Ali has previously served as a junior ambassador in Germany for the State Department's Congress Bundestag Youth Exchange for Young Professionals Program.

Nick Cohen is a historical researcher, currently at Schmidt Futures. He is also an advisor to the Wilson Center's Cold War Archives Research Institute. A former Schepp Scholar, he holds an MA from Columbia University, where he studied transatlantic diplomatic history, and a BA from Carleton College in International Relations.

Ayana Dootalieva is a lawyer at the Brussels Bar where she practices European and Belgian public and environmental law. She is trained in law and social sciences and holds degrees from Ghent University (Belgium) and Columbia University (NY, USA). Ayana is interested in the interplay between law, governance, and policy.

Faïz El Mamoune holds an MA from Columbia University, where he studied EU politics and economics, the state of transatlantic relations, and the geopolitics of Europe's international affairs. Originally from Paris, he holds degrees from Canadian and French universities and has worked for international organizations and governments in the United States and Canada.

Max Ferrer is a PhD candidate in History at King's College London. He holds a BA with Honors in History and Philosophy from Bucknell University and an MA in European History, Politics, and Society from Columbia University. His areas of interest include cultural commodification, national identity, transatlantic history, gender, tourism, and colonialism.

Emma Flaherty received her MA from Columbia University, where her research focused on RT, Eastern Europe, and media framing. She obtained a BA in International Studies and Political Science from Elon University, where she was an Honors Fellow and elected to *Phi Beta Kappa*.

Adam Frick obtained an MA from Columbia University's European Institute. He is interested in worker movements, labor unions, and contemporary labor activity in Britain and the United States. Originally from Pennsylvania, he earned a BA in Global Studies from Temple University.

Floris Maria Rijssenbeek is the founder of DE/MO, a European civil society organization that encourages youth political engagement. He was a Fulbright scholar at Columbia University. He holds an MA in History of Politics and Society from Utrecht University and a BA in History and Economics from the University of Amsterdam.

Ruben Tjon-A-Meeuw holds a bachelor's degree in European Studies from King's College London and a Master's degree in European History, Politics, and Society from Columbia University. He is interested in European issues surrounding economics, security, and geopolitics, particularly as they relate to Russia.

Introduction

European Unity, from Crisis to Integration: Perspectives from the Next Generation of Europe's Thinkers

Nick Cohen and Ayana Dootalieva

1 Introduction: The EU's Crisis-Integration Cycle

Born in the tension between grandiose visions and complicated legal structures, the European project endeavored to go further than anyone thought possible. In the aftermath of the Second World War, a battered and war-weary Europe set off on a path of unprecedented political, economic, and social integration that ultimately led to today's European Union. Even Europe's earliest and most ardent advocates, including Jean Monnet, Robert Schuman, Winston Churchill, and Paul-Henri Spaak, could not have envisioned today's Union that not only represents a large single economic market but also stands as a symbol of the triumph of multilateralism in the post-war world. Europe's visionary idea to achieve peace on the continent through integration, outpacing in practice even the greatest theories put forward at its start, was enough to earn it the 2012 Nobel Peace Prize. It was and remains the only Nobel recipient with state-like functions.

Beginning with the small seed of economic integration planted by the creation of the European Coal and Steel Community (ECSC) in 1951, the European project has since blossomed into a multiethnic, multi-confessional union of sovereign states participating in a level of cooperation unparalleled in any other multilateral organization. From its humble beginnings as a coal and steel organization between six European states,[1] the European Union today has transformed into the model *par excellence* of multilateralism and supranational governance, with 27 members comprising much of the European continent. Emerging slowly but surely, the structures of political and social integration evolved through methods of economic integration, leading to today's Union that, while not being strictly sovereign, holds much of the workings of a federal entity.

Yet, the seemingly unstoppable success of the European project has never been guaranteed. Existential crises have arisen with striking regularity, threatening to derail the formation of an ever closer union. The breakdown of the European project has been forecast more than once a generation; repeating that cycle, gloomy headlines on the future of Europe now seem to grace covers on an almost daily occurrence. The goal of an ever closer

DOI: 10.4324/9781003182344-1

Union[2] has been complicated by persistent obstacles, pervasive criticism, and periodic pushback, all of which work to disintegrate Europe from the inside out. This can be explained by the simple logic that, in moments of crisis, Member States habitually defer to domestic interests rather than entrust a supranational organization to pursue a collective interest. In other words, states frequently favor the short-term comfort of tending to their own needs rather than investing in long-term solutions that most likely benefit all members of the European community, including individual states. This is why integration is a very lengthy process, with bursts forward and inevitable periods of stagnation, as states learn to suppress nationalist tendencies in moments of tension and adjust to the reality of their membership in a tight knit regional organization.[3] Philippe Schmitter first theorized this phenomenon in the 1970s, arguing that a regional organization normally operates in a "zone of indifference" and in accordance with its mandates and assigned competencies up until the occurrence of a crisis forces the regional organization to challenge and rethink its habitual processes.[4] Political, economic, or legal crises therefore force the European Union to face difficult questions and to start conversations on the development of tools that would equip it to prevent, or seamlessly tackle, similar shocks in the future. This is why recurrent crises have – seemingly paradoxically – incrementally contributed to a deeper form of regional integration and an expansion of the EU's competencies and authority as a supranational organization.[5]

1.1 First Steps toward Union: The European Coal and Steel Community

Indeed, the very origin of the Union stemmed from crisis. In the late 1940s, many in Europe and the United States wished to avoid the destructive reparation system that followed the First World War. Instead of following the beggar-thy-neighbor policies of the interwar years, visionary European leaders sought sustainable peace through integration. Economic reconstruction was the low-hanging fruit, with mutual assistance benefitting all in the wake of Europe's most destructive war. This was particularly true when it came to coal and steel production, two industries that had been at the heart of the breakdown of peace prior to the Second World War. From the crisis of Europe's 'second Thirty Years' War' came the European Coal and Steel Community, French businessman Jean Monnet's idea to integrate Europe's coal and steel resources into one shared pool so as to stave off economic chauvinism and nationalism. The formal treaty governing the ECSC, negotiated through 1950 and signed in April 1951, established not just the grounds for economic integration in Europe but the institutional framework for the European Union some four decades later. The ECSC not only made a common market for coal, steel, and iron, it established executive and judicial authorities to oversee implementation and ensure members' compliance with ECSC regulations. This first delegation of state control to supranational bodies began the chain of events leading to today's European Union.[6]

Yet, no sooner had Europe taken its first steps toward integration than the forces of disintegration emerged. Building on the success of the ECSC treaty process, Monnet and his fellow Europhiles proposed a European Defense Community (EDC). Meant to integrate decisions on defense and begin laying the groundwork for a single European army, the EDC endeavored to harmonize not just Europe's economics but its politics. Although Europe's great post-war statesmen celebrated such a proposal, its citizens did not. French parliamentarians rejected the EDC treaty, scuttling the proposal for fear of incursions upon French sovereignty. At the time, many feared that the project of a united Europe was over before it even began.[7]

1.2 Out of the EDC's Ashes Rose the First Common Market

But as is the cyclical nature of European integration, the failure of the EDC energized Europe's founding fathers to search for alternative mechanisms of cooperation that would satisfy interests in national parliaments. By 1957, just five years after the EDC's rejection, ECSC signatories came together to establish the European Economic Community (EEC), a far more wide-ranging free-trade and integrated market mechanism than the ECSC. Established with the ratification of the Treaty of Rome, the EEC created the first internal transnational market in European history. For all EEC signatories, there would be no restrictions on the movement of goods, services, people, or capital. Mirroring the administrative structure of its predecessor, which emphasized a strong executive, the EEC endowed the European Commission, its executive body, to enact and implement Community legislation. The president of this Commission, acting on behalf of a single market, was delegated the authority to speak on all members' behalves in negotiations within the framework of the General Agreement on Tariffs and Trade, at that point the main international body regulating international trade. The EEC also extended the authority of the representative body (then called the Common Assembly) and the judicial arm, the European Court of Justice. In so doing, the EEC radically expanded the scope of economic integration in Europe and the supranational governance needed to regulate that expanded economic zone while keeping, in modified form, the successful structure of the ECSC. Thus, the crisis of integration brought about by the failure of the European Defense Community translated into a functional extension of European integration just five years later.

1.3 Cyclical Contraction and Expansion through the 1970s and 1980s

This pattern of disintegrative crisis leading paradoxically to further integration has continued to drive the European Union since its first cycle in the 1950s. In the mid-1960s, shortly after the common market governed by the EEC had been completed, French President Charles de Gaulle protested against what he saw as sovereign overreach by the European Commission. He resisted further efforts at integration and coordination and even went so far as to veto the United Kingdom's first accession attempt to the Community. Without strong support from France, one of Europe's great political and cultural powers, many again foresaw the demise of the European project. Yet, by the end of the 1960s, the economic success of the single market was enough to attract new members and to override French skepticism.[8] In 1973, the European Community enlarged for the first time in its roughly 20-year history, adding Denmark, Ireland, and Great Britain.

Just as the European Community grew for the first time, it was buffeted by gales of economic destabilization from abroad. The 1970s were marked by a series of global financial recessions, sparked first by the crisis of the US dollar and the subsequent end of the Bretton Woods fixed exchange rate regime. The financial instability caused by the transition to flexible exchange rates was exacerbated by a widespread oil embargo from major oil-producing states in the Middle East as a response to the 1973 Arab-Israeli War. Together, these dual crises produced the stagflation of the mid-1970s, which threatened national governments across Europe and encouraged economic nationalism to a degree unseen since the end of the Second World War. The integrated European economy built over the previous 20 years tottered on the edge of collapse as national governments implemented national solutions to inflation, unemployment, and low growth.[9] It was during these ongoing financial crises that the terms 'Euro-pessimism' and 'Euro-sclerosis' were first coined, reflecting the deep anxiety that many felt toward sustained European integration.[10]

Yet, the ultimate solution to Europe's immense financial problems was not national but supranational. It was recognized at the time that the most efficient mechanism through which to stabilize national currencies and to strengthen the performance of the European market was to develop an adjustable exchange rate that would prevent massive fluctuations in value between European currencies. This mechanism, called the European Monetary System (EMS), emerged in 1979. The EMS established a single European currency metric, the European Currency Unit (ECU), which pegged national currencies to a weighted average of the currencies of all participating states. This innovation, born of the deep financial crisis of the 1970s, successfully stabilized internal European monetary policy and allowed for new growth within the EEC.[11] Equally as important, the establishment of the EMS demonstrated the success of greater fiscal integration, with the ECU later becoming a physical and official currency: the euro.

By 1985, when former French minister of finance Jacques Delors took over as president of the European Commission, the lesson of the 1970s and the success of the EMS was clear: in order to avoid future stagflation, the single European market would need to further integrate.[12] Delors thus launched a comprehensive reform program, ultimately culminating in the Single European Act (SEA), that would eliminate the national idiosyncrasies built into the EEC system from 1957. The SEA promised two major steps forward in the process of European integration. First, it identified not just economic cooperation but social cohesion as a key priority for European Community policies. In essence, this was the first major step toward European social policy, meant to account for the major geographic and sectoral discrepancies between European countries. Second, the SEA required a restructuring of the internal market by 1992, including the full elimination of national capital controls and internal visa requirements for migrating workers.

The SEA's "relaunch" of European cooperation, as Delors dubbed it, culminated in the 1992 Treaty of Maastricht, which created the European Union as we know it today. Anticipating the completion of the single market as mandated under the 1985 SEA, the Maastricht Treaty implemented two proactive changes to European cooperation. First, it transformed the European Community into the European Union, endowing it with additional political and social policy functions. Specifically, the European Commission, which had for a long time been a site for policy coordination in the economic integration sphere, was now endowed with responsibilities in the fields of European citizenship, pan-European justice, and home affairs. Second, the Maastricht Treaty created the single European currency (later to be called the euro) and determined the process through which nations would surrender their national currencies in favor of the common European one. Although the ECU was already effectively a common European currency, the establishment of the euro granted the new European Union significant normative value, as it represented the largest modern currency union on the European continent.

1.4 From the Maastricht Treaty to a United States of Europe?

The Maastricht Treaty came at a moment of immense Euro-optimism, fueled in part by Delors' unique ability as a statesman but in large part by the collapse of the Soviet bloc and the perceived triumph of Western multilateralism. As communist nations in Eastern Europe transitioned to democracy throughout the early 1990s, it was widely considered that Europe's experiment would extend across the continent, ultimately leading to a United States of Europe. As early as the mid-1990s, newly independent Eastern European states began accession negotiations to the freshly minted European Union. In 1995, Austria, Finland, and Sweden joined the Union, the first round of accessions following the 1993 Copenhagen summit in which existing EU Member States agreed that Eastern European nations could join after completing their transitions to democracy and a market economy.

By the end of the decade, not only had the single market been completed and the euro inaugurated, but ten key Eastern European states had begun their accession negotiations.[13] From the crises of financial collapse in the 1970s and political collapses in the late 1980s came the most extensive expansion of European unity in the history of the continent.

Amidst this euphoria of democratic and multilateral triumph, European statesmen attempted an even more concrete step toward European integration: the creation of a European Constitution. In late 2001, the European Council launched a European Convention that likened itself to the eighteenth-century constitutional conventions in prerevolutionary America. Over the course of 16 months, this Convention drafted a constitution that endowed the European Union with the ability to act on behalf of its members internationally. Celebrated by Europhiles across the continent, the draft constitution was sent to national parliaments for ratification in 2004 and was endorsed through referendums in Spain and Luxembourg. But in the now-familiar cycle of integration-disintegration, this constitution was rejected by several national electorates for fear of sovereign intrusion, led chiefly by France and the Netherlands. These nay votes sparked an extended constitutional crisis, in which many predicted the twilight years of European construction to be nigh.

The constitutional crisis lasted for several years, with negotiations never leading to acceptable compromise. After years of unsuccessful attempts to salvage the constitutional project, the idea was abandoned altogether in 2007. However, the EU did adopt the Treaty of Lisbon, which allowed for greater national parliamentary involvement in EU affairs. Yet, even as it accepted greater national involvement at the expense of a further Europeanization of internal policy, the Lisbon Treaty established a new EU executive office: the European External Action Service (EEAS). The EEAS was to function as a European foreign ministry alongside, rather than as a replacement for, national diplomatic corps. In this way, even this most acute crisis of European identity and existence, punctuated by a general failure of greater Europeanization, still resulted in the expansion of EU authorities – a fitting example of the dialectic of European disintegration-integration.

1.5 National Resentments Born from Financial Crisis

The denouement brought about by the Treaty of Lisbon was short-lived. In the wake of serious economic upheavals from the 2008 financial crisis, a new form of politics emerged across the continent that would challenge unity and shift narratives about the desirability of European cooperation for more than a decade. Europe's financial crisis was far deeper and longer than its counterpart in the United States. The European sovereign debt crisis started in Iceland and reached the Eurozone when Greece became unable to fulfil its financial obligations. Due to the interconnectedness of the European banking system, the sovereign debt crisis quickly spread to

Portugal, Ireland, Cyprus, and Spain, leaving these countries unable to repay their debts or bail out their biggest financial institutions from bankruptcy. Sparked by a currency crisis in countries heavily dependent on foreign borrowing, the financial crisis was exacerbated by high labor costs and the inability of individual states to devalue their currency, given the fact that membership in the Eurozone prohibited individual states from resorting to this otherwise efficient monetary policy.[14] The subsequent European loans, bailouts, and austerity measures for the most affected countries resulted in recessions, a limit on government spending, and lingering effects on labor and employment markets that most of these countries are still experiencing today.[15] As Zoe Lefkofridi and Philippe Schmitter aptly noted, "citizens in all 28 EU MSs found themselves sharing anxieties and reflecting on the same issues. For some, more regional integration seemed an opportunity – even a necessary part of the solution; for others (and there were far more of them), it was perceived as a serious threat to its very existence."[16] The European Central Bank (ECB) was criticized for its slow response to prevent the several recessions which occurred from the onset of the biggest economic crisis in nearly a century, as well as for the perceived unfairness of both austerity measures and financial transfers from northern to southern Europe.[17]

A deeper reflection on the sequence of these events, however, allows one to draw slightly more optimistic conclusions. The financial crisis, and the renewed awareness of the interconnectedness of Member States' economic and financial structures, prompted all stakeholders to engage in a joint restoration of the economy, mainly with tools requiring a deeper level of cooperation and solidarity between Member States. It became clear that the management of the Eurozone requires a more integrated federal fiscal union that goes beyond the minimal competences of the ECB.[18] A fiscal union would allow EU institutions to decide on matters of taxation, national government spending, and to resolve collective debt with so-called Eurobonds, which would be issued by all members of the Eurozone. While these conversations are promising for more integration in the economic and fiscal areas, the reality remains that the idea of solidarity with other members of the European community is still too abstract to fathom, especially for strong economies like Germany.

The fallout from the financial crisis led directly to the resurgence of identity politics. Narratives of 'fortress Europe' dovetailed with a dramatically changed international environment: Russia reemerged on Europe's doorstep as a major geopolitical interlocutor just as the United States began to pivot away from its long-standing post-war commitment to transatlantic unity. Globalization, once seen as an inherent good and beneficial for all, became a bogeyman for communities struggling to adjust to changing labor markets, made all the more dire in Europe from periods of wage stagnation, increased levels of unemployment (especially in southern Europe), and a deepening of class divisions.

Euroscepticism did not solely occur in southern Europe but found fertile soil in the United Kingdom, an economic powerhouse, and a country with a complicated and often antagonistic relationship with the EU. The memory of its former hegemonic power made the United Kingdom vehemently and deeply skeptical of its fitness in a supranational organization like the EU. Britain's eventual vote to leave the bloc in 2016 posed perhaps the most fundamental challenge to the European project in its history, one many deemed to be the beginning of the collapse of the Union altogether. Years of tense negotiations and reconciliation with the future of UK–EU relations seemed to confirm the damage wrought to the European project. Although Brexit's ultimate impact on the EU will only be known in the future, it has already served to reinvigorate the discussion of European unity. From the chaos of Brexit has come a heightened awareness of the need to reform the current institutional functioning of the EU and renewed calls for the consideration of multispeed integration between a small number of participating countries.[19]

In the same period, an unprecedented level of migration followed in the wake of humanitarian crises in the Middle East. This massive migration flow challenged Union cohesion on social and identitarian levels in a manner wholly distinct from previous crises. The "one stop policy" of the Dublin III Regulation, which was enacted to prevent asylum seekers from filing multiple asylum applications in different Member States, resulted in added strain for border countries' asylum systems. Under that Regulation, the country of first entry was required to assess subsequent claims for asylum, resulting in countries at the eastern and southern borders to bear most of the responsibility of welcoming refugees. The 2015 migration crisis was marked by intense xenophobia, with countries like Hungary rejecting refugees altogether on the claim of maintaining Europe's Christian unity. Opposition to hosting migrants from states like Hungary led to the controversial migration agreement between Turkey and the EU, in which Turkey, a country often criticized for its human rights violations, agreed to prevent migrants from entering the EU without prior screening. Nevertheless, the migration crisis did lead to enhanced cooperation between many Member States' migration agencies, including proposals for a system of redistribution of refugees across all geographical areas, an amendment of the Dublin II Regulation, and most concretely through an expanded role for the EU border control agency Frontex.

1.6 Pandemic Politics: The Return of Europe?

These tensions, which already seemed to threaten European unity, have been exacerbated by the crushing economic, political, and social consequences of a global pandemic, making the potential for rupture on the European continent higher than ever before. At the start of the pandemic, there seemed to be a perfect storm of nationalist forces, galvanized by medical chauvinism and the closure of borders. Ultimately, the impact of the pandemic on European unity is yet to be seen, but in an echo of past cycles of European boom and bust, there are signs that the present crisis will result in a strengthening of the European project rather than its demise. The proposal for the issuance of so-called 'corona bonds' in July 2020, drawing inspiration from the Eurobonds proposed nearly a decade earlier, in addition to the joint procurement of COVID-19 vaccines and entry into force of the EU COVID Certificate, demonstrates that crises continue to exert centripetal force on the Union, bringing its members closer together through policy if not through rhetoric. If Europe truly is to become stronger and more unified, it will occur precisely in this moment of existential unease.

Each of Europe's existential crises have been overcome through the implementation of new thoughts, new perspectives, and new visions dreamt up by a new cohort of European thinkers. Today, Europe is again at an existential crossroads. As in the past, it must rely on the thoughtfulness, ingenuity, and energy of its next generation of thinkers to overcome its present crises and expanding zone of indifference. The essays in this volume, written by emerging scholars and policy practitioners in the service of the European idea, grapple with these diverse yet interconnected themes of challenge through interdisciplinary analyses. In so doing, this volume opens a generational conversation by showcasing how Europe's next generation of thinkers identifies, analyzes, and begins to resolve the crises of contemporary Europe.

2 How to Read This Volume – a Message from the Editors

The purpose of this volume is twofold, at once analytic and epistemic. From an analytic perspective, the volume is an interdisciplinary and explicitly intersectional approach to understanding Europe's many challenges. As any astute observer of contemporary politics would acknowledge, issues and their responses never occur within a disciplinary silo. Yet, too many studies of politics, economics, culture, and more – and particularly those studying Europe and the European Union – treat their subjects as standalone entities of inquiry. This is naturally partly from the necessity for concision – no volume, no matter how expansive or exhaustive, could ever adequately incorporate every perspective and approach that bears on a question. Nevertheless, the seeming futility of this ultimate goal should not stop us from pursuing it as best we can. Perhaps reflecting the notorious optimism and vigor of young people, the analyses put forward by Europe's new generation presented in this volume attempt to demonstrate the richness of discovery that can be attained through interdisciplinary analysis, no matter how non-exhaustive it may be.

By placing seemingly disparate approaches in direct conversation with one another, the reader should see clearly how intimately and inextricably linked various political, economic, and social fields are with each other in practice. This volume presents a holistic view of Europe's challenges, marrying a variety of humanities and social sciences disciplines to showcase the complexity of contemporary European studies. In doing so, the volume also demonstrates the necessity of using interdisciplinary approaches when attempting to resolve any of these challenges, as each issue necessarily interplays with another.

2.1 Chapter Overview

The volume opens with a historical discussion of the growing distance between Europe's social democratic parties and the working class those parties claim to represent. Using the example of the British Labour Party's attempted Social Contract in the 1970s, Adam Frick demonstrates in Chapter 1 that as the Labour Party became more institutionalized within British politics, it came to represent elite interests and follow the contours of leadership struggles rather than promote the voice of Britain's laborers. In so doing, the previously tight connection between Britain's labor unions and its Labour Party began to erode, punctuated by the failure of the Social Contract. Although today's social democratic parties in Europe do not have an explicit social contract, as Labour attempted in the 1970s, they nevertheless are experiencing a similar breakdown in cohesion between party politics and objectives and the working class on whose behalf they claim to advocate. Frick tells a story of caution for Europe's social democratic left, suggesting that without strong cohesion between parties and their main demographics of support, politics across Europe will be increasingly likely to experience the crisis that Labour went through in the 1980s.

In a by-now well-trodden narrative, globalization, digitization, the disappearance of the middle class and subsequent lack of social cohesion and trust between political parties and their electorate has led directly to the emergence of antiestablishment, anti-Europe far-right parties.[20] As Ali Cain demonstrates in Chapter 2, far-right populist parties capitalize on crisis moments by adjusting their narrative to respond to societal anxieties. She examines this phenomenon through the case of Germany's *Alternative für Deutschland* party during the COVID-19 pandemic, showing through the party's official rhetoric on social media that it deftly adjusted its political messaging throughout the pandemic to respond to crises in ways that would alienate voters from traditional parties. This not only included the sustained alienation of 'Others,' notably Muslims and immigrants, but renewed attacks on the idea of Europe as a positive entity for Europeans. As ongoing and future crises continue to change the social and political environments across Europe, Cain argues that far-right parties will continue to exacerbate divisions and moments of crisis for electoral gain.

Challenges to the narrative of a common European identity – based on liberal values and principles of democracy and the rule of law – do not come solely from antiestablishment far-right parties. Max Ferrer argues in Chapter 3 that disintegrative narratives are becoming increasingly prevalent through the proliferation of subregional tourism industries. He looks to the case of Catalonia, which in the last 30 years shifted its out-ward-facing identity from a unified Spanish tourist attraction of sand, sun, and beaches to an explicitly self-referential one emphasizing a unique *Catalanisme*. By demonstrating that this unique Catalan identity has been successful in creating a standalone tourist 'brand,' Ferrer shows that sub-regional tourist narratives can successfully challenge dominant narratives of national identity. He further suggests that at least some subregional narratives can challenge the entire project of the construction of a European identity. In the Catalan case, there is a renewed celebration of Catalonia's former empire, the idea of which runs counter to Europe's self-presentation as a champion of human rights, human freedoms, and self-determination. Although Ferrer is not quick to dismiss the prospects of a successful European identity, he rightly cautions that the project is doomed to failure if it does not reconcile with Europe's non-humanitarian, non-free, and non-self-determined history.

Although the forces of disintegration are many, and although they have gained speed through today's myriad crises, not all among Europe's emergent generation are skeptical of further integration. Floris Rijssenbeek argues in Chapter 4 that this new generation, namely those born after the early 1990s, represents a new cohort of decidedly pro-Europe Europeans. For this emergent Maastricht Generation, as he coins it, a united Europe is all they have ever known and will remain a guiding force for good. To demonstrate this, he looks to Hungary's Maastricht Generation. In one of the leading anti-European EU Member States, Rijssenbeek finds that the youth cohorts in recent years have grown more attached to democratic and European principles than their predecessors in the late 2000s and early 2010s. Of note, he finds that young Hungarians increasingly engage with democratic processes in extra-parliamentary ways such as protests, thereby adding complexity to our conception of contemporary democratic practices. Rijssenbeek is optimistic for the future of Europe, suggesting that as Hungary's Maastricht Generation comes to political adulthood, they will invest heavily in protecting and strengthening the European Union.

One particularly salient challenge to the optimism of the Maastricht Generation is the rise of digital disinformation. Particularly for a generation raised in the Information Age, the growth of targeted disintegrative media narratives by aggressive actors such as Russia poses a unique challenge to European cohesion. This is the argument that Emma Flaherty makes in Chapter 5 by documenting the shifting strategic narratives of the Russian-funded media outlet RT. Looking at RT's coverage of the EU's Central and Eastern European states, Flaherty demonstrates that the media outlet actively modulates its news stories to promote targeted country-dependent narratives tailored to Russian interests in each and every state.

This is not just hybrid warfare; it is highly complex, historically informed, and competitively flexible hybrid warfare. Even for the pro-European Maastricht Generation, it may be difficult to resist the anti-EU rhetoric of targeted misinformation and disinformation. As Flaherty warns, Europhiles must understand Russia's flexible disintegrative media strategy if it hopes to counter it.

Yet, although Russia actively attempts to destabilize the foundations of the European project, it remains one of Europe's key strategic partners, and one on which Europe heavily depends for its economic and technological growth. There are few fields in which this is more true than energy. Ruben Tjon-A-Meeuw makes the case for a new gas and oil *Ostpolitik* in Chapter 6, examining the politics of Nord Stream 2 and German–Russian gas relations. He argues that the construction of the contested Nord Stream 2 pipeline largely followed political calculations rather than economic and commercial ones. For Germany at least, Nord Stream 2 offers an opportunity to 'keep your enemy closer,' under the logic that states with complexly integrated commercial networks are less likely to go to war with each other. Tjon-A-Meeuw further contends that the controversial pipeline is not likely to decrease Eastern European security and energy independence. If anything, he claims, their uproar over the pipeline highlights Europe's need to invest in greater energy security and flexibility, a process that would ultimately result in a more interconnected Europe rather than a fragmented one.

As the ongoing debate over Nord Stream 2 underlines, it is impossible to separate European states' domestic politics from Europe's attempt to act as a unified voice in global politics. In the concluding chapter to this volume, Faïz El Mamoune considers the argument made by many Europhiles that the EU should occupy a single seat on the United Nations Security Council. Although such an idea would be the logical extension of much of the language encoded in the EU's treaties governing foreign policy, El Mamoune argues that it would be disintegrative to the future of Europe as it would destabilize the complex interplay between specifically French and German relations. Franco-German cooperation has driven European integration since the early days of the European Coal and Steel Community; the maintenance of a perceived cohesion or national balance of power between the two is essential for the short-term survival of the Union, El Mamoune argues. In a poignant close to the volume, he makes clear that Europe's domestic politics and its foreign identity are, and have been from the beginning of the idea of Europe, inextricably coupled.

*****

Taken together, these essays demonstrate the variety of challenges that face Europe in the 2020s and beyond. As has been the case throughout contemporary Europe's history, it will be the interplay of social, economic, political, and legal questions that will determine to what degree European structures integrate or disintegrate. Understanding these myriad challenges, and seeing how they interplay with each other in practice, is crucial in developing appropriate responses. By placing seemingly disparate disciplinary analyses side by side, it is the intention of this volume to excavate the subtle connective thread between these issues, putting that thread on full display for the reader.

2.2 Situating This Volume as Its Own Object of Study

The volume also serves an epistemic function: to bring to the fore the analysis, concerns, and solutions of the Maastricht Generation. The authors and the editors are themselves all members of this generation, Europeans and Europhiles born after the creation of the European Union. The idea of the volume was incubated at Columbia University, in the European Institute's seminar on European Studies, where the editors and authors first met to exchange thoughts and perspectives on Europe. Those initial conversations revealed that, despite disagreements on the normative or potential future of Europe, there is much for Europe's next generation to contribute to discussions on these subjects.

No generation or cohort of individuals, no matter how neatly defined, is a homogeneous grouping, and the contributors to this volume are no exception. There is a roughly equal number of European and American contributors (and one American and one European editor), with a wide geographic background ranging from Switzerland to the Netherlands, New York to North Carolina. By no means do the seven contributing authors represent the entire Maastricht Generation, nor do the essays presented in this volume claim to offer an exhaustive view of the future of Europe. Rather, they serve to showcase the breadth, depth, and complexity of issues facing contemporary Europe as seen through the eyes of those who will inherit them. The disciplinary approaches vary, as does each author's perspective on the future of European integration, reflecting in part the diversity that this group of young scholars brings to bear.

Because of the dual function of this book, both analytic and epistemic, the volume stands as a unique contribution to the study of Europe. It should not be seen just as an analytical and interdisciplinary exploration of Europe's pressing problems, but also as an object of study in its own right. Young scholars, policy practitioners, and participants in the European project must be included in discussions of Europe's future. In order to do so, their perspectives must be heard. It is our hope that this volume will spark a larger debate within the community of European Studies, with greater emphasis placed on the analytical voices of Europe's emergent thinkers.

Notes

1 France, Luxembourg, Italy, Belgium, the Netherlands, and West Germany.
2 This goal is set in the preamble to the Treaty on the Functioning of the European Union.
3 Armin Cuyvers, "The Road to European Integration," in *East African Community Law. Institutional, Substantive and Comparative EU Aspects*, eds. Emmanuel Ugirashebuja, John Eudes Ruhangisa, Tom Ottervanger and Armin Cuyvers (Brill, 2017), 22–23.
4 Philippe C. Schmitter, "A Revised Theory of Regional Integration," *International Organization* 24, no. 4 (Autumn 1970): 836–68.
5 Ibidem.
6 John Gillingham, *Coal, Steel, and the Rebirth of Europe, 1945–1955: The Germans and French from Ruhr Conflict to Economic Community* (Cambridge: Cambridge University Press, 1991).
7 Kevin Ruane, *The Rise and Fall of the European Defence Community: Anglo-American Relations and the Crisis of European Defence, 1950–1955* (Palgrave Macmillan, 2000); Renata Dwan, "Jean Monnet and the European Defence Community, 1950–1954," *Cold War History* 1, no. 1 (2001): 141–60.
8 John van Oudenaren, "European Integration: An Uncertain Prospect," in *Europe Today: A Twenty-first Century Introduction, Fifth Edition*, eds. Ronald Tiersky and Erik Jones (Rowman & Littlefield, 2014), 300–301.
9 John Gillingham, *European Integration, 1950–2003: Superstate or New Market Economy?* (Cambridge: Cambridge University Press, 2003). See especially Part II.
10 van Oudenaren, "European Integration: An Uncertain Prospect," 303.
11 Peter Nyberg, Horst Ungerer, and Owen Evens, *The European Monetary System: The Experience, 1979–1982* (International Monetary Fund, 1983); Michele Fratianni and Jürgen von Hagen, *The European Monetary System and European Monetary Union* (Routledge, 1992).
12 van Oudenaren, "European Integration: An Uncertain Prospect," 302–303.
13 These countries are: Hungary, Poland, Bulgaria, Czechia, Romania, Slovakia, Estonia, Latvia, Lithuania, and Slovenia.
14 Andreas Nölke, "Economic Causes of the Eurozone Crisis: The Analytical Contribution of Comparative Capitalism," *Socio-Economic Review* 14, no. 1 (January 2016): 141–61; Jeremy J. Siegel, "Devaluation – Last Option to Save the Euro," *Financial Times*, May 22 2012, https://www.ft.com/content/8626a02e-a35d-11e1-988e-00144feabdc0.
15 Olivier Blanchard and Lawrence Summers, *Rethinking Stabilization Policy. Back to the Future* (Peterson Institute for International Economics, 2017); Antonio Fatás and Lawrence H. Summers, "The Permanent Effects of Fiscal Consolidations," *Journal of International Economics* 112 (2018): 238–50.
16 Zoe Lefkofridi and Philippe C. Schmitter, "Transcending or Descending? European Integration in Times of Crisis," *European Political Science Review* 7, no. 1 (2015): 3.
17 Reint Gropp, Hans-Helmut Kotz, Jan Pieter Krahnen, Christian Odendahl, Beatrice Weder Di Mauro, Guntram B. Wolff, and Marcel Fratzscherand, "Mere Criticism of the ECB is No Solution," *Bruegel*, April 10, 2016, https://www.bruegel.org/2016/04/mere-criticism-of-the-ecb-is-no-solution/.
18 James Caporaso, Warren Durrett, and Min Kim, "Still a Regulatory State? The European Union and the Financial Crisis," *Journal of European Public Policy* 22 no. 7 (2014): 889–907. doi:10.1080/13501763.2014.988638. S2CID 153684746.
19 Michelle Cini and Amy Verdun, "The Implications of Brexit for the Future of Europe," in *Brexit and Beyond. Rethinking the Futures of Europe*, eds. Benjamin Martill and Uta Staiger (UCL Press, 2018), 70–71.

20 Dani Rodrik, "Populism and the Economics of Globalization," *Journal of International Business Policy* 1, no. 1 (2018): 13–19.

Bibliography

Blanchard, Oliver and Lawrence Summers. *Rethinking Stabilization Policy. Back to the Future*. Washington, DC: Peterson Institute for International Economics, 2017.

Caporaso, James, Warren Durrett, and Min Kim. "Still a Regulatory State? The European Union and the Financial Crisis." *Journal of European Public Policy* 22, no. 7 (2014): 889–907. doi:10.1080/13501763.2014.988638. S2CID 153684746.

Cini, Michelle and Amy Verdun. "The Implications of Brexit for the Future of Europe." In *Brexit and Beyond. Rethinking the Futures of Europe*, edited by Benjamin Martill and Uta Staiger, 70–71. London: UCL Press, 2018.

Cuyvers, Armin. "The Road to European Integration." In *East African Community Law. Institutional, Substantive and Comparative EU Aspects*, edited by Emmanuel Ugirashebuja, John Eudes Ruhangisa, Tom Ottervanger, and Armin Cuyvers, 22–23. Brill, 2017.

Dwan, Renata. "Jean Monnet and the European Defence Community, 1950–1954." *Cold War History* 1, no. 1 (2001): 141–60.

Fatás, Antonio and Lawrence H. Summers. "The Permanent Effects of Fiscal Consolidations," *Journal of International Economics* 112 (2018): 238–50.

Fratianni, Michele and Jürgen von Hagen. *The European Monetary System and European Monetary Union*. New York: Routledge, 1992.

Gillingham, John. *Coal, Steel, and the Rebirth of Europe, 1945–1955: The Germans and French from Ruhr Conflict to Economic Community*. Cambridge: Cambridge University Press, 1991.

Gillingham, John. *European Integration, 1950–2003: Superstate or New Market Economy?* Cambridge: Cambridge University Press, 2003.

Gropp, Reint, Hans-Helmut Kotz, Jan Pieter Krahnen, Christian Odendahl, Beatrice Weder Di Mauro, Guntram B. Wolff, and Marcel Fratzscherand. "Mere Criticism of the ECB is No Solution." *Bruegel*, April 10, 2016, https://www.bruegel.org/2016/04/mere-criticism-of-the-ecb-is-no-solution/.

Lefkofridi, Zoe, and Philippe C. Schmitter. "Transcending or Descending? European Integration in Times of Crisis." *European Political Science Review* 7, no. 1 (2015): 3.

Nölke, Andreas. "Economic Causes of the Eurozone Crisis: The Analytical Contribution of Comparative Capitalism." *Socio-Economic Review* 14, no. 1 (January 2016): 141–61.

Nyberg, Peter, Horst Ungerer, and Owen Evens. *The European Monetary System: The Experience, 1979–1982*. Washington, DC: International Monetary Fund, 1983.

Rodrik, Dani. "Populism and the Economics of Globalization." *Journal of International Business Policy* 1, no. 1 (2018): 13–19.

Ruane, Kevin. *The Rise and Fall of the European Defence Community: Anglo-American Relations and the Crisis of European Defence, 1950–1955*. London: Palgrave Macmillan, 2000.

Schmitter, Philippe C. "A Revised Theory of Regional Integration." *International Organization* 24, no. 4 (Autumn 1970): 836–68.

Siegel, Jeremy J. "Devaluation – Last Option to Save the Euro." *Financial Times*, May 22 2012. https://www.ft.com/content/8626a02e-a35d-11e1-988e-00144feabdc0.

van Oudenaren, John. "European Integration: An Uncertain Prospect." In *Europe Today: A Twenty-First Century Introduction, Fifth Edition,* edited by Ronald Tiersky and Erik Jones, 300–301. Lanham: Rowman & Littlefield, 2014.

1 The Disintegration of the Center-Left Labor Consensus

Lessons from the Labour Party's Social Contract Failure

Adam Frick

1 Introduction

Since the Second World War, social democratic parties have been mainstays in Western European governments. The roots of social democracy can be found in labor movements, extending back far before the contours of contemporary Europe emerged. As labor movements grow and thrive, they in turn cultivate the social democratic ideology. The relationship between a certain sect of the population – in this case a broadly defined, sometimes changing but ubiquitous 'working class' – and a particular political party has long been a subject of study, in part because this relationship lies at the heart of political discourse within the history of Europe's democracies. Both sides seek concessions from the other: political parties want their constituents' support and advocacy, and the constituents expect legislation supporting them, their livelihoods, and general societal prosperity. Whether it is stated or implied, this is a form of contract between political party and constituent. As long as the political order is beneficial for those citizens opting into this type of social contract, they may find the benefit outweighs what has been given up in terms of alternative political opportunities. But when legislation stalls or political parties back down from promises, that contract may be broken; citizens – in this case, specifically workers – leverage their labor and will cease to uphold their end of the agreement, be it by finding another party to partner with or by attempting to change the societal structure through revolution.

Today, established democracies find themselves challenged by a rise in far-right, anti-EU parties. Often taking advantage of a frustrated working class unsure of where to put their political allegiance, this rise in far-right support has coincided directly with a loss in support for social democratic parties on the left or center-left. The current state of these social democratic parties is precarious: long-reliant on the working class in their respective countries, an increasingly globalized world and flattened Europe have presented troubles for these parties. Low-skill work that is able to be done remotely is outsourced to other countries; worker mobilization across the EU is causing an increasing number of jobs to be occupied by Europeans

DOI: 10.4324/9781003182344-2

that cannot vote elsewhere besides their home country; and the volatility of labor markets – especially in wake of the COVID-19 pandemic – all contribute to a disgruntled working class, one that is frustrated with their supposed allies in social democratic parties. Without cohesion between social democratic parties and workers, the future of European integration is threatened, as workers will continue to shift their party allegiance to Eurosceptic, far-right parties. If the working masses turn against the EU and their allies and neighbors, then the entire continent's social order and prosperity may be threatened.

In order to understand the mechanism and long-term effects of the breakdown of worker–social–democratic consensus, we can look instructively to the British Labour Party in the late 1970s. The Labour Party, while internally struggling over European Economic Community (EEC) membership as a party-wide policy stance, was simultaneously dealing with heavy, outside criticism of their 'preferential' relationship to union members, as opposed to the nonunion members of society. Their attempts at formalizing a social contract between themselves and the Trade Unions Congress (TUC) came not only at the same time as further European integration, but also during shakeups in the strength of industries at home, with a modernizing workforce and increasing diversity throughout the UK labor market, especially in white-collar jobs. Labour was confronted with a crossroad: should they stay true to their old union allies, who were made up of primarily male, public blue-collar workers, or adapt to the new British working class and listen to their vocal demands?

An amicable relationship between center-left, national political parties and a broadly defined working class is consistently sought after, if not required by social democratic parties in order to achieve electoral success. While Labour's relationship with unions should be considered fairly unique in comparison to other European political parties, their up-and-down partnership with their working class voter base has similarities across the continent. As social democratic parties' voter base continues to shed supporters to alternative options, Labour's disastrous electoral collapses in 1979 and 1983 serve as cautionary tales for the price that comes with failing to adapt to a changing working class.

This chapter will follow the development and history of Labour's attempt at a formal agreement between the party and unions from 1970 to 1983 in the form of the 'Social Contract.' Intended to be an explicit document, this outlined the exact concessions needed from Labour in order to enter a voluntary cap on union members' wages. Concerned that the worker's annual wage increases were a cause for rising inflation, the agreement not only hoped to assist the prosperity of the British economy, but also help the public image of Labour and their long-standing, occasionally imbalanced relationship with unions. As will be shown below, this Social Contract utterly failed to satisfy the changing demands of the British working class; its failure then led to nearly two decades in opposition for Labour.

Although the historical specificities are unique, there are broad contemporary lessons to extract from this specific attempt at a formal contract between party and the working class. Today, social democratic parties are experiencing a breakdown in cohesion between their goals and politics and the changing working class whose success they claim to prioritize. Without reflecting the make-up and ideology of their supporter base, these parties' positions are threatened by the growing disconnect workers seem to have with them.

This chapter will first detail the political and economic situation that led to Labour's attempt at a Social Contract. In the United Kingdom, the decade contained their entrance into the European Communities as well as their 1975 Referendum on membership of the EEC, resulting in a 2:1 yes to no ratio – a resounding confirmation that the general populace wanted integration. Second, this chapter will cover the fine details of the Social Contract, including the negotiations leading to enacting an agreement; how the policies were interpreted across the ideological spectrum; and what its eventual collapse demonstrates for how outdated European social democratic parties relate to workers. Finally, the chapter will cover how Labour's relationship with all workers – not just those that were union affiliated – degraded swiftly during and shortly after the decade. As the party failed to update their visions of what a typical worker looked or acted like, the broad working masses began to resent Labour for not fighting for them with the same ferocity as they did union members – despite several opportunities to back nonunion workers in their struggles or strikes.

By piecing together a diverse number of perspectives from Labour and union leaders alongside existing academic works, I assemble an encompassing view on how Labour lost the confidence of workers, and what effect that has had on the party's success. Although it is necessary to emphasize the uniqueness of Labour's relationship with unions, the lessons learned from the complete collapse in coherency with their working class voter base can and should be viewed as a cautionary tale, one that stresses how powerful and decisive the working masses can be. The failure of the Labour Party to properly respond to their constituents must inspire introspection for other similar social democratic parties' relationships with workers. Workers today are already frustrated with their purported representatives in their electoral systems, as mass worker defections to far-right parties indicates.[1] If this frustration continues, social democratic parties will continue to flounder, as Labour did, benefitting only the far-right just as they did neoliberal parties in the 1980s.

2 A New Deal: How to Repair a Fractured Relationship with Communication

To understand Labour's situation in 1970, it is necessary for a brief historical overview of the party and their electoral successes – or lack thereof.

At the turn of the twentieth century, unionized British workers realized they needed a representation of themselves and their interests in the UK Parliament. A long-standing organization, the TUC, passed a resolution in 1899 to form a Labour Party – a party by workers, for workers. Throughout their hundred plus years' existence, Labour and the working class had what can only be described as a contentious alliance. Unions have consistently had massive influence over the party: not only are they responsible for a significant amount (and at times, most) of the party's funding, they have historically held an important portion of votes for internal leadership elections as party affiliates. This has meant favor toward unions – be it by individual leaders or through Labour's platform. Attempts at removing or reducing unions' association by party leadership would lead to a corresponding drop in electoral viability and votes. Labour's relationship with unions often comes under criticism by their Conservative opponents or the general British media, who accuse unions of running the party and, at times, gripping the nation with their alleged militancy or disregard for the prosperity of the British economy. Throughout the twentieth century, Labour has frequently fought for and sought out an agreement between themselves and workers, seeking to give the party legitimized power over their supporters in exchange for concessions, such as capping wage increases at a set annual figure, or by reducing strike opportunities that could have the outcome of making Labour appear badly in the eyes of their opponents and the media.

From their origins in 1899 through 1945, Labour failed to secure a majority place in parliament. They were close in 1929 with a minority government, but ultimately could not cross the final threshold and suffered an internal collapse shortly after. Their first chance at leadership came on 5 July 1945 with Clement Attlee leading the party to their first majority. Yet, even when experiencing success as a genuine national party in the post-war period, their electoral successes seemed less an endorsement of their policies and union allies and rather a rejection of other political parties. Wartime conditions during the Second World War proved to make the Conservative Party unpopular. Once the Second World War was brought home via Dunkirk and the failed Norway campaign, the Conservative's firm grip on the electorate quickly faded; as historian Ross McKibben has said, "Labour would have won any election held after July 1940."[2]

While the Social Contract was the longest standing attempt at a formal agreement between the TUC and Labour, it was not the first time the unions were forced into a wage cap despite their vocalized commitment against it. During the Attlee Administration, they were forced into an average 2.8% wage cap, far below what union leadership could have negotiated with leaders in their respective industries. In February of 1948, the cabinet proposed a national 'wages policy,' wherein guidelines were suggested for negotiated wage increases – against the long-standing wishes of the TUC that Labour needed to stay committed to their historically unfettered collective bargaining status.[3] As economic conditions continued to worsen in 1949, protectionist measures for workers at home were failing to raise export prices and lessen international competition; one year later, in June of 1950, the TUC renounced their commitment to Labour's policy, by a thin margin of 3.89 million votes for 3.52 against. This came just months after the February 23rd election, when Labour won a slim majority of just five seats. Due to the lack of TUC support and campaigning, Labour lost their subsequent election on 25 October 1951, yielding their majority to the Conservatives. As will be illustrated, Labour's fights with unions during their times in governments would cost them electorally.

In the following elections, Labour not only failed to perform as expected, but demographic breakdowns proved their voter base was occupying an increasingly smaller share of the general electorate. In 1959, Gallup polls following a loss showed their support dropping among all demographics except the 'very poor' and the elderly; analysts predicted Labour would remain out of office until it reflected the interests of well-off, younger workers, women, and white-collar employees.[4] Internally, the party remained split. The more moderate faction – led by party leader Hugh Gaitskell – felt it was time to become more of a national party, focused on a wider breadth of support and more centrist policies. On the opposite end, leftist Labour members felt a 'catch-all' approach was what led to their 1959 election failure, and that the party's relationship with the working class was a high priority.[5] These internal disagreements were persistent as the two wings of the party became increasingly fractured. Their 1964 election victory was with a slim majority and saw voter share losses in the working class and the aforementioned 'very poor', albeit correlated with a small increase in middle class support. Gallup polls showed that the general public still thought the Conservatives were better for the country's 'prosperity' than the Labour Party.[6] Although it came with a much larger majority, their subsequent 1966 electoral victory had more to do with the British electorate's rejection of the Conservatives as well as underfunding for the Liberal Party. While the Conservative Party lost two million members in a seven-year span prior, Labour's membership gains were less than half that at 800,000.[7] This led to concerns about the long-term viability of Labour due to their ingrained ties with unions as well as their perceived inability to acquire new voters.

Coming off six years of government, in 1970, Labour led opinion polls and seemed in direct control of the election campaign that cycle. Yet, when election day came on 18 June, the Conservative Party – helmed by Edward Heath – secured a majority of 30 seats over Labour. Although Harold Wilson remained on as Leader of Opposition, reactions across the ideological spectrum of Labour ranged from blaming him and his cabinet to excusing the administration due to the alleged difficulties of the economic and political situation Wilson and his cabinet had faced. Those on the left of Labour felt a radical overhaul of their policy plans was not only electorally viable, but paramount to the future economic success and prosperity for all of Britain. Opposition generally meant a time for policy and platform redrafting; while national governments had to be concerned with the whole British populace, the work that goes into running Britain and the actual implementation of policies, Labour in opposition could prepare to form new answers to existing problems and campaign their way back into power.[8] Heath had a comfortable lead in the House, meaning Labour did not need to prepare for the possibility of a snap election being called shortly after 1970. The subsequent three-year, eight-month period of opposition between the 1970 and February 1974 elections is of critical importance to understanding the breakdown of the Labour–labor alliance in the latter half of the decade and after.

2.1 Labour in Opposition, 1970–1974: Origins of the Social Contract

Labour's first priority in opposition was to repair their heavily damaged relationship with unions. During the Wilson administration, Labour had become increasingly confrontational toward unions, as unions had risen to arguably their strongest, most aggressive position since 1945. In what is now an infamous document, Wilson and then-Secretary of State for Employment Barbara Castle laid forth their grievances in the 1969 White Paper *In Place of Strife*. This side of Labour had grown frustrated with the general populace's perception of their 'imbalanced' alliance with unions. As summarized in the paper:

> At present individual unions can and do connive at the abuse of market power by individual firms or industries where this brings sectional advantages to their members. Equally they can and do connive at inefficiency spring from wage systems no longer relevant to present day conditions, from reluctance to link pay settlements to change in working methods, and from leap-frogging inflationary pay settlements.[9]

Labeling their biggest supporters as 'abusing' power is quite a departure from Labour's origins. As long as the party has existed, they have relied on unions for funding, campaigning, and general success. Given the strain of their relationship at this time, it should be no surprise that Labour lost 75 seats by the June 1970 General Election. Both sides saw a need for reconciliation, as the newly elected Heath administration threatened the hard-earned rights workers and unions had successfully fought for the last three decades.

Emerging out of this dependence on one another came a new collaboration tool between the Labour Party and the TUC, known as the TUC-Labour Liaison Committee. One of several new avenues for policymaking in the 1970s, it is through this channel that the TUC and the Labour Party reconciled with one another and sought greater coordination with their actions.

Although the original goal of the committee was focused on resisting the Heath Government and repealing the Industrial Relations Act, [10] by late 1972, the Liaison Committee turned to broader matters and general policies. Central to their discussions was an important and recurring policy area: the control of inflation. In 1973, Labour and unions reached a tentative, loosely defined agreement over inflation handling.[11] The Government would offer price controls and reflation tactics in exchange for a voluntary wage restraint on the side of unions; this framework provided the basis for what became the Social Contract.

Incomes policies took many forms, not just in the United Kingdom but in quite a number of post-war countries. As such, there is little in the way of a formal definition or collective agreement for what qualities incomes policies need to or should include.[12] Nevertheless, the idea of the policy is relatively simple. In times of full or near full employment – either in general or in specific industries – workers have exponentially increased leverage due to a lack of available replacement workers. Because of this, they are often in a strong position to negotiate massive raises and increases to their wages. This can cause inflation, be it for the economy in general, or for the rate of pay in a particular industry. Highly skilled, specialized workers – especially those that are unionized – enjoy demand for their employment and tend to use the opportunity for raises far above average rates. Incomes policies are formal or informal agreements for these workers to cap their wage increases at less than market value – say 5% as opposed to what could be 20% annual raises. Though this was a direct interference to unions' unfettered commitment to collective bargaining, some party members felt that not only would an agreement for wage controls help save the economy, but that such an agreement would help their image of being 'unable' to control their union allies.

Internally throughout Labour, arguments broke out over the issue. On one side, Revisionists – the less radical end of the party – saw explicit, formal incomes policies as an indispensable policy tool.[13] From their viewpoint, this was the only way to avoid a wage–price spiral that would lead to ballooning inflation. Labour members that were sympathetic to workers as well as the TUC felt that either incomes policies were insufficient to solve inflation or that other problems (like the rising unemployment rate) were more critical and had to be tackled first. Union leaders, on the other hand, were quite direct in how much of a barrier mandatory incomes policies were for their relationship with Labour. The TUC – which had recently seen several radicals rise to leadership, notably including Jack Jones of the Transport and General Workers' Union (TGWU) and Hugh Scanlon of the Amalgamated Engineering Union (AEU) – made clear in a 1970 resolution that they were committed to "opposing any policy which restricts the right of trade unions to defend and improve the living standards of their members... and indeed to any restriction on bargaining, whether legally enforced or otherwise."[14]

The TUC passed this resolution unanimously; the party had to accept that there would be no agreements with unions if it included formal incomes policies, so the issue was dropped until Labour returned to government.[15]

Most integral to understanding the party–union relationship of the 1970s is the Social Contract. The idea started to emerge out of the afore-mentioned problem with rising inflation, with the viewpoint that price controls were essential to curbing the rise. During the Liaison Committee meetings, Parliamentary Labour representatives argued they could not ap-proach a general election with some 10% rising inflation, at least not without specific ideas and promises to address this. The TUC agreed but claimed the problem was low demand and output, meaning any solutions should emphasize reducing unemployment as their priority.[16] In contrast to Labour Revisionists and most leadership, the more radical Labour members did not believe in formal incomes policies; since their viewpoint concluded inflation was the result of rising monopolies and unfettered capitalism, wages need not be targeted.[17] This was also supported by unions, which of course main-tained a hardline commitment to any government interference on wages or incomes, as it would interfere with their bargaining ability.

The TUC and unions were initially hesitant to work with Labour and did not necessarily trust them to stay with any promises made in oppo-sition once the party returned to power. Initially, unions attempted to work amicably with the Heath Government. The Conservative Party from 1972 onwards recognized the need for some level of cooperation with the TUC if they were to avoid collapsing in upcoming elections. There were several early meetings between the TUC General Council and the Heath Government via the National Economic Development Council (NEDC). Here, the TUC reiterated its position that there could be no discussions on pay or wage caps without a wider strategy covering rent control, possibil-ities of profit sharing, and greater worker control initiatives, such as work councils or voting procedures.[18] Unions wanted a 'contract' of sorts, some level of guarantee in industrial policy and a promise of a well-deserved seat at the decision-making table. A number of concessions and promises were proposed by Heath, but ultimately he was unwilling to negotiate any repeal of the Industrial Relations Act. Once negotiations fell apart, so ended the uneasy amicable relationship between Heath and the unions. Jack Jones gave support to this viewpoint:

> Had we a firm agreement to repeal the Industrial Relations Act, had we a firm agreement to apply statutory controls over prices, freeze price increases and rents... there would have been a basis on which we could have said to our movement well we ought to exercise some form of re-straint, we ought to be prepared to cooperate providing that we can see clearly that prices are going to be held down the cause of our concern is going to be eased.[19]

Admitting that temporary incomes policies were on the table, Jones showed how difficult it would be to enforce any kind of wage or income cap on the unionized workers. However, these talks were not a total loss. Much of the negotiating gave experience to the TUC in order to solidify their ideas and demands; Jones' view of the Liaison Committee was to use the committee to create a clearly understood, well-defined program uniting the party and the labor movement together. Whether this took the form of a formal agreement had yet to be determined.

In 1970, British economist and House of Lords member Thomas Balogh called for a 'contract social;' Wilson, future party leader James Callaghan, and Revisionist economist Stuart Holland echoed this call.[20] The term social contract came into formality with the 1973 Programme as well as the TUC-Labour Party Liaison Committee's 1973 release, *Economic Policy and the Cost of Living*. The latter emphasized price controls: "the key to any alternative strategy to fight inflation is direct statutory action on prices."[21] At the launch of this document, TUC General Secretary Vic Feather said, "if you get the prices right, the rest will follow."[22] The TUC was claiming that if price controls could be effective, then there would be no necessary demand for large wage increases by the workers. If that demand didn't exist, then there was no need for organized wage caps or restraints – the volunteer-ism on the part of unions would be sufficient.

Labour's goals for the Social Contract were initially lofty. The 1973 Programme called it "a fundamental and irreversible shift in the balance of power and wealth in favour of working people."[23] But problems arose shortly after the agreement was formalized: there were multiple interpreta-tions across the party and the TUC, a lack of concrete goals and specifics for the policy, and it seemed to be more focused on the spirit of an agree-ment between Labour and the TUC rather than forming an actual working partnership. Party Leader Harold Wilson believed that the contract was "a way of life based on economic and social justice, aimed at replacing conflict and confrontation with cooperation and conciliation." This stood in contrast to radical Tony Benn's definition of "a joint commitment to social, industrial and economic reform," with Benn later adding "...but for him [Wilson], it was the route that led back into *In Place of Strife* and a pay policy."[24] Judith Hart noticed the imprecise proposals as well, saying in respect to Wilson that "vague commitments can and do mean all things to all people."[25] This was arguably intentional, largely to gather support for the agreement.

Despite the imprecise details, Labour was putting forth an image of control over the TUC. Campaigning on a collaborative relationship with unions to fix the economy – rather than the combative nature the Conserv-atives had taken – Wilson and leadership wielded the Social Contract as a potential tool of control over their union allies. This was to help change the perception of their 'imbalanced' relationship with unions, who were currently being blamed for worsening economic conditions. As inflation continued to grow, Heath and the Conservatives called for a February 1974 snap election under the question of 'Who Governs Britain?' which meant to argue the government was in a power struggle with unions for 'control' of the country. The election took place while a strike by the National Union of Mineworkers crippled the UK's logistics, in response to which the Heath Government had to implement a three-day work week. February's election therefore can be considered more or less a referendum on which major party the public felt was better equipped to work with the unions; for now, faith was placed in Labour.

Wilson and the Labour Party – much as they were with their abject defeat in 1970 – were surprised to see their opposition of three years and eight months end with an electoral win of 301 seats compared to the Conservative Party's 297. This was not an overall majority, and the Party would quickly call another General Election for October of the same year. This time Labour took 319 seats (the Conservatives had 277), enough for a majority of just three seats – the slimmest majority margin in UK history.

2.2 Labour in Power, 1974–1979: The Social Contract Implemented

Although Wilson and his cabinet felt too weak strategically to impose any type of wage restraint, there was hope the TUC would follow their public assurance returning to orderly collective bargaining rather than unruly wage demands.[26] Implementing the Social Contract – a loosely defined handshake agreement – now became central to both the Labour–TUC relationship in office as well as the perception of how the party was 'dealing' with the unions. While a Minority Government, Labour attempted to implement the contract in face of worsening economic conditions as best they could. Price and rent freezes were imposed while food subsidies were introduced, an independent, impartial advisory forum for industrial relations was established, and permanent commissions (Health and Safety at Work, Manpower Services), which were very much supported by unionists like Jack Jones, became established and worked well.[27]

Some perspectives on Labour's first year in office from March 1974–1975 direct their criticism not toward the party, but instead toward unions for not fulfilling their end of the contract. In response to his own question of "what were the trade unions doing in return?", Robert Taylor said the following:

> The answer was — not much and never enough. During the winter of the 1974—5 inflationary wage settlements did not suggest many unions were willing to exercise much self-restraint in their collective demands, whatever verbal promises they might make to reassure increasingly anxious ministers. The deterioration in economic conditions did not even lead the Cabinet to initiate at least a discussion about the merits of

a national wages policy after Labour's narrow general election victory in October 1974. Ministers were still reluctant to confront the TUC with any such attempt if it threatened the existence of the Social Contract.[28]

This sentiment was similarly felt by Labour leadership. Labour had inherited a number of economic crises that had served to collapse the Heath Government.[29] Formalizing the Social Contract became central to the party's economic strategy during this Government. This was an idea spurred primarily by Denis Healey, who served as Chancellor of the Exchequer for the entirety of the Labour Government. Healey and leadership focused on securing voluntary wage restraint, though as will be demonstrated, they much preferred a nonvoluntary policy to combat inflation. Still, in 1974, hands were tied. Therefore, the plan which came into fruition was a trade-off of redistribution and reflation in exchange for voluntary wage restraint; Healey's first budget (March 1974) was neutral but his second that July helped to reflate the economy.[30] To a slight defense of Labour's leadership, voluntary restraint alone had indeed proven to be insufficient in combating the rising inflation. In 1974, wages increased by over 29%, and by the spring of 1975 inflation was peaking at over 25%.[31]

That summer, the pressure on an inflating sterling was bubbling on the surface of a currency crisis. Healey adjusted his economic strategy accordingly: the volunteerism of the social contract was replaced by a formal incomes policy which was a flat rate increase of 6 sterlings per week, with nothing for those earning more than 8,500 sterlings a year.[32] Revisionist economic strategy shifted to a reduction in public spending, and trade union leaders reluctantly accepted the policy, spurred on by leaders like Jack Jones. There was plenty of dissent: the TUC General Council had only approved it narrowly, Left MPs voted against it in parliament, and Hugh Scanlon's own union campaigned against it – despite Scanlon personally supporting the policy.[33]

Dealing with this problem stoked the flame of internal politics throughout the TUC as well as Labour itself. The situation only soured after Harold Wilson announced his resignation as party leader in March 1976. The subsequent leadership election churned out James Callaghan as his successor. Within the ideological spectrum of Labour, Callaghan could be considered a centrist; while he was a harsh critic of the radical 'Alternative Economic Strategy' proposals and the MPs supporting it, he did not consider himself a Revisionist nor a socialist. Now, as party leader and PM, he was ready to lead Labour into a successful Government. His first step was to tackle the inflation crisis. The pay policy with unions expired in August 1976, but was shortly then replaced with another tight incomes policy. While wage settlements did significantly fall from 1975–1977, it is ambiguous how much the income policies played a role in this; rising unemployment was perhaps more significant.[34] Inflation had actually been reduced from its peak rate of 26% down to 12.9% in July 1976, but the sterling remained in a dire state.

The Callaghan administration, with a rising number of policy failures deemed inadequate to handle the economic crises, had no choice but to pursue a loan with the International Monetary Fund (IMF). Met with bipartisan unpopularity, the conditions for the bailout meant massive cuts in public spending. On 29 September, the Government applied for a loan of $3,900 million and the IMF demanded £5,000 million in public expenditure cuts. Over autumn, discussions with the IMF continued and on 2 December, the cabinet supported the loan. There were admittedly fewer cuts than originally proposed: £1,500 million in the public sector borrowing requirement (PSBR) for 1977–1978 was cut, and there were further expenditure cuts of £1,000 million in the following two years.[35] Public industry unions were the strongest and loudest in the TUC, and fewer public workers meant less opportunities, money, and strength. Leftwing Labour members naturally sided with unions and balked at any reductions in public spending, but the social democratic, Revisionist wing was hurt the most.

The party had won in 1974 on somewhat radical programs containing public spending and nationalization. The relationship between public expenditure and economic prosperity was therefore challenged with the IMF loan and subsequent budget cuts, as this went directly against Revisionist beliefs of compatibility between a market economy and high public spending. It also marked a clear end to any beliefs that this administration would be a radical or transformative one. Certain MPs were aware of this but failed to come up with an alternative. Crosland in particular was the voice around which Revisionists rallied. He noted that there was "now no sense of direction and priorities, only pragmatism, empiricism, safety first."[36] During the December 2nd meeting, Crosland stated he was "absolutely unconvinced by the economic arguments" but that it was his 'duty' to support Callaghan.[37]

Perhaps the most peculiar takeaway of this situation is that the IMF loan was not really necessary. Original PSBR estimates by the Treasury had been overestimated, and Healey only ever had to draw about half of the total amount loaned to the Government. In April 1978, he was able to introduce a reflationary budget, and by the end of Labour's tenure in Government in 1979, the IMF received its money back in full.[38] The incomes policies for unions held steady, and in August 1977, it was agreed to have a third policy with a 10% maximum limit, held through June 1978. In June 1977, inflation reached a new low point at 7.4% with unemployment falling back from this point forward. It seemed that for all the party's squabbles, the economy was on the path to recovery.

The cuts to public spending and loaning from the IMF seemed a direct violation against Keynesian principles the party often endorsed. Without public expenditure, delivering on social programs or goods became a much more difficult promise, and it became hard to see the party as Keynesian or one that prioritized combating unemployment. Callaghan, speaking at the Labour Party Conference in 1976, provided the death blow:

> We used to think you could spend your way out of recession, and increase unemployment by cutting taxes and boosting government spending. I tell you in all candour that option no longer exists, and that in far as it ever did exist, it worked on each occasion since the war by injecting a bigger dose of inflation into the economy, followed by a higher level of unemployment... that is the history of the last twenty years.[39]

Pragmatism remained the theme for Callaghan's economic strategy. Labour's shift to more moderate, liberal economic policies away from their social democratic ways brought forth confusion. In retrospect, it seems possible that Wilson and Callaghan sensed a public opinion shift back toward the right. They may have predicted the broader demise of social democracy across Europe, as neoliberal parties gained in the wake of social democratic parties' poor electoral performances.[40] The legitimacy and efficiency of public sector firms were being challenged. During the 1970s, social policy scholars were "...more likely to question the prevailing social democratic assumption that the state was an instrument for good."[41]

Regardless of whether or not Labour foresaw this ideological shift, their worldview and perception of how to best champion the working class was shamefully outdated. The Social Contract had been deemed insufficient by an increasing number of Labour leaders to deal with the union 'problem'. It was still a skeleton of what it originally endeavored to be, and every annual new 'Phase' introduced was a temporary solution to a long-standing problem. There was little more left of the contract beyond the wage caps that Callaghan and his allies in Labour felt necessary to implement. Len Murray spoke of the sacrifices they were sick of making:

> We are familiar with the message from Governments, that we must make sacrifices in the short term in order to reap the rewards in the longer term. This is sometimes true. But if words are not to lose their meaning, the short term cannot last forever.[42]

Labour's insistence on continuing a pay policy despite increasing unemployment and improving economic conditions drew hostile attitudes. The union's right to unfettered collective bargaining was impeded by the very party that claimed to be their ally, the same party whose origin came directly out of the labor movement. More unions started to oppose Labour even if the TUC did not. In 1977, the Fire Brigades Union approached the General Council to campaign against the government's 10% pay limit and wage settlements. In December of 1977, the council voted 21-19 to oppose the firefighters' strike and subsequent demands.[43] It became clear to smaller union and rank-and-file members that the TUC leadership was more concerned with appeasing Labour so as to avoid embarrassment than they were with helping workers.

By February 1978, inflation had come down to 10% for the first time in five years and public borrowing was comparatively down.[44] Wages were down too. Between 1975 and 1978, real wages fell by over 13%, with workers having the largest reduction in purchasing power since 1931.[45] Labour was in a decent position electorally and the economy, if not recovering, at least seemed to be on the upswing. Yet, the Callaghan administration persisted in carrying out their version of the Social Contract. In July of 1978, Labour published a new White Paper chiefly written by Denis Healey. Mainly about pay and wages, the Labour Government agreed that while pay was not the sole cause of inflation (which remained steady at 7–8% throughout 1978), further economic developments did depend on wage restraint.[46]

Callaghan therefore proposed a fourth phase of the Social Contract, with a 5% wage cap and a 'promise' to return to unfettered collective bargaining in early 1979. Unions and the TUC were appalled: their historic commitment against incomes policies had been upset for nearly the entirety of this Labour Government, and yet even when economic conditions improved, a repressive wage cap was still proposed. The TUC refused to back it and their members were furious. In some ways, this was entirely an electoral strategy by Labour. As British historian Andrew Thorpe elaborates:

> Most observers felt that the new pay policy was not intended seriously; rather, given the apparently favourable electoral signs, it was seen as a piece of pre-election window-dressing.[47]

The policy was also rejected by the actual Labour Party Conference, which even went so far as to reject all of the Government's economic policy proposals.[48] The policy – even if it could theoretically aid in the election – was unpopular and unions flat-out refused to cooperate with it. The administration's mistake was pushing forward with the pay policy regardless of the TUC's support, which was given in all other 'phases' of the Social Contract the past few years. Callaghan's decision appalled other Labour members; as he freely admits in his memoirs, the 5% wage ceiling was conceived in an attempt to blame unions for any further inflation.[49] Yet, Callaghan – along with then-Deputy Leader Michael Foot and Chancellor Healey – had doubts about a 1978 election. They thought it may only produce yet another minority Labour Government, a prospect which Callaghan – sick of compromising and parliamentary deals – detested.[50] Callaghan felt that if the 5% policy was maintained throughout the winter, then a Spring 1979 election would prove fruitful for Labour's electoral popularity.

To the universal shock of the TUC and the British media, Callaghan postponed calling for an election. Angered and feeling once again mistreated in their relationships, the unions and workers had lost their patience. Over the course of what was then the coldest winter in 16 years, hundreds of thousands of workers from a variety of unions, industries, and backgrounds took turns striking to protest the 5% wage cap Labour had been imposing. Ford workers won an astonishing 17% increase in income, and from then onwards, direct action exploded. Unions and workers demonstrated that their wage restraint for the last several years was well below what they could earn, and Labour looked more incompetent by the week. On 22 January, an estimated 1.50 million public sector workers engaged in a national 1-day strike, spreading disruption and drawing the country to an eerie halt.[51] Here, most of the infamous media imagery – of standstill train cars, National Health Service workers on strike, and a small number of gravediggers – is to be found. It was the largest single-day strike since the General Strike of 1926.

As late as November 1978, Labour was about five points ahead in polls; three months later, they trailed by more than 20%. On 28 March, the government lost a motion of no confidence as minority parties stopped supporting Labour in wake of Scottish and Welsh referendums on devolution. In what was the largest swing since 1945, the May 3rd General Election had Labour lose 51 seats while the Conservative Party gained a 43-seat majority. Over the course of these six months, the Winter of Discontent became etched into British history forever. Severe storms accompanied strikes in the transportation industry, conjuring the image of isolated regions throughout the United Kingdom, helpless to the critical workers on strike for higher pay. Truthfully, the situation was heavily exaggerated by the Conservatives and the media. Then-Secretary of State for Transport between 1976 and 1979, William Rodgers, later commented on the media frenzy:

> The strike produced more warnings of shortages and more signs of damage than actual disruption...The reporting of the strike by newspaper, radio and especially television was dramatic, and [had] much more impact on opinion than the public's own direct experience of the strike.[52]

Although the Social Contract was agreed upon by TUC leadership for each iteration, it was the rank-and-file workers that built up resentment toward Labour. The brunt of the burden that came with accepting incomes policies was felt by the workers themselves, as it was their wage increases that were being slowed in order to appease the party. Orders to stop striking by TUC leadership were ignored by union members; this only worsened as the large wage increases were won by Ford workers. Trade unionists went from voting for the Conservative Party at 25% in 1974 to 33% in the 1979 election.[53] Not only had Labour failed to capture the new British working class as their supporters, but they struggled to maintain their traditional union support base as well. The Social Contract had collapsed, the relationship between unions and Labour was more tenuous than ever, and the United Kingdom was soon to pivot to the Conservative Margaret Thatcher, who went on to dissect union strength and push a ferociously anti-worker agenda for years to come.

3   What Did Labour Get Wrong? Diversity, New Industries, and Non-Union Workers

Labour's inability to adapt and modernize its perspectives was ultimately the party's undoing. The collapse of the Social Contract and the disastrous Winter of Discontent brought forth heavy disapproval on the party for their inability to 'control' their union allies. Yet, criticism in line with labeling unions as too radical or strong ignores several key contributing factors to the negative result from the Social Contract. The first factor is that of Labour's outdated and ill-fitting definition of what a 'typical worker' looked or acted like. This was true not only of the general working class but of their union members as well. One of the most critical architects of the Social Contract was Tony Benn, a Labour MP and outspoken party member who had undergone a radical shift in ideology in 1970. Benn's speeches referenced a particular kind of worker that did not reflect what the contemporary workforce looked like nor the direction it was trending in. In 1968, Benn talked of how "when *a man enters the factory gate* in the morning he sheds much of his dignity with his overcoat." In 1971, Benn spoke on "the new grey flannel brigade with their degrees in business studies, familiar with the language of accounting and computers and their shiny office *away from the dirt and noise of the factory floor* are still often too remote."[54]

In 1973, Audrey Wise – who was a Labour MP after 1974 – brought insightful questions into the political discourse:

> Have you ever noticed that jobs threatened by closures are always 'men's jobs,' even when many are actually women's jobs? And that strikers are always 'the lads' and 'solid to a man' even when a good number of them are women? And that trade unionists always have 'wives and families' even though about a quarter of them are women?[55]

Perspectives taking this stance at the time were rare.[56] Pro-worker journals and publications were filled with images of white, male coal-miners and laborers in manual blue-collar industries; in one issue of the popular *Workers' Control Bulletin*, almost half of the paper's 12 pages were occupied by coal mining-related stories alone.[57] Overrepresentation of these traditional industries showcases the misconception Labour had with the makeup of the working class. Although emerging industries and diverse workers were ignored by Labour, their significance was increasing.

There are two key changes to the makeup of union members that need elaboration. The first is the upward surge in white-collar jobs, unionization, and affiliation. The Transport and General Workers' Union (TGWU), already among the largest union organizations, increased its membership by over 400,000 between 1958 and 1971; two million more white-collar members, of which 40% were new affiliations, also joined the TUC over the course of these years.[58] Corresponding with this membership increase were rapidly rising employment numbers in engineering, education, and professional service industries. Prior to this, white-collar organizing and unionization efforts had been lackluster and encountered numerous difficulties. The right to be recognized for union representation had to be fought for, and in the private industries, this was especially difficult.

Most efforts prior to the 1960s had been done in times of war, by the efforts of manual unions deciding to recruit nonmanual workers, and the attempts were limited almost entirely to large firms. Contrasting with manual industries, white-collar membership had risen by a third from 1948 to 1964 and achieved a somewhat higher density. After 1964, however, it skyrocketed: from about 1.7 million white-collar workers in TUC unions (900,000 in non-TUC unions) in 1964, those figures were raised to over 3 million and about 1 million in 1971, respectively.[59] Most of these membership numbers came from the public sector, where the recognition of unions and organizing attempts were usually more protected by law.

The second important demographic change stemmed from the increased recruitment of women workers. Women had slowly assumed a greater role in the workforce. Between 1948 and 1966, employment of women grew from around 33% to nearly 37%. Similar figures can be found in their union membership: women made up 18% of unions in 1948, 22% in 1966, and 25% in 1971. In 1971, 24% of TUC members were women, and they accounted for nearly 40% of all white-collar union members.[60] The rise came out of not only the number of women increasing in the workforce, but also by concentrated recruitment efforts. The two biggest and most general unions – the TGWU and the National Union of General and Municipal Workers – were among those making an emphasis on women membership at the end of the 1950s. Most of the membership growth for women between 1958 and 1971 was accomplished at the public sector level, and due to their prominence in white-collar work compared to blue-collar, were major impacts on the explosion of white-collar unions and membership increases.

Demonstrably, there was a disconnect between Labour's interpretation of a typical worker and the changing diversity and background of workers. What was the relationship like between these new workers and Labour? Using examples of direct action leading up to the Winter of Discontent, a clear pattern emerges of Labour caring little about nonunion (or even non-TUC affiliated) worker's struggles. On the contrary, the party frequently sought to distance itself from notable strikes – especially those that were not sanctioned or approved by the workers' union – so that they could avoid criticism of their association with those striking. The party constantly betrayed their constituents and the working class that they promised to fight for.

One prominent example of this was Labour's behavior during the two-year 'Grunwick Dispute.' In August of 1976, a handful of Asian, women workers walked out of Grunwick Film Processing Laboratories. This was a small place of work, at a white-collar, private-sector firm in North-West London. These workers, of which there were around 500 in total, sought to unionize against their millionaire boss George Ward. After having gone on strike, the workers were unsure how to actually unionize. They were advised to join the Association of Professional, Executive, Clerical and Computer Staff (APEX), which filed it as an official dispute about union recognition.[61] The workers' strike committee proposed mass picketing to raise solidarity, which turned into much more than they could have imagined. Solidarity boycotting of Grunwick mail started in November of 1976 and happened again in June 1977 by members of the Union of Post Office Workers (UPW).[62] Grunwick workers called for mass pickets in order to disrupt non-striking workers from entering the building and were met with heavy police presence. There was some legal action taken. Ward, joined by the National Association for Freedom (NAFF), raised issues surrounding the UPW boycott. When the Scarman Report (named after Lord Justice Scarman, who was called on by the government to investigate Grunwick) concluded that management had acted "within the letter but outside the spirit of law," it was outwardly rejected.[63] Labour had few actions available to them, as the legality of any intervention was not there.

Meanwhile, strikes and pickets continued largely as a result of nonworkers joining the line. The largest of these occurred on 11 July 1977, with 18,000 supporters from across the country blockading the plant and clashing with the police; even prominent union Secretary-Generals appeared on the picket line alongside the workers.[64] APEX reached out to the TUC, whose new General Secretary, Len Murray, came back asking for unions to give all possible assistance to Grunwick – not just in solidarity by showing up, but also through boycotts. Murray told them the TUC "are not just behind you. We are right alongside you."[65] General Secretary of APEX Roy Grantham was supported by the PM, who shared his pragmatic centrist opinions. APEX, Callaghan, and the TUC were worried in July about the ballooning imagery the press was pushing, that of 'anarcho-syndicalism' and riots. This only intensified following July 11th. Callaghan's hands were tied as they were reliant on the Liberal–Labour Pact to keep a majority in parliament. The PM never thought Grunwick could be 'won' in any sense: "the determining issue now was that of public order. Other matters were secondary."[66] Taking their cue, the TUC backed down. Pickets lobbied the September 1977 TUC Congress, asking for solidarity action in cutting off essential services and supplies for Grunwick. The General Council voted by a majority to avoid supporting any potential illegal actions, as they believed it would embarrass the Labour Government.[67]

The last point is necessary to dwell on. The Trade Unions Congress General Council – whose leaders represented millions of diverse workers across the United Kingdom – prioritized the image of the Labour Party over the thousands of striking women fighting for rights public industries have long enjoyed. This was not the first time the TUC had capitulated for Labour's reputation. They had during the previously mentioned 1977 Fire Brigades Union request and behaved equally similar to Grunwick during the 1926 General Strike and dock worker strikes in 1947 and 1948. The TUC had spent its earned goodwill among its workers, and as a result Labour suffered.

Labour lost the 3 May 1979 election, with the Conservatives winning on their campaign of 'Labour Isn't Working.' Following the collapse, James Callaghan swiftly announced his resignation pending a leadership election. In November of 1980, radical socialist Michael Foot became leader of the Labour Party. Months later, senior moderate party leaders split with Labour and went on to form the Social Democratic Party (SDP), which allied with the Liberals to form a coalition threatening Labour's electoral position. As leader, Foot represented the historical view of industries Labour clung to. Though there were a few years to prepare for the next election, the party continued to reinforce their obsolete beliefs. *Labour's Programme 1982* stated that the party's interest was to 'end the decline of steel' and sought "a highly competitive and efficient coal industry playing a central role in Britain's energy future."[68] In 1981, internal campaign strategy suggested that Labour needed to hold some responsibility for the public's perception that the party was "concerned only to defend the traditional or declining sectors of the economy."[69] The party's research wing concurred that there were issues. In November 1982, the party's Research Secretary Geoff Bish wrote on how Labour was approaching the upcoming election with "many policy gaps... with some of these—such as science and technology or consumer protection—the lack of content in our policies may prove to be embarrassing."[70] The warning signs, though plentiful, were ultimately ignored by Labour leadership.

The 1983 Election Manifesto, *New Hope For Britain,* can be considered an updated version of their election-winning 1976 Manifesto, a socialist statement endorsing another attempt at the Social Contract and industrial intervention. Foot, writing the foreword, spoke of the need to "rebuild our shattered industries."[71] The program stated that Labour's priority if elected would be to "save jobs and stop the further destruction of industry" while giving "priority to the coal industry."[72] Labour MP Gerald Kaufman infamously labeled the document as "the longest suicide note in history."[73] This was the last attempt at sticking to their roots, living and dying with the TUC and highly skilled unions. An abject failure, Labour was on the receiving end of the largest electoral thrashing since their own victory in 1945. Opponents of Labour leadership were confirmed in their beliefs. At the TUC's annual conference shortly following the election, Frank Chapple – TUC General Council member and general secretary of the Electrical, Electronic, Telecommunications and Plumbing Union (EETPU) – said Labour

> ...will have to stop wishing that the world was like it once was and face up to what it is...we will have to appeal to the new working class and not cling to old fashioned definitions from 50 years ago.[74]

Margaret Thatcher's Conservatives took a parliamentary majority, and although Labour kept their opposition status in defeat, the party was in its worst position in over 50 years. It would not return to the majority for 18 years.

4   Conclusion: Lessons Learned From Labour's Collapse

When Labour failed to properly understand their working class support base, it was reflected in their electoral defeats; it was only in 1997, after Tony Blair fundamentally changed the party's structure and relabeled it 'New Labour,' that the party would return to government. Their successes were built off the funding, campaigning, and votes of union members. The Social Contract, though presented as a mutually beneficial agreement between both unions and Labour, became nothing more than another attempt at interfering with workers' bargaining potential. It is a cautionary tale not only for political parties, but also for workers. Willingly signing away power – however little it may seem – runs the risk of disrupting organizing efforts or direct action attempts. The government and workers' alleged allies in Labour became barriers to success just as much as the Conservatives. The Party failed to understand the direction workers were taking in their demographics, their industries, or their organizing methods. As diversity continued to increase and the image of a 'union worker' began to change, Labour clung to its outdated views and lost opportunities to show solidarity with the British working class. No confidence has been placed in Labour to do right by the workers, and the suspicion that Labour will always relapse back to moderation or liberal tendencies remains a constant for a number of former and current supporters of the party.

The Labour Party did not successfully respond to a changing workforce and understand what the average worker now looked like. Coupled with their problems identifying and working with emerging industries, Labour's failures become lessons to other social democratic parties across Europe. Europe's working class is not only far more diverse than ever before, but increasingly non-blue-collar. With the rise of the gig economy, the usefulness of the binary, blue/white-collar classification starts to erode. The definition of the 'traditional' workers is too static for the rapidly changing economic landscape in the West. Drawing on the lessons of Labour's failures, Europe's social democratic parties must respond to a modernizing workforce. This means working with emerging industries to ensure workers have protections and the same rights previously fought for in older, more established sectors. Women and people of color should be actively protected, prioritized, and recruited by social democratic parties.

Although the fine details of the Social Contract and Labour's unique relationship with British unions may not translate into other European countries, their recurring tendencies and symbiotic relationship with workers should be considered. Workers were unafraid to protest against the wishes of their union representatives or leaders, and often did so when it came to matters of preserving Labour's reputation or image in the media. Far-right parties among European countries have seen a sudden surge in popularity and legitimacy, often taking advantage of workers who are frustrated with social democratic parties failing to respond to their needs. In harnessing this frustration, the power of the working class is threatening to be used to further nationalistic, anti-European policies and attitudes. Social democratic parties must regain the confidence of workers in their respective countries, as they may be the key to maintaining the prosperity and order the EU and its members have built over the last decades.

Notes

1 Increasingly so since the early 1980s. See S.D. Ashe, J. Busher, G. Macklin, and A. Winter, eds. *Researching the Far Right: Theory, Method and Practice* (Routledge, 2020), 17–28; 284–301.
2 Isser Woloch, *The Postwar Moment* (New Haven: Yale University Press, 2019), 143.
3 Ibid, 167.
4 Steven Fielding, "Rethinking Labour's 1964 Campaign," *Contemporary British History* 21, no. 3 (2007): 310.
5 Ibid 313.
6 Ibid, 319.
7 Ibid, 318.
8 On the importance of this period of opposition and shift in policy making, see Michael B. Brown, *From Labourism to Socialism: The Political Economy of Labour in the 1970's* (Nottingham: Bertrand Russell Peace Foundation, 1972); Patrick Bell, *The Labour Party in Opposition: 1970–1974* (London; New York: Routledge, 2004); Lewis Minkin, *The Contentious Alliance: Trade Unions and the Labour Party* (Edinburgh: Edinburgh University Press, 1991) with emphasis on the dynamics between unions and Labour, primarily chapter 6 (pp 159–191) and pp 106–127.
9 Harold Wilson, *In Place of Strife,* 2.
10 Introduced by the Conservative Party, this limited the legality of wildcat strikes; forced more 'no strike' clauses in union contracts; and attempted to funnel union strength to leadership and shop stewards, rather than the workers and general members. For further reading, see Sam Warner, "(Re)Politicising 'the Governmental': Resisting the Industrial Relations Act 1971," *The British Journal of Politics and International Relations* 21, no. 3 (August 2019): 541–558.
11 Mark Wickham-Jones, "The Political Economy of the Alternative Economic Strategy: An Analysis of Social Democracy and Economic Policy-Making in the Labour Party, 1970–1983." PhD diss., The University of Manchester, 1994, 192–194.

12 For further reading on definitions of incomes policies, see Jonathan Boston, "The Theory and Practice of Voluntary Incomes Policies with Particular Reference to the British Labour Government's Social Contract 1974–1979." PhD diss., University of Oxford, 1983, 1–25.

13 Wickham-Jones, "The Political Economy of the Alternative Economic Strategy," 354.

14 Quoted in Andrew Taylor, *The Trade Unions and the Labour Party* (London; Wolfeboro: Croom Helm, 1983), 13.

15 Ibid.

16 Ibid, 11.

17 Wickham-Jones, "The Political Economy of the Alternative Economy Strategy," 190.

18 Taylor, *The Trade Unions and the Labour Party,* 19.

19 Quoted in Ibid, 21.

20 Wickham-Jones, "The Political Economy of the Alternative Economic Strategy," 189–190.

21 TUC-Labour Party Liaison Committee, *Economic Policy and the Cost of Living,* 1973.

22 Quoted in Wickham-Jones, "The Political Economy of the Alternative Economic Strategy," 190.

23 Labour Party, *Labour's Programme 1973,* 7.

24 Quoted in Wickham-Jones, "The Political Economy of the Alternative Economic Strategy," 248–249.

25 Ibid, 248.

26 Robert Taylor, "The Rise and Fall of the Social Contract." In *New Labour, Old Labour: The Wilson and Callaghan Governments 1974–1979.* 76.

27 Ibid 77.

28 Ibid.

29 See Michael Artis and David Cobham, *Labour's Economic Policies 1974–1979* (Manchester: Manchester University Press, 1991); and Martin Holmes, *The Labour Government 1974–1979: Political Aims and Economic Reality* (London: Macmillan, 1985) for further reading on the economic situation Labour was elected into.

30 Wickham-Jones, "The Political Economy of the Alternative Economic Strategy," 375–376.

31 Ibid.

32 Ibid.

33 Andrew Thorpe, *A History of the British Labour Party* (Basingstoke: Macmillan, 1997), 177–178.

34 Ibid.

35 Ibid, 179.

36 Quoted in Wickham-Jones, "The Political Economy of the Alternative Economic Strategy," 270.

37 Thorpe, *A History of the British Labour Party,* 178–179.

38 Ibid, 180.

39 Quoted in Wickham-Jones, "The Political Economy of the Alternative Economic Strategy," 268.

40 Polly Toynbee and David Walker, "Social Policy and Inequality" In *New Labour, Old Labour: The Wilson and Callaghan Governments 1974–1979,* 118–120.

41 Quoted in Toynbee and Walker, "Social Policy and Inequality," 119.

42 Quoted in Taylor, *The Trade Unions and the Labour Party,* 96.

43 Ralph Darlington and Stephen Mustchin, "The Role of the TUC in Significant Industrial Disputes: An Historical Critical Overview," *Labor History* 60, no. 6 (2019): 635.

44 Wickham-Jones, "The Political Economy of the Alternative Economy Strategy", 377–378.

45 Colin Hay, "Chronicles of a Death Foretold: The Winter of Discontent and Construction of the Crisis of British Keynesianism," *Parliamentary Affairs* 63, no. 3 (2010): 450–451.

46 Taylor, *The Trade Unions and the Labour Party,* 100.

47 Thorpe, *A History of the British Labour Party,* 183.

48 Wickham-Jones, *The Political Economy of the Alternative Economic Strategy,* 378.

49 Hay, "Chronicles of a Death Foretold," 451.

50 Thrope, *A History of the British Labour Party,* 184.

51 Taylor, *The Trade Unions and the Labour Party,* 104–105; Hay, "Chronicles of a Death Foretold," 455.

52 Hay, "Chronicles of a Death Foretold," 455–456.

53 Toynbee and Walker, "Social Policy and Inequality," 105.

54 Quoted in Richard Jobson, "A New Hope for an Old Britain? Nostalgia and the British Labour Party's Alternative Economic Strategy, 1970–1983," *Journal of Policy History* 27, no. 4 (2015): 684.

55 Audrey Wise, "Women Want a Different Economy," *Workers Control Bulletin,* 1973: 3.

56 This perspective has since gained ground. For example, see Tara Martin López, *The Winter of Discontent: Myth, Memory, and History* (Liverpool: Liverpool University Press, 2014.)

57 Jobson, "A New Hope for an Old Britain?" 683.

58 Brown, *From Labourism to Socialism,* 156.

59 Ibid; G.S. Bain in *Royal Commission on Trade Unions and Employers' Associations* (1968), commonly referred to as the "Donovan Commission/Report" as it was chaired by Terence Donovan.

60 Brown, *From Labourism to Socialism,* 157; George Sayers Bain and Robert Price, *Profiles of Union Growth: A Comparative Statistical Portrait of Eight Countries* (Oxford: Basil Blackwell, 1980), 38–42 (Tables 2.1–2.3).

61 Jack McGowan, "'Dispute, 'Battle', 'Siege', 'Farce'? –– Grunwick 30 Years On," *Contemporary British History* 22, no. 3 (2008): 385.

62 Ralph Darlington and Stephen Mustchin. "The Role of the TUC in Significant Industrial Disputes: An Historical Critical Overview." *Labor History* 60, no. 6 (2019): 634.

63 McGowan, "Dispute, 'Battle', 'Siege', 'Farce?" 385.

64 Darlington and Mustchin, "The Role of the TUC in Significant Industrial Disputes," 634.

65 Quoted in Ibid.

66 Quoted in McGowan, "Dispute, 'Battle', 'Siege', 'Farce?," 392.

67 Darlington and Mustchin, "The Role of the TUC in Significant Industrial Disputes," 634–635.

68 The Labour Party, *Labour's Programme 1982* (London, 1982), 48.

69 Jobson, "A New Hope for an Old Britain?" 677.

70 Quoted in Ibid, 678.

71 The Labour Party, *The New Hope for Britain: Labour's Manifesto 1983* (London, 1983), 4.

72 Ibid, 14.

73 Nyta Mann, "Foot's Message of Hope to Left," *BBC News*, July 14, 2003. http:// news.bbc.co.uk/2/hi/uk_news/politics/3059773.stm Retrieved October 4, 2021.
74 Quoted in Jobson, "A New Hope for an Old Britain?" 678.

Bibliography

Artis, Michael, and David Cobham, eds. *Labour's Economic Policies 1974–1979.* Manchester: Manchester University Press, 1991.

Ashe, S.D., Joel Busher, Graham Macklin, and Aaron Winter, eds. *Researching the Far Right: Theory, Method and Practice.* London: Routledge, 2020.

Bain, George Sayers, and Robert Price. *Profiles of Union Growth: A Comparative Statistical Portrait of Eight Countries.* Oxford: Basil Blackwell, 1980.

Barratt Brown, Michael. *From Labourism to Socialism: The Political Economy of Labour in the 1970's.* Nottingham: Bertrand Russell Peace Foundation, 1972.

Bell, Patrick. *The Labour Party in Opposition: 1970–1974.* London; New York: Routledge, 2004.

Boston, Jonathan. "The Theory and Practice of Voluntary Incomes Policies with Particular Reference to the British Labour Government's Social Contract 1974– 1979." PhD diss., University of Oxford, 1983.

Darlington, Ralph, and Stephen Mustchin. "The Role of the TUC in Significant Industrial Disputes: An Historical Critical Overview." *Labor History* 60, no. 6 (2019): 626–645.

Fielding, Steven. "Rethinking Labour's 1964 Campaign." *Contemporary British History* 21, no. 3 (2007): 309–324.

Hay, Colin. "Chronicles of a Death Foretold: The Winter of Discontent and Construction of the Crisis of British Keynesianism." *Parliamentary Affairs* 63, no. 3 (2010): 446–470.

Holmes, Martin. *The Labour Government 1974–1979: Political Aims and Economic Reality.* London: Macmillan, 1985.

Jobson, Richard. "A New Hope for an Old Britain? Nostalgia and the British Labour Party's Alternative Economic Strategy, 1970–1983." *Journal of Policy History* 27, no. 4 (2015): 670–694.

López, Tara Martin. *The Winter of Discontent: Myth, Memory, and History.* Liverpool: Liverpool University Press, 2014.

Mann, Nyta. "Foot's Message of Hope to Left," *BBC News*, 14 July 2003. http:// news.bbc.co.uk/2/hi/uk_news/politics/3059773.stm. Accessed 4 October 2021.

McGowan, Jack. "'Dispute', 'Battle', 'Siege', 'Farce'? – Grunwick 30 Years On." *Contemporary British History* 22, no. 3 (2008): 383–406.

Minkin, Lewis. *The Contentious Alliance: Trade Unions and the Labour Party.* Edinburgh: Edinburgh University Press, 1991.

Seldon, Anthony, and Kevin Hickson, eds. *New Labour, Old Labour: The Blair, Wilson and Callaghan Governments.* London; New York: Routledge, 2004.

Taylor, Andrew. *The Trade Unions and the Labour Party.* London; Wolfeboro: Croom Helm, 1987.

The Labour Party. *Labour's Programme 1982.* London: Labour Party, 1982.

The Labour Party. *The New Hope for Britain: Labour's Manifesto 1983.* London: Labour Party, 1983.

Thorpe, Andrew. *A History of the British Labour Party.* Basingstoke: Macmillan, 1997.

TUC-Labour Party Liaison Committee. *Economic Policy and the Cost of Living.* London: Labour Party, 1973.

Warner, Sam. "(Re)Politicising 'the Governmental': Resisting the Industrial Relations Act 1971." *The British Journal of Politics and International Relations* 21, no. 3 (August 2019): 541–558.

Wickham-Jones, Mark. "The Political Economy of the Alternative Economic Strategy: An Analysis of Social Democracy and Economic Policy-Making in the Labour Party, 1970–1983." PhD diss., The University of Manchester, 1994.

Wilson, Harold and Barbara Castle. *In Place of Strife.* London: Labour Party, 1969.

Wise, Audrey. "Women Want a Different Economy." *Workers Control Bulletin,* 1973.

Woloch, Isser. *The Postwar Moment.* New Haven: Yale University Press, 2019.

2 State of Pandemic

Opportunity or Challenge for Far-Right Populist Parties? The Case of the *Alternative für Deutschland* Party

Ali Cain

1 Introduction

On 29 August 2020, over 38,000 Germans protested coronavirus lockdown measures in Berlin. Demonstrators were from various and intersecting groups, including anti-vaxxers, devoted QAnon followers, and far-right extremists. Many were supporters of the *Alternative für Deutschland* (AfD) Party, Germany's leading far-right populist party.[1] They attempted to storm the Reichstag, the meeting place of the German Parliament (Bundestag) but were blocked by police and barricades. Not only did these protestors attack a prominent symbol of German democracy but many did so carrying red, black, and white imperial flags that are the new symbol of the far-right. Some made Nazi salutes while trying to get into the Reichstag.

It is almost unthinkable that the far-right would make such a blatant attack on democracy in Germany, a country so connected to the crimes it committed during the Second World War that it was one of the last states in Western Europe where the most recent wave of far-right parties gained popularity. However, the AfD has followed other right-wing groups in making extremism, racism, and xenophobia a rallying cry against contemporary Western civil and political norms. Throughout the coronavirus pandemic, the party criticized Chancellor Angela Merkel's handling of the crisis, arguing that national lockdowns hurt the economy and that mask mandates infringe on Germans' constitutional rights.[2] Subsequently, it encouraged its supporters through social media to protest lockdown measures and reclaim their civil and political liberties.

Although support for European far-right populist parties has surged since the refugee crisis in 2015, the pandemic challenged their appeal.[3] An October 2020 YouGov poll found that positive attitudes toward populists in eight different European countries – including Germany – significantly decreased in 2020.[4] Throughout the COVID-19 crisis, the global far-right towed similar lines: criticism of government lockdowns, skepticism of masks and vaccines, and the embrace of common conspiracy theories. Its efforts to discredit scientific experts is part of the populist crusade to challenge the

DOI: 10.4324/9781003182344-3

'elite.' It is unclear how the pandemic will shape populists' political trajectory long term but state elections in Germany in both 2020 and 2021 demonstrated that there continues to be support for traditional ruling parties.[5] In Baden-Württemberg and Rhineland-Palatinate, the Greens and Social Democrats, respectively, kept their leadership positions while the AfD lost a third of its total voting share in each state.[6] In Sachsen Anhalt, the AfD was expected to become the ruling party but fell behind Merkel's Christian Democrats. Populists' falling popularity may not be permanent, however. As the pandemic wanes in the West, issues like migration will resurface as top political priorities for voters.[7] We should therefore see populists, especially on the far-right, as being down but not entirely out.[8]

The coronavirus pandemic is one case study that serves to answer the larger question of how populists change their political strategies during times of crisis. Since the AfD entered office in 2017, no crisis has presented as big of a challenge to the party's appeal as the pandemic. As government criticism and migration issues are core tenets of the far-right's platform, the COVID-19 crisis presents an important opportunity to assess whether these ideological pillars remain intact or if parties rely on additional grievances to maintain support. In answering the question of how far-right populist parties change their political strategies during a crisis, I define a party's political strategy as the content of a party's public communication with potential supporters. Utilizing the AfD as a case study within the larger COVID-19 crisis, I analyzed all 1,012 posts shared on the party's Facebook page before the pandemic began on 2 January 2020, and until the end of the crisis' first year on 30 December 2020. Although the AfD has various Facebook accounts to serve its different regional branches, I chose its federal party's account to analyze since all material posted to its page is relevant to the whole party and not a specific branch.

Generally, I selected Facebook as the unit of analysis as social media is the preferred communication medium for populists and allows them to circumvent the traditional media, ignore criticism, and speak directly to voters. My research explores not only the issues that the AfD has focused on during the pandemic, but also how they utilize social media to communicate with their supporters, particularly during times of crisis. By analyzing their strategies during crises, we can better understand how electorates respond to far-right populists and, in turn, how these parties incorporate new issues to try to appeal to more potential voters.

As is demonstrated below, during the coronavirus crisis, the AfD not only maintained government criticism and migration issues as main strategies, it added grievances over culture issues that invoke partisan divides, historical memory, and loss of identity as new tools to attract broad support. This finding is an important contribution to the understanding of far-right populist parties' short- and long-term trajectories in Europe. It is crucial to understand these trajectories, as far-right populist parties have increasingly come to challenge both democratic stability in individual European states as well as the political cohesion of the European Union (EU) as a whole.

2 Far-right Populism

In order to make sense of the narrative put forward by the AfD during the coronavirus crisis, it is important to first understand its operation as a far-right populist party. To define populism, I rely on Cas Mudde's ideational approach that populism is "an ideology that considers society to be separated into two homogeneous and antagonistic groups, 'the pure people' versus 'the corrupt elite'...which argues that politics should be an expression of the general will of the people."[9] Mudde and others believe that populism is a thin-centered ideology in which the party's platform "can evolve fitfully and quickly, is incoherent and contradictory, and made up of various ideological fragments."[10] The thin-centered nature of populist ideology is evident in many parties, including the AfD, as they incorporate emotionally charged issues into their rhetoric and strategy as new problems arise.[11]

When looking at differences among right-wing and left-wing populists, each side's interpretation of the in- and out-group supports Mudde's ideational approach. Despite regional differences or various approaches to domestic issues, far-right and far-left populists have their own ideas of who composes the in- and out-groups. Left-wing populists "champion the people against an elite or establishment" and view the bottom and middle classes together against the corrupt upper class.[12] Far-left populists usually view multinational corporations, wealthy individuals, and supranational institutions as enemies. Traditional parties are chastised for being too moderate, upholding the status quo, and being beholden to outside powers, including corporations, lobbying groups, and international institutions. Right-wing populists believe that the elite coddles out-groups such as immigrants and minority communities. Compared to the left, they attack not only the ruling class but groups that are outsiders and receive special privileges from elites.[13] Although left-wing populism in Europe gained increased popularity following the Eurozone crisis in 2010, right-wing populism is currently more prevalent.[14]

The far-right's authoritarian reflexes pose tangible threats to many European democracies.[15] Despite claims that they will reinstate a democracy that is representative of the will of the people, many right-wing populists adopt authoritarian stances and policies. Pippa Norris and Ronald Inglehart argue that they demand conformity, security, and loyalty which lead to authoritarian impulses.[16] These parties employ authoritarian approaches to not only attract voters but to validate the abolishment of institutional constraints that empower them while slowly eroding democracy. This chapter focuses on the far-right rather than the far-left, as its popularity poses a significant threat to democratic norms throughout Europe, particularly given that there are over 50 European political parties currently classified as authoritarian populists.[17]

2.1 Direct Voter Contact: Social Media Strategies of the Far-Right

An important strategy of the far-right, especially those with authoritarian reflexes, is to circumvent the traditional media. Popular social media platforms, especially Facebook and Twitter, allow populists to bypass mainstream news outlets and communicate directly with supporters.[18] Many view the media as an extension of the establishment and argue that traditional media outlets are biased in not giving their party sufficient attention or, when they do, publishing negative or untrue coverage. Yves Mény and Yves Surel believe that some populists, like former United Kingdom Independence Party (UKIP) leader Nigel Farage, utilize the media for attention by feeding journalists provocative statements that attack opponents.[19] Most far-right populists, though, see the media as a threat, with some using the Nazi-era term 'Lügenpresse' (lying press) to discredit mainstream outlets.[20]

Due to their distrust of the media, populists rely on social media platforms to disseminate their messages. Donald Trump is a prime example of a far-right populist who used Twitter to his advantage; during his presidential campaign and term in office, he amassed 88 million followers, most of whom espoused his viewpoints. Trump criticized his enemies and announced policies in 280 characters or less. Far-right populists in Europe have adopted Trump's strategy, relying on social media to communicate with voters. Benjamin Krämer argues that populists favor social media because they are largely uncensored and do not face challenges to their claims. If someone questions information in a post, the comment can either be ignored or deleted.[21] Platforms like Facebook and Twitter allow for popularity cues and provide the notion that the party's beliefs and statements are correct and well supported. Informal approval through likes or positive reactions usually outnumber critical comments.[22] If there is negative feedback, it can be manipulated to argue that the party and the 'true people' are under attack.[23]

Populists also use social media to deepen echo chambers. Facebook and Twitter further entrench populist viewpoints, limit genuine debate, and advance political and societal polarization. False information is additionally spread through social media as many groups repost articles from far-right news sources or promote common conspiracy theories, augmenting support. Hate speech has significantly proliferated through online platforms as well, challenging basic civic values and normalizing racism, xenophobia, and misogyny. The echo chamber, created by online sites, helps to justify hateful beliefs and viewpoints.[24] Social media grants far-right populists a platform to test, refine, and project their political strategies.

Far-right populism has taken a hold throughout Europe partly through social media platforms that allow parties to speak directly with voters.

By using Facebook and Twitter, populists reinforce the belief that they are the only ones who have a direct connection with constituents and will therefore always fight for them. The far-right's reliance on social media as a strategic tool normalizes authoritarian reflexes. Although the parties present themselves as the protectors of democracy, they employ sites like Facebook to deepen societal divisions that may later allow for democratic backsliding.

3 Maintaining the Status Quo or Leveraging a Crisis? Theorizing Populist Parties' Crisis Response

Given the existing literature on how populist parties utilize social media during times of normalcy, I sought to answer how these parties change their political strategies during a crisis. By analyzing the AfD's Facebook posts throughout the coronavirus pandemic, I assess how the party utilizes Facebook to communicate issues to supporters. My analysis is grounded in the following three hypotheses:

> *H1: During a crisis, one of the main strategies of populist parties will continue to be government criticism and presenting themselves as outsiders.*

Government criticism is foundational to populist ideology, especially in terms of upholding the appearance of being an outsider. By distancing themselves from the political establishment, populists argue that they have new solutions to old problems and blame the political establishment for failing to implement the will of the true people. Tom Louwerse and Simon Otjes conclude that populist parties in national parliaments but not part of ruling governments are more likely to scrutinize the government than engage in policymaking.[25] Although it is possible for them to both scrutinize the government and propose legislation, Louwerse and Otjes' case study of Dutch populist parties concluded that those on the far-right and far-left mainly criticized the ruling government. They argue, "many parties do not seek a role of constructive opposition and just want to expose failures and limitations of the incumbents."[26] Representation is more important than policymaking, as cooperation and the passing of legislation would legitimize the system that populists are supposedly against.

Populists' concentration on government criticism will continue and, in fact, heighten during a crisis. To maintain their popularity, parties will criticize the ruling government for taking either too benign or too drastic action. Doing so allows populists to advance negative feelings toward the political establishment and sustain favorability with their supporters. During the pandemic, those on the far-right have attacked ruling governments for implementing lockdowns and mask mandates. At times, they have also criticized the government for not implementing lockdowns or closing borders fast enough. Instead of offering pragmatic solutions to a crisis, far-right populists instead condemn ruling politicians and present themselves as the only party that can mitigate current problems. They seek to retain their outsider image by arguing that the establishment is failing to properly address citizens' concerns and cannot handle the crisis. By criticizing the government and maintaining ambiguous policies, far-right populists try to use their outsider status to appeal to all.

> *H2: Populist parties will continue to criticize the government even when the government adopts a particular issue of the populist party as part of their agenda.*

At times, ruling parties may adopt populist parties' positions to maintain power. Takis Pappas' populist democracies theory concludes that traditional parties incorporate populist positions into their policies to appeal to estranged voters and cultivate public support.[27] He found that traditional parties in both Greece and Hungary became more populist after the Pasok and Fidesz parties, respectively, gained power. Pappas argues that traditional parties' acceptance of populist policies often leads to higher political instability as competition between both groups hardens two-party systems and intensifies polarized pluralism.

During a crisis, far-right policies such as the closing of borders may receive more support among the ruling parties. In Europe, politicians like Marine Le Pen of the French National Rally[28] have consistently called for borders to be closed to asylum seekers and migrants, particularly during the refugee crisis. Throughout the pandemic, Europe's external borders have been shut to non-EU residents to decrease travel and combat rising infection rates. Far-right positions were therefore adopted with border closures. When governments assume these positions, populists have three possible options: take credit for the policy, criticize the government for stealing their proposal, or move on to different issues in order to distance themselves from the political establishment and uphold their outsider image. Since borders remain closed to asylum seekers and migrants, far-right populists will shift their focus from condemning migration influxes to criticizing the government for disregarding concerns related to integration, abuse of the state's welfare system, and national security issues. Although cultural grievances related to migration have traditionally been at the center of the far-right's platform, their focus will increase. Right-wing populists will argue that even in the middle of a pandemic, the coalition government still caters to migrants and asylum seekers, at the expense of its citizens.

> *H3: Populist parties will continue to focus on the issues that have made them popular.*

During the pandemic, support for populists decreased while approval ratings for ruling politicians increased throughout Europe. To stay relevant, populist parties pushed issues that were seen as directly impacting voters to appeal to their supporters' viewpoints. Previous literature theorizes that economic grievances drive populism as globalization has stagnated wages, eliminated traditional industries, and increased inequality, leading to a displacement of low-wage workers. Norris and Inglehart's cultural backlash theory challenges the narrative that economic grievances are responsible for populism. They argue a shift in post-war values from the prioritization of economic security to individual freedom is provoking a significant identity crisis among Europe's older generations that cultivates fears of societal and cultural displacement.[29]

As Norris states, "many socially conservative people feel that their basic values are being eroded by rapid cultural change, a feeling reinforced by growing ethnic diversity and the specter of Islamic terrorism."[30] The adoption of more liberal values by younger generations, structural changes like urbanization and access to higher education, and increasing diversity are deepening cultural cleavages and pushing older generations toward conservatism. Far-right populists manipulate these concerns, as Norris argues:

> the grievances and resentment exploited by Authoritarian-Populists has helped legitimize xenophobic and misogynistic forces, making bigotry respectable in some circles and providing an avenue for its expression at the ballot box. The perceptions of threat among traditionalists have been activated by the message of Authoritarian-Populists, emphasizing fears of threats from 'outsiders' and criticizing the establishment for not responding to genuine public concerns.[31]

Taking into account Norris and Inglehart's cultural backlash theory and the in-group versus out-group divide that is fundamental to populist ideology, it can be assumed that populists will continue to concentrate on traditional issues – especially cultural grievances – during crises to sustain support. Given that the AfD rose to power by tapping into Germans' fears related to newly arrived migrants and asylum seekers, the party is expected to maintain its focus on cultural issues connected to migration.

If confirmed, all three hypotheses would demonstrate that during times of crisis, the AfD targets the issues that made it popular, especially government criticism and cultural anxieties around migration. Understanding the issues that the AfD and far-right populist parties incorporate into their strategies is important in assessing the long-term viability and direction of Europe's far-right. Discourse that justifies hatred and violence toward asylum seekers and heightens distrust toward the government may facilitate deeper political divisions, societal discord, and larger democratic instability in different European states that pose a threat to the EU's future.

3.1 Far-Right Parties in Times of Crisis: The Evolution of the AfD Party's Political Strategy From the Eurozone Crisis to the Coronavirus Pandemic

In assessing parties that may change their political strategies during a crisis, and particularly the coronavirus pandemic, the AfD stands out as a case study for three reasons. First, the party already changed its political strategy between the Eurozone and refugee crises.[32] As will be discussed below, the AfD was founded out of resistance to the Eurozone crisis bailouts. However, it quickly transformed into Germany's main opposition against the traditional parties and specifically against immigration. The party has successfully used social media to communicate with voters and has the largest social media following of all of Germany's six political parties.[33] Second, Germany initially handled the COVID-19 outbreak well, leading to increased support for the Merkel government. Although it experienced multiple infection waves, Merkel's approval rating remained above 83% at the time of writing.[34] The AfD's favorability among the German electorate has fallen to a steady 10%, its lowest approval rating since entering the Bundestag, indicating that the pandemic has decreased its support.[35] Finally, the AfD is significant in looking at the threat that far-right populism poses to Germany's political status quo. The party is not the first right-wing party to emerge in Germany after the Second World War, but it is the most successful thus far.[36] Germany was one of the last countries in which the far-right was able to establish a foothold, as its history with national socialism had hitherto prevented such parties from gaining popularity.[37] The AfD's success raises questions about whether the memory of the Second World War will continue to define and shape Germany's approach to future national and EU politics.

The AfD has transformed from a group of elites who wished to pose a 'conservative challenge' to the Christian Democratic Union of Germany (CDU) to an Islamophobic party that embraces populist far-right ideology. It was founded by former CDU supporters, academics, and economists who were opposed to the EU's bailouts and reforms during the Eurozone crisis. The party was not as Eurosceptic as traditional populists; it supported the EU as an institution but wished for Germany to exit the Eurozone.[38] It also claimed that Merkel moved the party too far to the left on socially conservative issues like gay marriage, and sought to attract CDU voters who believed the chancellor was "gradually eroding the CDU's ideological distinctiveness."[39] Some AfD members, including Alice Weidel, stoked cultural grievances and laid the foundation for the party's current platform. In 2013, Weidel's published emails revealed significant xenophobic rhetoric such as, "The reason why we are overrun by culturally foreign people such as Arabs, Sinti and Roma is the systematic destruction of civil society as a possible counterweight from the enemies of the constitution by whom we are governed."[40] At the time, immigration, and therefore cultural concerns, were not a defining voting issue. Neither the AfD's more extreme members like Weidel nor the party's anti-bailout platform struck a chord with Germans, resulting in the party narrowly missing the 5% threshold needed to enter the Bundestag in the 2013 election. The AfD's lack of popularity and party infighting led to a substantial leadership and structural transformation between 2014 and 2017.[41]

Although government criticism had always been a part of the AfD's strategy, immigration became the second pillar of its revised platform for the 2017 election. Most notably, the AfD capitalized on fears over cultural differences and became the primary opposition voice against Merkel's open-border policies during the refugee crisis. When the crisis began, former party leader Frauke Petry stated, "police should have the right to shoot illegal migrants at the border if necessary," while former party deputy Beatrix von Storch wrote on Facebook that the German Border Guards should use weapons against female refugees with children.[42] According to Dilling, "the AfD draws a picture of a German nation whose inner security, welfare system and identity are threatened by the spread of Islam and mass migration."[43] The party connects refugees and Muslims with terrorism and crime. For example, the AfD referenced the New Year's Eve assaults in Cologne in 2015, when men of migrant background attacked German women at a public celebration, to argue that all refugees are dangerous.[44] The party also believes that Islam is incompatible with the German identity.[45]

When comparing the AfD's 2013 and 2017 manifestos, it is hard to believe that they represent the same party. For example, the 2013 manifesto has three points on migration that includes improving integration and reforming Germany's asylum system to ensure that those facing persecution will receive protection.[46] In comparison, the 2017 manifesto has five pages on migration issues. The AfD calls for the closing of the EU's external borders, controls along Germany's borders, and the creation of asylum centers near countries of origin.[47] The 2017 manifesto demands minimum annual deportation quotas, restrictions on Islamic practices, and the denial of citizenship opportunities, including permanent residence status, for refugees. [48] Considering Dilling's conclusion that voters who believed immigration was a cultural threat to the German identity were almost 4.5 times more likely to vote for the AfD, we can consider this strategy to be largely successful.[49] Exit polls from the 2017 election show that 44% of German voters believed that refugees and integration were the most important voting issue.[50] By manipulating violent incidents and nurturing concerns over cultural differences, the AfD deepened xenophobia into its larger strategy alongside its criticism of the mainstream parties.

The AfD's anti-immigrant and anti-establishment platform succeeded in recruiting voters from different parties and sources during the 2017 election. A study found that 31% of voters came from former nonvoters, 26% from previous CDU and Christian Social Union (CSU) supporters, [51] and

12% from former Social Democratic Party of Germany (SPD) voters, among other groups.[52] The AfD is supported throughout Germany but has its largest base in the East.[53] Its popularity among voters forced the traditional parties to reconfigure their coalition design, allowing the AfD to also become the biggest opposition party in the Bundestag. After the election, Merkel's CDU tried to form a coalition with two minority parties, the Greens and the Free Democrats (FDP). Although the SPD received the second highest number of votes after the CDU, it wanted to remain outside of the coalition government to become the largest opposition party and challenge the CDU's policies in an effort to bolster its declining support.[54] When coalition talks collapsed between the CDU and FDP over migration, the SPD was forced out of opposition. It took five months to create the current government, the longest formation period in Germany's history.[55] The 2017 election results, and the difficulties in creating a coalition government after, demonstrate the AfD's growing significance to voters and establishment parties. Despite being outside of the coalition government, the AfD still disrupted traditional politics and may do so in the future.

While adopting a xenophobic and highly conservative platform, the party's success is also a result of presenting itself as professional and legitimate. According to Frankland, the AfD has been more successful than other populists because it is well-organized, invests in a public relations strategy, and focuses on popular issues.[56] The AfD's founders and subsequent leaders have political experience and professional contacts, as they were previously members of the CDU, universities, and nongovernmental organizations. The party's membership expanded from 17,687 in 2013 to 34,751 in 2019, demonstrating that its efforts reached more voters.[57]

Scholars also debate the role of historical memory in the AfD's platform and voter support. Some argue that many Germans, especially in the East, are beginning to revolt against institutionalized taboos on voting for far-right candidates and parties. Although the AfD appeals to those on the far-right who may hold antisemitic beliefs, the party's federal leadership makes a concrete effort to distance itself from antisemitism. It has posted various declarations of support for Israel and decries attacks against Jews. State leaders including Andreas Kalbitz, former party head in Brandenburg, have been ousted for holding membership in a neo-Nazi group.[58] Björn Höcke, the AfD's most controversial and right-wing leader, has been condemned various times by the party as well. Höcke has made incendiary comments regarding the Holocaust and led the AfD's former radical branch *die Flügel* before it was dissolved in March 2020.[59] Distancing itself from its extreme branches allows current party leaders Jörg Meuthen and Tino Chrupalla to claim plausible deniability and separate the AfD from antisemitism and, therefore, the taboo of national socialism. Although the AfD distances itself from antisemitism, many party members argue that Germany needs to be free from its 'guilt' around the Holocaust and should be proud of its long history. For example, at an AfD youth group's conference in 2018, former party leader Alexander Gauland stated, "Germany has a glorious history and one that lasted a lot longer than those damned 12 years. Hitler and the Nazis are just a speck of bird shit in over 1,000 years of successful German history."[60] The AfD challenges Germany's historical memory as part of its political strategy.[61]

The AfD gained significant support since its founding in 2013, although its popularity has waned since the 2017 election. A Bertelsmann Foundation study concluded that populist support began to decline in 2019 and that only 20% of voters identified as populist in 2020 due to more Germans returning to the political center. The decrease in populist support may continue for three reasons. First, the AfD's growing entanglement with extremism could turn more moderate voters off. In March 2021, Germany's Federal Office for the Protection of the Constitution announced that it was placing the party's federal branch under official watch. While under surveillance, the party's communications and financial transactions will be observed due to its "attacks on human dignity, rejection of the rule of law and anti-democratic positions."[62] The Office also previously announced that three state branches would undergo surveillance as well. Historical memory may be under discussion in Germany, but it still has a significant presence and could increasingly deter voters from supporting a party that is deemed a threat to democracy.

Second, the coalition government has implemented policies that appeal to voters, especially those on the center-right. It has enacted tougher immigration policies by increasing deportations, especially of those with criminal backgrounds, which is a favorable policy among those concerned about migration and crime.[63] With Merkel's retirement, former CDU voters who voted for the AfD as a protest against Merkel may be more inclined to return to the CDU.

Finally, the COVID-19 crisis has increased support for the coalition government and decreased favorable opinions toward the AfD. During Germany's first wave of infections in April 2020, Merkel's approval rating was at an all time high of 82%.[64] Even in February 2021, when the country experienced its third infection wave, eight out of ten Germans reported that the government did a 'good' job managing the crisis.[65] Although Merkel retired in September 2021, her party's management of the crisis may continue to deter voters from supporting the AfD in the short and long term.

3.2 Measuring the AfD's Support through the Pandemic

In analyzing whether government criticism and migration issues continue to define the AfD's strategy during the pandemic, I collected the party's Facebook posts from 2 January 2020 to 30 December 2020. I was intentional about my timeline as I sought to gather posts that were right before the first coronavirus case was detected in Germany on 27 January 2020. Within this time period, I was able to analyze the evolution of the AfD's discourse slightly before and throughout the crisis.

In choosing which social media platform to analyze, I decided on the AfD's federal party's Facebook page. The AfD has different Facebook pages, including its Bundestag group, European Parliament group, regional branches, and party leaders. I selected the federal party's page as it has the most followers and also disseminates the AfD's main platform and strategy, as opposed to a specific branch or individual leader's interests.[66] Facebook was chosen because the party's page has five times as many followers as the AfD's Twitter account.[67]

I documented all of the AfD's posts and included each posts' date, text in German, text in English, and a category classification. I did not create prearranged categories but instead coded each by topic, which allowed 16 broad categories to emerge naturally. Most of the AfD's posts focused on multiple issues, which I categorized based on the themes presented. For example, if a post criticized Merkel for the COVID-19 lockdown, I coded the post as part of the 'COVID-19' and 'Government Criticism' categories. The AfD's content also produced four party leaders as categories: Jörg Meuthen, Tino Chrupalla, Alice Weidel, and Beatrix von Storch. The inclusion of these leaders was not predetermined; it emerged as a result of the AfD's reposting of their content on its main page. I also created an 'Other' category for posts that did not fit into the 15 other categories. Figure 2.1 contains my final analysis of the posts divided into the 16 categories.

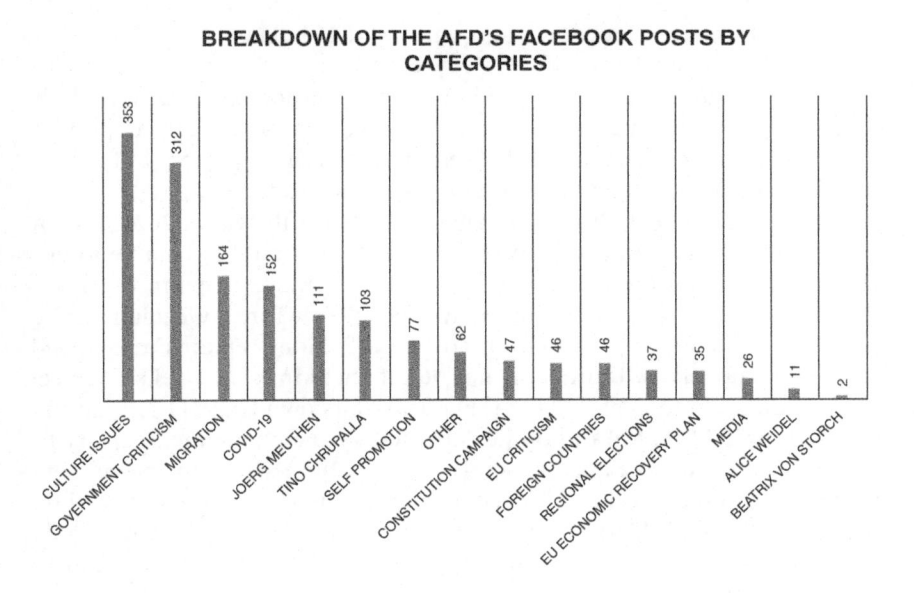

BREAKDOWN OF THE AFD'S FACEBOOK POSTS BY CATEGORIES

Figure 2.1 Breakdown of the AfD's Facebook Posts in 16 different categories.

3.3 Breaking Down the AfD's Political Strategies: Embracing Culture War Issues

The data reveals that the AfD maintained its two-pronged strategy of government criticism and criticism of migration throughout the coronavirus crisis. Additionally, it shows that culture issues became one of the central features of the party's platform. Below I analyze the data and draw conclusions in the context of my hypotheses.

H1: During a crisis, one of the main strategies of populist parties will continue to be government criticism and presenting themselves as outsiders.

The AfD's persistent criticism of the government throughout the analysis period demonstrated that the party still presents itself as an outsider and sustains its narrative that the coalition government is not implementing the will of the true people. Most of its criticism centered on Merkel. This is not totally surprising as her position as Chancellor makes her the obvious target. More concretely, her 16-year tenure as Chancellor deepened the AfD's portrayal of Merkel as an establishment politician who cannot be trusted. Other AfD targets included the grand coalition government, members of Merkel's party like Health Minister Jens Spahn, and SPD leaders.

The COVID-19 crisis was the biggest issue for which the AfD criticized the government, with the party consistently finding fault with government action toward the pandemic. However, its criticism shifted from blaming Merkel and Spahn for failure to act against COVID-19 sooner to denouncing the government-imposed lockdown and questioning the medical and scientific communities. This change in strategy correlates with rising support for Merkel's coronavirus policies as public opinion responded positively to the government's pandemic management. By focusing on socially unpopular issues like mask wearing, the AfD faulted Merkel's government to keep animosity toward elites high and preserve its outsider appeal.

The AfD's first post about the pandemic was on 10 March 2020. It complained that those who had COVID-19 symptoms would be unable to visit doctors because of the lockdown.[68] The party criticized Spahn for downplaying the virus and not acting sooner. Meuthen wrote, "Germany is facing a catastrophe: If the growth of corona infections remains unchanged, ventilation capacity will probably not be sufficient in a few weeks. We need an immediate shutdown!"[69] The AfD released its own COVID-19 plan that included: protection for all families affected by the pandemic; security for the self-employed, freelancers, small- and medium-sized businesses, and craftsmen; a rescue package for the tourism industry; fast internet without price increases for all citizens; and ensuring the food supply for the population and agriculture.[70] Some posts additionally called for more financial aid and tax cuts for businesses.

At the pandemic's onset, the federal government increased its 'Kurzarbeit' program which subsidizes workers' wages for lost hours to maintain employment and alleviate the pandemic's economic consequences.[71] The ruling coalition also provided financial aid and tax cuts to companies and gave cash handouts to vulnerable groups.[72] Although Germany's economy contracted by 1.8% in the first quarter of 2021, the European Commission predicted strong economic growth throughout the EU for the remainder of the year.[73]

Merkel played an important role not only in steering the German economy through the coronavirus crisis but in negotiating the EU's €750 billion economic recovery plan as well. The plan gave aid to states hurt most by the pandemic and deepened economic integration by allowing the European Commission to borrow money off of the international market.[74] It also pooled together the different EU Member States' securities in what has been called 'corona bonds.' Germany is eligible to receive 25.6% of funds from the plan, which will further strengthen its pandemic recovery.[75] The AfD criticized the EU and disagreed with the recovery funds in 35 posts, taking a similar line to its 2013 rhetoric criticizing the use of German tax funds for other countries' recoveries. For instance, Meuthen posted,

> Various countries are now demanding that Germans should be held liable for their next debt orgy, which has already begun. What the media likes to hide from citizens: The average citizens in these countries are much wealthier than the Germans![76]

Meuthen expressed further outrage over corona bonds by commenting, "Thanks to Merkel, there are now corona bonds... the debt-addicted Mediterranean countries can continue to distribute social benefits to their citizens on pumps, and we Germans are now being held directly accountable for this."[77] Although 65% of Germans opposed corona bonds in a March 2020 survey, the government's acceptance of and leadership in finalizing the plan did not hurt Merkel, as her approval ratings remained between 70% and 82% throughout spring and summer 2020.[78] The AfD's critique of the economic recovery plan receded as the party turned to more controversial issues that impact daily life like mask wearing.

Comparing the AfD's posts from March 2020 to November 2020, it is apparent that its approach changed from criticizing the government for not doing enough to doing too much. After March, most of its commentary condemned Merkel for imposing lockdowns, assuming too much power, infringing on human rights, and hurting the economy. On 31 March 2020, Chrupalla posted,

> The unlimited corona laws are a blatant interference with our fundamental rights...those responsible will have to ask themselves later

whether all this would not have been at least largely avoidable. Together with the responsible bodies of the party, we are already developing an exit strategy for Germany.[79]

Many of its posts claimed that Merkel created a 'corona hysteria' and argued that the German economy must remain open. The party also incorporated common right-wing misinformation: masks do not work, the imposition of masks is an infringement on Germans' civil and political liberties, and everyone should question the vaccine. The AfD additionally praised countries which did not initially mandate a lockdown and wanted to rely on herd immunity, such as Sweden.

The party used Merkel's response to COVID-19 to heighten its appearance as an outsider party. For example, Chrupalla wrote,

> For weeks, hundreds of emails and letters from citizens have reached me regarding the planned Civil Protection Act. Everyone is writing that they have concerns and now even fears for our constitutional state, democracy, and the economic and social future of our country. We, the AfD, are the only party that gives these citizens a credible and consistent voice in public and parliaments.[80]

The data therefore confirms the first hypothesis that, during a crisis, far-right populist parties continue to rely heavily on government criticism as a political strategy and present themselves as outsiders. Doing so allows them to shape frustration with emergency measures into opposition to the ruling party or parties.

> *H2: Populist parties will continue to criticize the government even when the government adopts a particular issue of the populist party as part of their agenda.*

In determining whether this hypothesis holds true, it is useful to look at the data regarding migration. Since opposition to migration propelled the AfD into its current prominent position, one would assume that the party would keep posting about it. However, with Germany's borders closed because of COVID-19, the coalition government indirectly adopted an AfD policy. Nevertheless, the data makes clear that the party maintained its xenophobic strategy despite the coalition government's restrictions on migration. In fact, the number of posts about migration were higher than the number of posts about COVID-19. The AfD criticized the government for the ongoing refugee crisis and for agreeing to accept refugees from Greece in September 2020. Most of its posts focused on crime among migrant communities and cultural grievances. As the government adopted a closed border policy, the AfD increased its written attacks against asylum seekers and migrants by expounding on cultural concerns.

There were two main themes in posts about migration: fear of future refugee influxes and the challenge immigrants pose to German culture and society. The party wrote the most about migration in September 2020 (30 posts) after fires occurred in the Moria and Samos refugee camps in Greece. The AfD argued that refugees intentionally set the fires so they would be moved to Germany. For example, the party wrote,

> While politicians across the old party spectrum overburden themselves with the numbers of refugees from Moria and Samos, Greece keeps a cool head in coping with several crises and does not think about rewarding asylum seekers for arson and obstruction. Greece's prime minister in particular stands out: "If you give in to arsonists, you will reward criminals and like in 2015, many new young men will follow." We say: THANK YOU Mr. Mitsotakis![81]

The AfD further criticized Merkel for taking in 150 minors from Moria. Many posts reiterated Merkel's open border policy during the refugee crisis and warned that Moria would create greater migration influxes. One post specifically condemned the government by stating, "The CDU and CSU want to take on 5,000 migrants from Moria. This is the wrong signal for migrants and smugglers! It sends a message that whoever burns down his camp will be evacuated to Germany."[82] The language in this post indicates that the party tried to use the Moria fire to invoke anger over the refugee crisis and foment greater criticism of Merkel and the establishment parties.

Another point of contention around migration in September 2020 was the European Commission's release of its New Pact on Migration and Asylum. The Pact, under consideration at the time of writing, would allow each country to contribute to 'burden sharing' by accepting refugees or funding the return of those who do not qualify for asylum.[83] After the Pact's release, Meuthen wrote,

> This new EU migration pact is a fight for our entire Western way of life: for our social states already at its end, for our internal security, for our free society and, of course, for our Christian culture, which is incompatible with most migrants with an Islamic worldview.[84]

The AfD also published a petition to collect one million signatures of those in opposition to the Migration Pact.[85] In line with populists' failure to provide pragmatic solutions, the AfD did not offer any alternatives to the government's response to the Moria fires or the Commission's Migration Pact.

The pandemic strengthened waning concerns about migration. A poll found that apprehension over migration fell significantly; only 6% of Germans identified migration as the most important voting issue in 2021 compared to

88% in 2016.[86] Yet, multiple AfD posts invoked cultural concerns and security threats, focusing on future influxes of migrants. The main themes were crime, Islam, and culture issues. For instance, the AfD wrote,

> Riots occurred in a refugee home in Suhul after a confirmed corona case and the following quarantine. Children were used as shields and police had to stop attempts to leave the facility while residents showed the ISIS flag. Punishable behavior can only be accepted with immediate deportation.[87]

Another post read, "Murder attempt at police officer in Frankfurt am Main – African throws flower buckets off bridge! A quick conviction and an even faster deportation would be obvious for the AfD."[88] The party's emphasis on refugees and migrants being violent criminals is important in demonstrating that the party continued to utilize the two-group dichotomy foundational to populism.

By arguing that refugees and migrants pose security threats, the AfD inflamed negative sentiments about migration at a time when the issue was becoming less important to Germans. The AfD's response to Germany's border closures suggested that populist parties will continue to find ways to criticize the government even when ruling parties adopt policies that align with the populist's own agenda.

H3: Populist parties will continue to focus on the issues that have made them popular.

I assessed not only the salience of migration and government criticism but also the prominence of other issues in the AfD's platform. As demonstrated in relation to the second hypothesis, the party maintained its concentration of cultural grievances surrounding migration. What is striking, though, is that 'Culture Issues' is the largest category. As displayed in Figure 2.2, the AfD's focus on culture issues decreased as the pandemic began while its government criticism increased. However, its posts related to cultural grievances increased in June 2020 when the Black Lives Matters (BLM) protests occurred after George Floyd's murder in the United States.[89] After decreasing its commentary on culture issues in July 2020, the AfD's posts on culture issues peaked in October 2020 after a French teacher was beheaded by a Muslim. It then receded as Germany entered its second infection wave in November 2020, prompting the AfD to revert back to government criticism.[90] Figure 2.2 demonstrates that the issue of migration peaked in September 2020 when the Moria fires occurred. Although migration is important to the AfD's strategy, the data exhibits that government criticism and culture issues took precedence on the party's social media.

The 'Culture Issues' group contains seven subcategories that connect with the loss of traditions and identity prevalent among the global far-right's

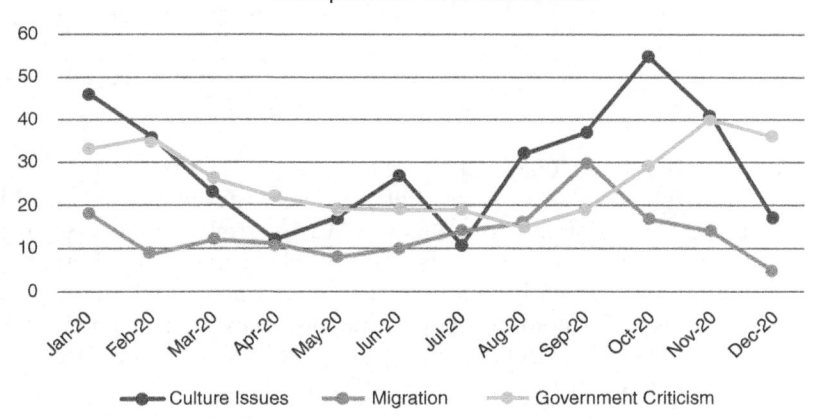

Figure 2.2 Comparison of three biggest categories.

cultural grievances: (1) crime, (2) opposition to the left, (3) protests, (4) police, (5) Islam, (6) climate change, and (7) the AfD's reunification campaign regarding the former East Germany. The 'Culture Issues' category challenges Hypothesis 3, as it demonstrates that the AfD incorporates new issues into its discourse to grow its support among those dissatisfied with the changing world. Throughout its posts, the party instills political divisions through the exacerbation of historical memory and perceived loss of the German identity, exemplifying that it is trying to appeal to cultural grievances. Below I address each subcategory.

The AfD's posts on crime were most commonly associated with migration and the left. In line with other far-right actors, the AfD crusades against 'Antifa' and presents left-wing activists as violent threats. One example is a post that referred to 'Antifa' as a terrorist organization after the burning of an Antifa community house.[91] Another stated,

> Today, the Bundestag rejected the application submitted by the AfD to examine an Antifa ban....In large German cities and universities, these groups [Antifa] are omnipresent and continue to be tolerated, although they have shown their willingness to be violent several times...It is shameful that violent groups and networks that defame and intimidate citizens with non-compliant views can continue to control and manage the spectrum of opinion in our democracy as they please.[92]

Crime was also invoked in discussing government agencies; for example, the AfD wrote, "Intelligence wants access to WhatsApp & Co! What do you think? Should intelligence be allowed to access Messenger when prosecuting terrorists and criminals or is the state going too far with its interference in private chats and surveillance?"[93] The AfD not only used refugees as targets of its fear mongering tactics but the left and government agencies as well.

In tandem with depicting the left as violent, the AfD tied leftists to communism and German history. One post stated,

> Get your hands off Bismarck! A real storm has evolved in the racism hysteria that the American Leftists have developed worldwide. Monuments of Columbus or George Washington become the target of blind destruction rage. This wave is now carried by Leftists to Germany. They actually take Bismarck monuments into the focus of their confused ideology as they argue Bismarck was responsible for German colonialism. But the left should sweep at its own doorstep. The worst racist and anti-Semite was Karl Marx.[94]

The party also demonized political correctness; in another post about Marx, it wrote,

> Bismarck monument soaked in blood red color: Learn from history instead of blindly destroying it! Even in Germany, the left-wing demonstrations against racism are turning more and more into hate, hustle and blind destruction rage. Apparently in connection with the death of African American George Floyd, a Bismarck monument in Hamburg has now also been smeared with red...What continues to be hidden: Monuments of conflicting personalities can serve as memory and for learning from the light and dark sides of history.[95]

The AfD's posts about the left also criticized leftist politicians and judges. One stated,

> CDU votes for far-left constitutional Judge Borchardt! On Friday, the CDU faction in Mecklenburg-Vorpommern voted for the extremist constitutional Judge Borchardt, together with the parties of the left-wing block...Borchardt had downplayed the construction of the Berlin Wall several times...It is a slap in the face of the victims of the [SED] regime[96] – and the CDU strikes along. The former anti-communist union has finally abandoned the democratic consensus and, for power-political reasons, does not shy away from electing a woman to a high judgement office who mocks the victims of a murderous and contempt regime.[97]

In displaying leftists as extreme, the AfD categorized anyone who identifies as left as part of the out-group, thus deepening partisan divides.

The AfD's anti-left discourse was also exhibited in its commentary on protests, which demonstrates its increasing conservatism and explicit racism. Most posts were primarily about the BLM movement and refusal to recognize global racism. The AfD mocked the movement and the current historical reckoning regarding racism and colonialism's legacy throughout the world. One post stated,

> Learn from history instead of destroying it...the political left wants to overthrow monuments because of 'racism.' However, racist Karl Marx does not fall into their minds. In order to draw attention to these double standards, Beatrix von Storch has covered the Karl Marx bust at Straussberger Platz #blm.[98]

In denying racism, the AfD attempted to manipulate Germans' fear of losing their identity by criticizing political correctness and furthering a historical narrative that shines a more positive light on German history.

The party's posts on the BLM protests were also often tied to support for the police. The AfD took a very pro-police position, using the BLM and leftist movements to advocate for 'law and order.' Its pro-police stance tied into two important discussions occurring in Germany. The first is whether the country should increase its military capabilities. Germany's history has fostered the popularity of a pacifist approach when it comes to developing a strong military and defense presence. Donald Trump's calls for Germany to bolster its defense spending and contributions to the North Atlantic Treaty Organization (NATO) intensified public conversation on Germany's military future that has been ongoing since the Cold War.[99] Germany's EU leadership, especially after Brexit, raises new questions about the future of its defense capabilities. The AfD supported a military buildup, writing several posts demanding new weapons and equipment for troops, possibly exhibiting a commitment to the resurgence of German military power. The second reason for its pro-police stance is that the police have increasingly visible connections to far-right extremism. Katrin Bennhold, Berlin bureau chief for the *New York Times*, has reported extensively on the proliferation of far-right extremism within the police and military.[100] The AfD's pro-police stand exemplifies how the party attracts those with extremist viewpoints.

The AfD's posts about Islam were tied to government criticism and migration. In October 2020, 10 of the AfD's 98 Facebook posts focused on Islamic attacks. After a French schoolteacher was beheaded in October 2020, the AfD applauded French President Emmanuel Macron for his swift imposition of restrictions on Islam. It also criticized Merkel for not responding to the attacks by posting,

> Islamist beheads teachers in France: Where is the outcry? Where are those who always talk about the threat of democracy when it comes to undoubtedly abhorrent right-wing extremism? While there are major demonstrations in France and the Interior Minister orders the expulsion of 231 "suspected" Islamists, Germany remains silent.[101]

Another post read, "After beheading: France closes Islamist mosque – and us? In Germany: Silence, embrace of the Islamic background, transition to the left-wing green agenda. In France, on the other hand, mass demonstrations against Islamism and expulsion of hundreds of Islamists."[102] By comparing different countries' handling of terrorist attacks, the AfD offered more criticism toward Merkel and further instilled fears about refugees and Muslims.

The party's commentary on climate change tied into government criticism as well as a challenge to scientific expertise. It posted 58 times on climate change issues and is skeptical of global warming and new energy sources. Many posts critiqued rules including procedures for electric cars, changing of speed limits on highways, and Germany's wind energy developments. One post exclaimed, "Germany has the most expensive electricity in the WORLD! Stop it! Vote for the AfD!"[103] The party mocked Swedish activist Greta Thunberg; Meuthen criticized Merkel for meeting with Thunberg by stating,

Instead of worrying about the real problems of our corona-bagged economy, the chancellor meets Greta & Co.! All the chancellors before her have avoided inviting an extra-parliamentary protest movement to the Chancellery – but of course, that's no problem for Ms. Merkel in her constant search for beautiful pictures![104]

The AfD's efforts to challenge climate change connect with the global far-right's efforts to deny science and facts. Again, the AfD offered no solution for how to deal with climate change's detrimental consequences.

Finally, the AfD had a social media campaign celebrating Germany's reunification. Its posts targeted eastern voters by claiming,

Even after 30 years of German unity, the social division has not been overcome. Polls show that one in five East Germans do not feel welcomed in the Federal Republic and are not satisfied with what they have achieved. The AfD is not satisfied with the achievement either. There is a lot to catch up on both sides after 30 years of German unity. The AfD is the first real all German party![105]

It also plays into the victim narrative that many in the former East Germany and various Central and Eastern European states have adopted when discussing the aftermath of the Second World War and Soviet occupation. In a post, the AfD wrote,

Well over 100,000 citizens of the GDR tried to escape the injustice regime over the inner German border. More than 600 Germans lost their lives in the process. We mourn everyone who had to give up their lives just because they wanted to transfer from one part of Germany to another.

Its reunification campaign appealed to its eastern supporters as the party condemned traditional parties for not addressing inequalities between the east and west after reunification as well as the Soviet Union's repression of East Germans.

Overall, the data reveals that the AfD used the coronavirus crisis to broaden its platform to include those who are not only angry about immigration but feel like their identity is threatened by changes within Germany and in the world. Its embrace of culture issues demonstrates that, although the party still relies on immigration as its trigger for cultural anxieties, the AfD simultaneously adopted the same platform as other far-right parties, especially that of the Republican Party in the United States. In criticizing the BLM movement, the left, and violence against the police, it catered to those who may hold extreme views.

4 Conclusion

I have sought to answer the question of how populist parties change their strategies during a crisis. Although the coronavirus pandemic is ongoing, far-right parties throughout Europe and the world have adopted similar stances, allowing for insight into their political platforms.[106] It is too early to determine how the AfD's criticism of Merkel's handling of the pandemic and embrace of conspiracy theories will impact its support in the long term, but favorable opinions toward the party and populism in general is declining in Germany and may continue to do so.

The data confirms previous literature on populists' strategy of government criticism and cultural grievances. Louwerse and Otjes' study of populist parties in the Netherlands, in which they found that parties rely on government criticism instead of passing legislation, is supported by Hypothesis 1. The AfD's consistent disapproval of the Merkel government's handling of the coronavirus pandemic and its lack of strategy demonstrates that it would rather concentrate on exacerbating voter dissatisfaction with the coalition government instead of working with the ruling parties to find solutions to the pandemic.

Norris and Inglehart's theory of cultural grievances is heavily supported by the data, as the AfD's social messaging during the pandemic concentrated chiefly on cultural grievances relating to migration, protests, and Islam. Importantly, it was only once the AfD embraced a strategy of xenophobia that tapped into these cultural grievances that it garnered enough supporters to become the third-largest party in Germany.

Pappas' theory of populist democracies is not strongly supported by my research. Merkel's government adopted harsher stances on migration in response to pressure from CDU and CSU party members stemming from the AfD's popularity. Prior to and throughout the pandemic, it increased deportations, limited the number of asylum seekers allowed to enter Germany, and worked with other countries in 'counter-smuggling' efforts to patrol the Mediterranean and return those trying to enter Europe. These, as well as the closing of Germany's borders, are all policies that the AfD supports. However, it is important to remember that Germany's borders – and Europe's collective external borders – were closed because of COVID-19. Since this policy was enacted five years after the refugee crisis, it can be assumed that the Merkel government did not adopt this policy to try to appease the AfD or bring back former voters. It did so out of public health concerns. Post-pandemic research should analyze Pappas' theory in relation to whether post-Merkel governments, particularly that immediately following her tenure, adopt the AfD's policies.

There are three important conclusions to draw from this data. First, the AfD fits the populist prototype of using government criticism as a political strategy. The AfD views and presents itself as an eternal outsider to the political establishment, despite being ingrained in the Bundestag and state governments. Second, although Germany's borders closed for over a year, migration remained a salient issue for the AfD. This suggests that the party attempted to manipulate anger and fear over Merkel's former open border policies to illicit support. Finally, the most surprising and yet the most important conclusion from the data is that culture issues outside of migration became central to the AfD's platform. The party's adoption of far-right stances on culturally sensitive issues surrounding race and racism, historical memory, and identity loss exhibits the party's use of cultural grievances for its own political gain. It can be inferred that 'culture wars' will become incorporated even more into the AfD's political platform in the future and that the attempted storming of the Reichstag may not be the last public measure taken by the far-right to reclaim its civil and political liberties.

The AfD is just one of many examples of far-right populist parties in Europe that are challenging the liberal world order. Future research should analyze other right-wing populist parties' social media strategies during crises. It should analyze the AfD's social media, especially its Facebook page, in the months leading up to different federal elections. Such a time frame would further the analysis of populist strategies by seeing what type of issues the party communicates as important elections near. Additional avenues for further research include a comparative study of different far-right populist parties' strategies throughout Europe or between right-wing and left-wing parties in a particular country during the coronavirus crisis, specifically. As social media is prominent among populists, scholars should also analyze how traditional parties' utilization of social media has changed over time to try to appeal to more voters and compete with populist parties. Although the surge of populist support after the refugee crisis is alarming, it provides an opportunity to better define, study, and analyze populist parties' strategies.

Nevertheless, what is clear, particularly as the pandemic wanes, is that support for ruling governments will likely decrease. Other non-pandemic issues will become political priorities, potentially opening space for right-wing populists to regain lost support. Throughout the COVID-19 crisis, parties like the AfD demonstrated that they are more interested in causing chaos and disarray than governing. The far-right prioritizes false information, conspiracy theories, and increasing partisanship over saving lives, ensuring that correct information is disseminated, and putting the safety and well-being of society first. We can anticipate that this trend will continue, especially during future crises.

This is not merely a concern for state-level cohesion; the continued success of far-right populist parties' disruptive narratives threatens the future of European integration. Despite recent polls revealing that Europeans want the EU to gain greater powers, the AfD and other far-right populist parties still promote falsehoods about the EU, most notably by criticizing purported losses to national sovereignty. In their 2021 campaign manifesto, the AfD listed Germany leaving the EU and Eurozone as priorities, exhibiting a major shift from its 2013 platform (in which it advocated leaving the Eurozone but not the EU).[107] As with the COVID-19 crisis, we can expect that in future crises, populist far-right parties will continue to blame EU bureaucracy and loss of national sovereignty for current problems. Euroscepticism has become part of the 'culture war' platform that the far-right embraces.

Notes

1 The Party's name in English is the "Alternative for Germany Party."
2 Alice Weidel, "Merkel's Lockdown-Forever Halting ist ein offenbarungseid für Offenbarugnseid für unsere Demokratie," *Alternative für Deutschland,* February 9, 2021, https://www.afd.de/alice-weidel-merkels-lockdown-forever-haltung-ist-ein-offenbarungseid-fuer-unsere-demokratie/
3 Bernd Riegert, "World Refugee Day: Migration Problems Help Populists Prosper in Europe," *Deutsche Welle,* June 19, 2018, https://www.dw.com/en/world-refugee-day-migration-problems-help-populists-prosper-in-europe/a-44263784.
4 Jon Henley and Pamela Duncan, "European Support for Populist Beliefs Falls, YouGov Survey Suggests," *The Guardian,* October 26, 2020, https://www.theguardian.com/world/2020/oct/26/european-support-for-populist-beliefs-falls-yougov-survey-suggests.
5 To see approval ratings toward European governments throughout the pandemic, see Politico's "Poll of Polls." https://www.politico.eu/europe-poll-of-polls/.
6 Ben Knight, "German State Elections Deepen Troubles for Angela Merkel's CDU," *Deutsche Welle,* March 15, 2021, https://www.dw.com/en/german-state-elections-deepen-troubles-for-angela-merkels-cdu/a-56879941.
7 Pepijn Bergsen, "Why the Pandemic and Populism Still Work Together," *Chatham House,* November 24, 2020, https://www.chathamhouse.org/2020/11/why-pandemic-and-populism-still-work-together.
8 Louise K. Davidson-Schmich, "The Alternative for Germany," (Panel, American Institute for Contemporary German Studies, March 1, 2021).
9 Cas Mudde, "Populism: An Ideational Approach," in *The Oxford Handbook of Populism,* eds. Christóbal Rovira Kaltwasser, Paul Taggart, Paulina Ochoa Espejo, and Pierre Ostiguy (Oxford: Oxford University Press, 2017), 3.

10 Eric Langenbacher, "Germany's Memory Culture and the Alternative for Germany," *American Institute for Contemporary German Studies,* February 2, 2021 and Mudde, "Populism," 4.

11 For alternative definitions of populism, see *The Oxford Handbook of Populism,* Noam Gidron and Bart Bonikowski, "Varieties of Populism: Literature Review and Research Agenda," *Weatherhead Center for International Affairs Harvard University Working Paper Series,* no. 13-0004, 2014; Jan Jagers and Stefaan Walgrave, "Populism as a Political Communications Style: An Empirical Study of Political Parties' Discourse in Belgium," *European Journal of Political Research* 46, no. 3 (2007): 319–345; Benjamin Moffitt and Simon Tormey, "Rethinking Populism: Politics, Mediatisation, and Political Style," *Political Studies* 62, no. 2 (2014): 381–397; and Matthjis Rooduijn, "The Nucleus of Populism: In Search of the Lowest Common Denominator," *Government and Opposition* 49, no. 4 (2013): 573–599.

12 John B. Judis, *The Populist Explosion: How the Great Recession Transformed American and European Politics* (New York: Columbia Global Reports, 2016), 15.

13 Judis, *Populist Explosion,* 23.

14 See the Populist project for more information on the rise of far-right and far-left parties in Europe at https://popu-list.org/.

15 Pippa Norris and Ronald Inglehart, *Cultural Backlash: Trump, Brexit, and Authoritarian Populism* (New York: Cambridge University Press, 2019).

16 Norris and Inglehart, *Cultural Backlash,* 71.

17 Norris and Inglehart, *Cultural Backlash,* 1–10.

18 Sven Engesser et al., "Populism and Social Media: How Politicians Spread a Fragmented Ideology," *Communication & Society* 20, no. 8 (2017): 1109–1126.

19 Yves Mény and Yves Surel, "The Constructive Ambiguity of Populism," in *Democracies and the Populist Challenge,* eds. Yves Mény and Yves Surel (London: Palgrave Macmillan, 2002), 126.

20 Jeff Nesbit, "Donald Trump Supporters Are Using a Nazi Word to Attack Journalists," *TIME,* October 25, 2016, https://time.com/4544562/donald-trump-supporters-lugenpresse/.

21 Benjamin Krämer, "Populist Online Practices: The Function of the Internet in Right-Wing Populism," *Communication & Society* 20, no. 9 (2017): 1293–1309.

22 Krämer, "Populist online practices," 1300.

23 Krämer, "Populist online practices," 1300.

24 Lars Rensmann, "The Noisy Counter-Revolution: Understanding the Cultural Conditions and Dynamics of Populist Parties in Europe in the Digital Age," *Politics and Governance* 5, no. 4 (2017): 131.

25 Tom Louwerse and Simon Otjes, "How Populists Wage Opposition: Parliamentary Opposition Behaviour and Populism in Netherlands," *Political Studies* 67, no. 2 (2019): 479–495.

26 Louwerse and Oties, "Populists Wage Opposition," 481.

27 Takis S. Pappas, "Populist Democracies," *Government and Opposition* 49, no. 1 (2014): 18–19.

28 The French National Rally was formerly known as the French National Front. It changed its name in 2018.

29 Norris and Inglehart, *Cultural Backlash,* 32–56.

30 Norris and Inglehart, *Cultural Backlash,* 175.

31 Norris and Inglehart, *Cultural Backlash,* 52.

32 For more information on the Eurozone crisis, see Christopher Alessi and James McBride, "The Eurozone in Crisis," *Council on Foreign Relations,* accessed July 12, 2021. https://www.cfr.org/backgrounder/eurozone-crisis and Rebecca M. Nelson et al., "The Eurozone Crisis: Overview and Issues for

Congress," *Congressional Research Service,* September 26, 2012. https://fas.org/sgp/crs/row/R42377.pdf. For information on the refugee crisis see, William Spindler, "2015: The Year of Europe's Refugee Crisis," *UNHCR,* December 8, 2015, https://www.unhcr.org/en-us/news/stories/2015/12/56ecleb-de/2015-year-europes-refugee-crisis.html; Jeanne Park, "Europe's Migration Crisis," *Council on Foreign Relations,* accessed July 12, 2021. https://www.cfr.org/backgrounder/europes-migration-crisis; and Phillip Connor, "Number of Refugees to Europe Surges to Record 1.3 Million in 2015," *Pew,* August 2, 2016. https://www.pewresearch.org/global/2016/08/02/number-of-refugees-to-europe-surges-to-record-1-3-million-in-2015/.

33 As of August 12, 2021, the Alternative for Germany had 538,416 Facebook followers; the Greens had 226,477 Facebook followers; the Christian Democratic Union had 225,713 Facebook followers; the Christian Social Union had 221,659 followers; and the Free Democratic Party had 168,072 Facebook followers. The Social Democratic Party did not have a Facebook page.

34 "Wie macht Angela Merkel ihre Arbeit als Bundeskanzlerin alles in allem gesehen?" *Statista,* accessed July 13, 2021, https://de.statista.com/statistik/daten/studie/675140/umfrage/bewertung-der-arbeit-von-angela-merkel-als-bundeskanzlerin/#professional.

35 To see approval ratings toward the AfD throughout the pandemic, see Politico's "Poll of Polls," https://www.politico.eu/europe-poll-of-polls/.

36 The National Democratic Party of Germany (NPD) was founded in 1964 and is considered far-right and ultranationalist. It has been referred to as the most significant neo-Nazi party to emerge after 1945. Although it has gained representation in state governments 11 times, it has never passed the 5% voting threshold needed to enter the Bundestag. Since 2016, the NPD has no representation in any of Germany's 16 state governments. It also had one seat in the European Parliament that it lost in 2019. Germany's Federal Constitutional Court has tried and failed to ban the party in 2003 and 2017. For more information on NPD, see Manfried Schreiber and Yung Ping Chen, "Ideology of the National Democratic Party of Germany," *Journal of Thought* 6, no. 2 (1971): 88–104; John D. Nagle, *The National Democratic Party: Right Radicalism in the Federal Republic of Germany* (Berkeley: University of California Press, 1970); Angela K. Bourne, *Democratic Dilemmas: Why Democracies Ban Political Parties* (London: Routledge, 2018), 114–142; and Samuel Salzborn, "Discussion of New Right Elements in German Right-Wing Extremism Today," *German Politics & Society* 34, no. 2 (2016): 36–63.

37 Frank Decker and Philipp Adorf, "Coalition Politics in Crisis?: The German Party System Before and After the 2017 Federal Election," in *Twilight of the Merkel Era,* ed. Eric Langenbacher (New York: Berghahn Books, 2019), 42 and Marcel Lewandowsky, "Alternative für Deutschland: A New Actor in the German Party System," *Friedrich Ebert Stiftung,* March 2014. http://library.fes.de/pdf-files/id/ipa/10644.pdf.

38 "Walhprogram Parteitagsbeschluss vom 14.04.2013," *The Alternative for Germany Party,* accessed, April 18, 2021, https://manifestoproject.wzb.eu//down/originals/41953_2013.pdf.

39 Matthias Dilling, "Two of the Same Kind? The Rise of the AfD and its Implications for the CDU/CSU," in *Twilight of the Merkel Era,* ed. Eric Langenbacher, 193.

40 Rebecca Staudenmaier, "AfD's Alice Called German Government 'Pigs' in Racist Email," *Deutsche Welle,* September 20, 2017, https://www.dw.com/en/afds-alice--called-german-government-pigs-in-racist-email/a-40433932 and Sven-Felix Kellerhoff, Martin Lutz, and Uwe Müller, "Alice Weidel will Veröffentlichung rassistischer E-Mail stoppen," *Die Welt,* September 9, 2017,

https://www.welt.de/politik/article168489086/Alice--will-Veröffentlichung-rassistischer-E-Mail-stoppen.html.

41 "Official Provisional Result of the 2013 Bundestag Election," *The Federal Returning Officer,* September 23, 2013, https://www.bundeswahlleiter.de/en/info/presse/mitteilungen/bundestagswahl-2013/2013-09-23-vorlaeufiges-amtliches-ergebnis-der-bundestagswahl-2013.html.

42 "AfD Deputy Backpedals on Shooting at Refugee Children," *Deutsche Welle,* February 1, 2016, https://www.dw.com/en/afd-deputy-backpedals-on-shooting-at-refugee-children/a-19015194.

43 Dilling, "Two of the Same Kind," in *Twilight of the Merkel Era,* ed. Eric Langenbacher, 195.

44 "Germany Shocked by Cologne New Year Gang Assaults on Women," *BBC,* January 5, 2016, https://www.bbc.com/news/world-europe-35231046.

45 Elizabeth Schumacher, "German populists AfD adopt anti-Islam manifesto," *Deutsche Welle,* May 1, 2016, https://www.dw.com/en/german-populists-afd-adopt-anti-islam-manifesto/a-19228284.

46 "Walhprogram," *Alternative for Germany Party,* 4.

47 Dilling, "Two of the Same Kind," in *Twilight of the Merkel Era,* ed. Eric Langenbacher, 195–196 and "Programm für die Wahl zum Deutschen Bundestag am 24, September, 2017," *Alternative for Germany Party,* 16–20, accessed April 18, 2021, https://manifesto-project.wzb.eu/.

48 "Programm für die Wahl," *Alternative for Germany Party,* 25–30 and Dilling, "Two of the Same Kind," in *Twilight of the Merkel Era,* ed. Eric Langenbacher, 196.

49 Dilling, "Two of the Same Kind," in *Twilight of the Merkel Era,* ed. Eric Langenbacher, 202.

50 Eric Langenbacher, "Introduction: Merkeldämmerung," in *Twilight of the Merkel Era,* ed. Eric Langenbacher, 26.

51 The CSU is the CDU's sister party in Bavaria.

52 Dilling, "Two of the Same Kind," in *Twilight of the Merkel Era,* ed. Eric Langenbacher, 199.

53 Langenbacher, "Introduction," in *Twilight of the Merkel Era,* ed. Eric Langenbacher, 5.

54 Melissa Eddy and Katrin Bennhold, "Angela Merkel Averts Crisis, Forming Government with SPD Again," *The New York Times,* March 4, 2018, https://www.nytimes.com/2018/03/04/world/europe/germany-spd-merkel.html and Decker and Adorf, "Coalition Politics in Crisis," 48–52.

55 Eddy and Bennhold, "Merkel Averts Crisis."

56 Langenbacher, "Introduction," in *Twilight of the Merkel Era,* ed. Eric Langenbacher, 5. The AfD hired Harris Media, which formerly worked for the 2016 Trump campaign, to assist with its 2017 campaign.

57 "Anzahl der Parteimitglieder der AfD von 2013 bis 2019," *Statista,* August 3, 2020, https://de.statista.com/statistik/daten/studie/730862/umfrage/mitgliederentwicklung-der-afd/.

58 "AfD Panel Confirms Exclusion of Extremist from Party," *Deutsche Welle,* July 25, 2020, https://www.dw.com/en/afd-panel-confirms-exclusion-of-extremist-from-party/a-54318408.

59 Philip Oltermann, "Germany's AfD Thrown into Turmoil by Former Neo-Nazi's Expulsion," *The Guardian,* May 18, 2020, https://www.theguardian.com/world/2020/may/18/germany-afd-thrown-into-turmoil-by-former-neo-nazi-explusion-andreas-kalbitz; Guy Chazan, "Germany's Far-Right Firebrand Disturbs Allies and Opponents Alike," *Financial Times,* October 25, 2019, https://www.ft.com/content/3816a566-f597-11e9-a79c-bc9acae3b654; and "Germany's Far-Right AfD to Dissolve Extreme 'Wing' Faction," *Deutsche Welle,* March 20, 2020, https://www.dw.com/en/germanys-far-right-afd-to-dissolve-extreme-wing-faction/a-52864683.

60 Gauland bezeichnet NS-Zeit als "Vogelschiss in der Geschichte,'" *Die Welt,* June 2, 2018, https://www.welt.de/politik/deutschland/article176912600/AfD-Chef-Gauland-bezeichnet-NS-Zeit-als-Vogelschiss-in-der-Geschichte.html.

61 Langenbacher, "Germany's Memory Culture,"1–8.

62 On March 5, 2021, a court in Cologne temporarily blocked the surveillance of the AfD's federal party. "German Court Suspends Surveillance of Far-Right AfD, For Now," *Deutsche Welle,* March 5, 2021, https://www.dw.com/en/german-court-suspends-surveillance-of-far-right-afd-for-now/a-56785125. See Alex Berry, "German State Puts Regional AfD Branch Under Surveillance – Reports," *Deutsche Welle,* January 26, 2021, https://www.dw.com/en/german-state-puts-regional-afd-branch-under-surveillance-reports/a-56342789 and "AfD: Regional Branch of Far-Right Party Put Under Surveillance," *Deutsche Welle,* June 15, 2020, https://www.dw.com/en/afd-regional-branch-of-far-right-party-put-under-surveillance/a-53806958 for information on the initial decision.

63 Robert Vehrkamp and Wolfgang Merkel, "Populism Barometer 2020: Populist Attitudes Among Voters and Non-Voters in Germany 2020," *Bertelsmann Stiftung,* 2020, 8, https://www.bertelsmann-stiftung.de/fileadmin/files/BSt/Publikationen/GrauePublikationen/ZD_Populism_Barometer_2020.pdf.

64 Noah Porter, "Like Sands Through an Hourglass, So Are Angela Merkel's Approval Rating," *American Institute for Contemporary German Studies John Hopkins University,* August 12, 2020, https://www.aicgs.org/2020/08/like-sands-through-an-hourglass-so-are-angela-merkels-approval-ratings/ and Sabine Kinkartz, "Coronavirus: Angela Merkel's Approval Ratings Up Amid Health Crisis," *Deutsche Welle,* April 3, 2020, https://www.dw.com/en/coronavirus-angela-merkels-approval-ratings-up-amid-health-crisis/a-53001405.

65 Kat Devlin and Nicholas Kent, "As Pandemic Continues, More in U.S. and Europe Feel Major Impact on Their Lives," *Pew Research Center,* February 3, 2021, https://www.pewresearch.org/global/2021/02/03/as-pandemic-continues-more-in-u-s-and-europe-feel-major-impact-on-their-lives/.

66 See the Alternative for Germany's Facebook page at: https://www.facebook.com/alternativefuerde.

67 As of 12 August 2021, the Alternative for Germany had 171,500 followers on Twitter.

68 Alternative für Deutschland, "Wegen Corona: Krankschreibung ab sofort ohne Arztbesuch," Facebook, March 10, 2020.

69 Jörg Meuthen, "Liebe Leser, Deutschland steht vor einer Katastrophe. Nichts anderes sagen die Zahlen der letzten Tage, auch und gerade des gestrigen Tages," Facebook, March 20, 2020, https://www.facebook.com/554345401380836/posts/1577731682375531/.

70 Alternative für Deutschland, "Corona-Krise: AfD legt 5 Punkte Sofort-programm vor," Facebook, March 18, 2020.

71 Kate Connolly, "Kurzarbeit: Germany's Scheme for Avoiding Unemployment," *The Guardian,* September 24, 2020, https://www.theguardian.com/world/2020/sep/24/kurzarbeit-germanys-scheme-fo-avoiding-unemployment.

72 Michael Nienaber and Thomas Seythal, "Germany Avoids Record Economic Plunge in 2020 Despite COVID-19 Hit," *Reuters,* January 14, 2021, https://www.reuters.com/article/us-germany-economy-gdp/germany-avoids-record-economic-plunge-in-2020-despite-covid-19-hit-idUSKBN29J10T.

73 Raf Casert, "EU Economy to Expand, Bouncing Back from Pandemic Crisis," *AP,* May 12, 2021, https://apnews.com/article/europe-economy-health-coronavirus-pandemic-business-92cd5c307f3d24e38e71ce1aa279a439.

74 "Recovery Plan for Europe," *European Commission,* accessed April 18, 2021, https://ec.europa.eu/info/strategy/recovery-plan-europe_en and Silvia Amaro and Christine Wang, "EU leaders reach $2 Trillion Deal on Recovery Plan After

Marathon Summit," *CNBC,* July 20, 2020, https://www.cnbc.com/2020/07/21/eu-leaders-reach-a-breakthrough-on-the-regions-recovery-fund.html.

75 "Recovery and Resilience Facility: Maximum Grant Allocations," *European Commission,* accessed April 18, 2021, https://ec.europa.eu/info/sites/info/files/about_the_european_commission/eu_budget/recovery_and_resilience_facility_.pdf.

76 Jörg Meuthen, "Liebe Leser, bitte schätzen Sie einmal: Über wieviel Vermögen verfügt der mittlere (volljährige) Deutsche (also derjenige, der sich genau in der Mitte zwischen der ärmeren und reicheren Hälfte unseres Landes befindet)?" Facebook, April 18, 2020, https://www.facebook.com/554345401380836/posts/1604023103079722/.

77 Jörg Meuthen, "Liebe Leser, die Lobhudeleien nach dem desaströsen EU-Gipfel kannten keine Grenzen: Überall war nur von Gewinnern "die Rede," Facebook, July 23, 2020, https://www.facebook.com/554345401380836/posts/1694088050739893/.

78 "Mehrheit gegen "Corona-Bonds,"" *Cicero-Redaktion,* March 31, 2020, https://www.cicero.de/wirtschaft/corona-bonds-eu-schuldentilgung-corona-krise.

79 Tino Chrupalla, "Mit vereinten Kräften für unser Land!," Facebook, March 31, 2020, https://www.facebook.com/TinoAfD/photos/a.1758788034429462/2243317925976468/.

80 Tino Chrupalla, "Seit Wochen erreichen mich hunderte von E-Mails und Briefen von Bürgern zum geplanten 3. Bevölkerungsschutzgesetz," Facebook, November 17, 2020, https://www.facebook.com/TinoAfD/photos/a.1758788034429462/2416792031962389/.

81 Alternative für Deutschland, "Bravo Griechenland! "Europa hat einen neuen Grenzschützer!"," Facebook, September 23, 2020.

82 Tino Chrupalla, "CDU und CSU wollen 5000 Migranten aus Moria aufnehmen," Facebook, September 10, 2020, https://www.facebook.com/TinoAfD/photos/a.1758788034429462/2360964484211811/.

83 "New Pact on Migration and Asylum Package," *European Commission,* September 23, 2020, https://ec.europa.eu/commission/presscorner/detail/en/ip_20_1706 and "'Solidarity cannot be voluntary,' Portugal begins talks on EU migration pact," *Reuters,* January 5, 2021, https://www.reuters.com/article/us-portugal-europe-migration/solidarity-cannot-be-voluntary-portugal-begins-talks-on-eu-migration-pact-idUSKBN29A2SE.

84 Jörg Meuthen, "Liebe Leser, derzeit, also während der EU-Ratspräsidentschaft Deutschlands, versuchen die Endlos-Kanzlerin und ihre Schwester im Geiste von der Leyen mit aller Gewalt, die desaströse, Deutschland wie auch die EU tief spaltende Migrationspolitik der letzten Jahre auf Dauer festzuschreiben," Facebook, September 26, 2020, https://www.facebook.com/554345401380836/posts/1756731811142183/.

85 Alternative für Deutschland im EU-Parlament, "Der neue Migrations-und Asylpakt: Eine Million Europäer können die Migrantenflut aufhalten!," Facebook, September 24, 2020, https://www.facebook.com/AfDimEUParlament/photos/a.270760250212577/665187744103157/.

86 Forschungsgruppe Wahlen E.V., "Politik II," accessed April 18, 2021, https://www.forschungsgruppe.de/Umfragen/Politbarometer/Langzeitentwicklung_-_Themen_im_Ueberblick/Politik_II/.

87 Alternative für Deutschland, "In einem Flüchtlingsheim in Suhl kam es nach einem bestätigten Corona-Fall und der folgenden Quarantäne zu massiven Ausschreitungen," Facebook, March 18, 2020.

88 Alternative für Deutschland, "Mordversuch an Polizistin in Frankfurt/M. – Afrikaner wirft Blumenkübel von Brücke," Facebook, May 26, 2020.

89 Chris Graves, "The killing of George Floyd: What We Know," *MPR News,* June 1, 2020, https://www.mprnews.org/story/2020/06/01/the-killing-of-george-floyd-what-we-know.

90 Holly Ellyatt, "One Chart Shows How Bad Germany's Second Wave of the Coronavirus is," *CNBC,* December 1, 2020, https://www.cnbc.com/2020/12/01/germanys-second-wave-of-covid-19-has-been-worse-than-the-first.html.

91 Alternative für Deutschland, "Antifa gefährdet Menschenleben: Ehemals besetzte „Liebig 34" wohl von Linksextremisten angezündet!," Facebook, October 22, 2020.

92 Alternative für Deutschland, "Linksradikalismus bleibt salonfähig," Facebook, June 19, 2020.

93 Alternative für Deutschland, "Geheimdienste wollen Zugriff auf WhatsApp & Co! Ihre Meinung ist gefragt!," Facebook, October 21, 2020.

94 Alternative für Deutschland, "Hände weg von Bismarck! Schaut auf Marx – einen der übelsten Rassisten und Antisemiten," Facebook, June 21, 2020.

95 Alternative für Deutschland, "Farb-Attacke auf Bismarck-Denkmal: Aus Geschichte lernen, statt sie blindwütig zu zerstören," Facebook, June 15, 2020.

96 SED is the acronym for Sozialistische Einheitspartei Deutschlands (Socialist Union Party of Germany) which ruled East Germany between 1949 and1989.

97 Alternative für Deutschland, "CDU stimmt GEGEN die Abwahl der linksextremen Verfassungsrichterin Borchardt!," Facebook, June 13, 2020.

98 Alternative für Deutschland, "Marx verhüllt: Aus Geschichte lernen, statt sie zu zerstören," Facebook, July 15, 2020.

99 Elisabeth Braw, "Germany, Stop Worrying About Boosting Military Spending," *Politico,* December 21, 2020, https://www.politico.eu/article/germany-military-spending-nato-alliance-security-war/; Chris Bowlby, "Germany: Reluctant military giant," *BBC,* June 12, 2017, https://www.bbc.com/news/world-europe-40172317; and Rajan Menon, "The Story of Germany's Armed Forces," *Foreign Policy,* June 18, 2020, https://foreignpolicy.com/2020/06/18/trump-withdraw-troops-germany-military-spending/.

100 Katrin Bennhold, "Body Bags and Enemy Lists: How Far-Right Police Officers and Ex-Soldiers Planned for 'Day X,'" *The New York Times,* August 1, 2020, https://www.nytimes.com/2020/08/01/world/europe/germany-nazi-infiltration.html and Katrin Bennhold, "She Called Police Over a Neo-Nazi Threat. But the Neo-Nazis Were Inside the Police," *The New York Times,* December 21, 2020, https://www.nytimes.com/2020/12/21/world/europe/germany-far-right-neo-nazis-police.html.

101 Alternative für Deutschland, "Islamist enthauptet Lehrer in Frankreich: Wo bleibt der Aufschrei?," Facebook, October 20, 2020.

102 Alternative für Deutschland, "Nach Enthauptung: Frankreich schließt Islamisten-Moschee – und wir?," Facebook, October 21, 2020.

103 Alternative für Deutschland, "Deutschland hat den teuersten Strom WELTWEIT! Schluss damit!," Facebook, November 20, 2020.

104 Jörg Meuthen, "Liebe Leser, wenn die Coronakrise irgendetwas Gutes hatte, dann die Tatsache, dass die überdrehte Hysterie der freitäglichen Schulschwänzer-Bewegung mit einem Schlag von der Bildfläche verschwand," Facebook, August 22, 2020, https://www.facebook.com/554345401380836/posts/1722147484600616/.

105 Tino Chrupalla, "Die gesellschaftliche Teilung ist auch nach 30 Jahren deutscher Einheit nicht überwunden," Facebook, September 28, 2020, https://www.facebook.com/TinoAfD/photos/a.1758788034429462/2375577226083870/.

106 Giuliano Bobba and Nicolas Hubé, "Populism and Covid-19 in Europe: What We Learned from the First Wave of the Pandemic," *LSE,* April 20, 2021,

https://blogs.lse.ac.uk/europpblog/2021/04/20/populism-and-covid-19-in-europe-what-we-learned-from-the-first-wave-of-the-pandemic/.
107 Alternative fuer Deutschland, "Kurzwahlprogramm," accessed July 13, 2021, https://cdn.afd.tools/wp-content/uploads/sites/111/2021/06/Kurzwahlprogramm_DINlang_Webversion.pdf.

Bibliography

"AfD Deputy Backpedals on Shooting at Refugee Children." *Deutsche Welle*, February 1, 2016. https://www.dw.com/en/afd-deputy-backpedals-on-shooting-at-refugee-children/a-19015194.

"AfD Panel Confirms Exclusion of Extremist From Party." *Deutsche Welle*, July 25, 2020. https://www.dw.com/en/afd-panel-confirms-exclusion-of-extremist-from-party/a-54318408.

"AfD: Regional Branch of Far-Right Party Put Under Surveillance." *Deutsche Welle*, June 15, 2020. https://www.dw.com/en/afd-regional-branch-of-far-right-party-put-under-surveillance/a-53806958 for information on the initial decision.

Alessi, Christopher, and James McBride. "The Eurozone in Crisis." *Council on Foreign Relations*. Accessed July 12, 2021. https://www.cfr.org/backgrounder/eurozone-crisis

Alternative für Deutschland. "Antifa gefährdet Menschenleben: Ehemals besetzte 'Liebig 34' wohl vonLinksextremisten angezündet!" Facebook, October 22, 2020.

Alternative für Deutschland. "Bravo Griechenland! 'Europa hat einen neuen Grenzschützer!'" Facebook, September 23, 2020.

Alternative für Deutschland. "CDU stimmt GEGEN die Abwahl der linksextremen VerfassungsrichterinBorchardt!" Facebook, June 13, 2020.

Alternative für Deutschland. "Corona-Krise: AfD legt 5 Punkte Sofortprogramm vor." Facebook, March 18, 2020.

Alternative für Deutschland. "Deutschland hat den teuersten Strom WELTWEIT! Schluss damit!" Facebook, November 20, 2020.

Alternative für Deutschland. "Farb-Attacke auf Bismarck-Denkmal: Aus Geschichte lernen, statt sie blindwütig zu zerstören." Facebook, June 15, 2020.

Alternative für Deutschland. "Geheimdienste wollen Zugriff auf WhatsApp & Co! Ihre Meinung ist gefragt!" Facebook, October 21, 2020.

Alternative für Deutschland. "Hände weg von Bismarck! Schaut auf Marx – einen der übelsten Rassisten und Antisemiten." Facebook, June 21, 2020.

Alternative für Deutschland. "In einem Flüchtlingsheim in Suhl kam es nach einem bestätigten Corona-Fall und der folgenden Quarantäne zu massiven Ausschreitungen." Facebook, March 18, 2020.

Alternative für Deutschland. "Islamist enthauptet Lehrer in Frankreich: Wo bleibt der Aufschrei?" Facebook, October 20, 2020.

Alternative für Deutschland. "Kurzwahlprogramm." Accessed July 13, 2021. https://cdn.afd.tools/wp-content/uploads/sites/111/2021/06/Kurzwahlprogramm_DINlang_Webversion.pdf.

Alternative für Deutschland. "Linksradikalismus bleibt salonfähig." Facebook, June 19, 2020.

Alternative für Deutschland. "Marx verhüllt: Aus Geschichte lernen, statt sie zu zerstören." Facebook, July 15, 2020.

Alternative für Deutschland. "Mordversuch an Polizistin in Frankfurt/M. – Afrikaner wirft Blumenkübel von Brücke." Facebook, May 26, 2020.

Alternative für Deutschland. "Nach Enthauptung: Frankreich schließt Islamisten-Moschee – und wir?" Facebook, October 21, 2020.

Alternative für Deutschland. "Wegen Corona: Krankschreibung ab sofort ohne Arztbesuch." Facebook, March 10, 2020.

Alternative für Deutschland im EU-Parlament. "Der neue Migrations-und Asylpakt: Eine Million Europäer können die Migrantenflut aufhalten!" Facebook, September 24, 2020. https://www.facebook.com/AfDimEUParlament/photos/a.270760250212577/665187744103157/.

Amaro, Silvia, and Christine Wang. "EU Leaders Reach $2 Trillion Deal on Recovery Plan After Marathon Summit." *CNBC*, July 20, 2020. https://www.cnbc.com/2020/07/21/eu-leaders-reach-a-breakthrough-on-the-regions-recovery-fund.html.

"Anzahl der Parteimitglieder der AfD von 2013 bis 2019." *Statista*, August 3, 2020. https://de.statista.com/statistik/daten/studie/730862/umfrage/mitgliederentwicklung-der-afd/.

Bennhold, Katrin. "Body Bags and Enemy Lists: How Far-Right Police Officers and Ex-Soldiers Planned for 'Day X.'" *The New York Times*, August 1, 2020. https://www.nytimes.com/2020/08/01/world/europe/germany-nazi-infiltration.html

Bennhold, Katrin. "She Called Police Over a Neo-Nazi Threat. But the Neo-Nazis Were Inside the Police." *The New York Times*, December 21, 2020. https://www.nytimes.com/2020/12/21/world/europe/germany-far-right-neo-nazis-police.html.

Bergsen, Pepijn. "Why the Pandemic and Populism Still Work Together." *Chatham House*, November 24, 2020. https://www.chathamhouse.org/2020/11/why-pandemic-and-populism-still-work-together.

Berry, Alex. "German State Puts Regional AfD Branch Under Surveillance – Reports." *Deutsche Welle*, January 26, 2021. https://www.dw.com/en/german-state-puts-regional-afd-branch-under-surveillance-reports/a-56342789

Bobba, Giuliano, and Nicolas Hubé. "Populism and Covid-19 in Europe: What We Learned From the First Wave of the Pandemic." *LSE*, April 20, 2021. https://blogs.lse.ac.uk/europpblog/2021/04/20/populism-and-covid-19-in-europe-what-we-learned-from-the-first-wave-of-the-pandemic/.

Bourne, Angela K. *Democratic Dilemmas: Why Democracies Ban Political Parties.* London: Routledge, 2018.

Bowlby, Chris. "Germany: Reluctant Military Giant." *BBC*, June 12, 2017. https://www.bbc.com/news/world-europe-40172317

Braw, Elisabeth. "Germany, Stop Worrying About Boosting Military Spending." *Politico*, December 21, 2020. https://www.politico.eu/article/germany-military-spending-nato-alliance-security-war/

Casert, Raf. "EU Economy to Expand, Bouncing Back From Pandemic Crisis." *AP*, May 12, 2021. https://apnews.com/article/europe-economy-health-coronavirus-pandemic-business-92cd5c307f3d24e38e71ce1aa279a439.

Chazan, Guy. "Germany's Far-Right Firebrand Disturbs Allies and Opponents Alike." *Financial Times*, October 25, 2019. https://www.ft.com/content/3816a566-f597-11e9-a79c-bc9acae3b654

Chrupalla, Tino. "CDU und CSU wollen 5000 Migranten aus Moria aufnehmen." Facebook, September 10, 2020. https://www.facebook.com/TinoAfD/photos/a.1758788034429462/2360964484211811/.

Chrupalla, Tino. "Die gesellschaftliche Teilung ist auch nach 30 Jahren deutscher Einheit nicht überwunden." Facebook, September 28, 2020. https://www.facebook.com/TinoAfD/photos/a.1758788034429462/2375577226083870/.

Chrupalla, Tino. "Mit vereinten Kräften für unser Land!" Facebook, March 31, 2020. https://www.facebook.com/TinoAfD/photos/a.1758788034429462/2243317925976468/.

Chrupalla, Tino. "Seit Wochen erreichen mich hunderte von E-Mails und Briefen von Bürgern zum geplanten 3. Bevölkerungsschutzgesetz." Facebook, November 17, 2020. https://www.facebook.com/TinoAfD/photos/a.1758788034429462/2416792031962389/.

Connolly, Kate. "Kurzarbeit: Germany's Scheme for Avoiding Unemployment." *The Guardian,* September 24, 2020. https://www.theguardian.com/world/2020/sep/24/kurzarbeit-germanys-scheme-fo-avoiding-unemployment.

Connor, Phillip. "Number of Refugees to Europe Surges to Record 1.3 Million in 2015." *Pew,* August 2, 2016. https://www.pewresearch.org/global/2016/08/02/number-of-refugees-to-europe-surges-to-record-1-3-million-in-2015/.

Davidson-Schmich, Louise. "The Alternative for Germany." Panel, American Institute for Contemporary German Studies, March 1, 2021.

Decker, Frank, and Philipp Adorf. "Coalition Politics in Crisis?: The German Party System Before and After the 2017 Federal Election," In *Twilight of the Merkel Era,* edited by Eric Langenbacher, 42. New York: Berghahn Books, 2019.

Devlin, Kat, and Nicholas Kent. "As Pandemic Continues, More in U.S. and Europe Feel Major Impact on Their Lives." *Pew Research Center,* February 3, 2021. https://www.pewresearch.org/global/2021/02/03/as-pandemic-continues-more-in-u-s-and-europe-feel-major-impact-on-their-lives/.

Eddy, Melissa, and Katrin Bennhold. "Angela Merkel Averts Crisis, Forming Government with SPD Again." *The New York Times*, March 4, 2018. https://www.nytimes.com/2018/03/04/world/europe/germany-spd-merkel.html

Ellyatt, Holly. "One Chart Shows How Bad Germany's Second Wave of the Coronavirus is." *CNBC,* December 1, 2020. https://www.cnbc.com/2020/12/01/germanys-second-wave-of-covid-19-has-been-worse-than-the-first.html.

Engesser, Sven, Nicole Ernst, Frank Esser, and Floris Büchel. "Populism and Social Media: How Politicians Spread a Fragmented Ideology." *Communication & Society* 20, no. 8 (2017): 1109–26.

European Commission. "Recovery and Resilience Facility: Maximum Grant Allocations." Accessed April 18, 2021. https://ec.europa.eu/info/sites/info/files/about_the_european_commission/eu_budget/recovery_and_resilience_facility_.pdf.

European Commission. "Recovery Plan for Europe." Accessed April 18, 2021. https://ec.europa.eu/info/strategy/recovery-plan-europe_en

Forschungsgruppe Wahlen E.V. "Politik II." Accessed April 18, 2021. https://www.forschungsgruppe.de/Umfragen/Politbarometer/Langzeitentwicklung_-_Themen_im_Ueberblick/Politik_II/.

"Gauland bezeichnet NS-Zeit als "Vogelschiss in der Geschichte." *Die Welt,* June 2, 2018. https://www.welt.de/politik/deutschland/article176912600/AfD-Chef-Gauland-bezeichnet-NS-Zeit-als-Vogelschiss-in-der-Geschichte.html.

"German Court Suspends Surveillance of Far-Right AfD, For Now." *Deutsche Welle,* March 5, 2021. https://www.dw.com/en/german-court-suspends-surveillance-of-far-right-afd-for-now/a-56785125.

"Germany's Far-Right AfD to Dissolve Extreme 'Wing' Faction." *Deutsche Welle,* March 20, 2020. https://www.dw.com/en/germanys-far-right-afd-to-dissolve-extreme-wing-faction/a-52864683

"Germany Shocked by Cologne New Year Gang Assaults on Women." *BBC,* January 5, 2016. https://www.bbc.com/news/world-europe-35231046.

Gidron, Noam, and Bart Bonikowski. "Varieties of Populism: Literature Review and Research Agenda." *Weatherhead Center for International Affairs Harvard University Working Paper Series,* no. 13-0004, 2014.

Graves, Chris. "The Killing of George Floyd: What We Know." *MPR News,* June 1, 2020. https://www.mprnews.org/story/2020/06/01/the-killing-of-george-floyd-what-we-know.

Henley, John, and Pamela Duncan. "European Support for Populist Beliefs Falls, YouGov Survey Suggests." *The Guardian,* October 26, 2020. https://www.theguardian.com/world/2020/oct/26/european-support-for-populist-beliefs-falls-yougov-survey-suggests.

Jagers, Jan, and Stefaan Walgrave. "Populism as a Political Communications Style: An Empirical Study of Political Parties' Discourse in Belgium." *European Journal of Political Research* 46, no. 3 (2007): 319–45.

Judis, John B. *The Populist Explosion: How the Great Recession Transformed American and European Politics.* New York: Columbia Global Reports, 2016.

Kellerhoff, Sven-Felix, Martin Lutz, and Uwe Müller. "Alice Weidel will Veröffentlichung rassistischer E-Mail stoppen." *Die Welt,* September 9, 2017. https://www.welt.de/politik/article168489086/Alice--will-Veröffentlichung-rassistischer-E-Mail-stoppen.html.

Kinkartz, Sabine. "Coronavirus: Angela Merkel's Approval Ratings Up Amid Health Crisis." *Deutsche Welle,* April 3, 2020. https://www.dw.com/en/coronavirus-angela-merkels-approval-ratings-up-amid-health-crisis/a-53001405.

Knight, Ben. "German State Elections Deepen Troubles for Angela Merkel's CDU." *Deutsche Welle,* March 15, 2021. https://www.dw.com/en/german-state-elections-deepen-troubles-for-angela-merkels-cdu/a-56879941.

Krämer, Benjamin. "Populist Online Practices: The Function of the Internet in Right-Wing Populism." *Communication & Society* 20, no. 9 (2017): 1293–309.

Langenbacher, Eric. "Germany's Memory Culture and the Alternative for Germany." *American Institute for Contemporary German Studies,* February 2, 2021.

Langenbacher, Eric, ed. *Twilight of the Merkel Era: Power and Politics in Germany After the 2017 Bundestag Election.* New York: Berghahn Books, 2019.

Lewandowsky, Marcel. "Alternative für Deutschland: A New Actor in the German Party System." *Friedrich Ebert Stiftung,* March 2014. http://library.fes.de/pdf-files/id/ipa/10644.pdf.

Louwerse, Tom, and Simon Otjes. "How Populists Wage Opposition: Parliamentary Opposition Behaviour and Populism in Netherlands." *Political Studies* 67, no. 2 (2019): 479–95.

"Mehrheit gegen 'Corona-Bonds'." *Cicero-Redaktion,* March 31, 2020. https://www.cicero.de/wirtschaft/corona-bonds-eu-schuldentilgung-corona-krise.

Menon, Rajan. "The Story of Germany's Armed Forces." *Foreign Policy,* June 18, 2020. https://foreignpolicy.com/2020/06/18/trump-withdraw-troops-germany-military-spending/.

Mény, Yves, and Yves Surel. "The Constructive Ambiguity of Populism." In *Democracies and the Populist Challenge,* edited by Yves Mény and Yves Surel, 126. London: Palgrave Macmillan, 2002.

Meuthen, Jörg. "Liebe Leser, bitte schätzen Sie einmal: Über wieviel Vermögen verfügt der mittlere c(volljährige) Deutsche (also derjenige, der sich genau in der Mitte zwischen der ärmeren und reicheren Hälfte unseres Landes befindet)?" Facebook, April 18, 2020. https://www.facebook.com/554345401380836/posts/1604023103079722/.

Meuthen, Jörg. "Liebe Leser, derzeit, also während der EU-Ratspräsidentschaft Deutschlands, versuchen die Endlos-Kanzlerin und ihre Schwester im Geiste von der Leyen mit aller Gewalt, die desaströse, Deutschland wie auch die EU tief spaltende Migrationspolitik der letzten Jahre auf Dauer festzuschreiben." Facebook, September 26, 2020. https://www.facebook.com/554345401380836/posts/1756731811142183/.

Meuthen, Jörg. "Liebe Leser, Deutschland steht vor einer Katastrophe. Nichts anderes sagen die Zahlen der letzten Tage, auch und gerade des gestrigen Tages." Facebook, March 20, 2020. https://www.facebook.com/554345401380836/posts/1577731682375531/.

Meuthen, Jörg. "Liebe Leser, die Lobhudeleien nach dem desaströsen EU-Gipfel kannten keine Grenzen: Überall war nur von Gewinnern "die Rede," Facebook, July 23, 2020. https://www.facebook.com/554345401380836/posts/1694088050739893/.

Meuthen, Jörg. "Liebe Leser, wenn die Coronakrise irgendetwas Gutes hatte, dann die Tatsache, dass die überdrehte Hysterie der freitäglichen Schulschwänzer-Bewegung mit einem Schlag von der Bildfläche verschwand." Facebook, August 22, 2020. https://www.facebook.com/554345401380836/posts/1722147484600616/.

Moffitt, Benjamin, and Simon Tormey. "Rethinking Populism: Politics, Mediatisation, and Political Style." *Political Studies* 62, no. 2 (2014): 381–97.

Mudde, Cas. "Populism: An Ideational Approach." In *The Oxford Handbook of Populism,* edited by Christóbal Rovira Kaltwasser, Paul Taggart, Paulina Ochoa Espejo, and Pierre Ostiguy, 3. Oxford: Oxford University Press, 2017.

Nagle, John D. *The National Democratic Party: Right Radicalism in the Federal Republic of Germany.* Berkeley: University of California Press, 1970.

Nelson, Rebecca M. "The Eurozone Crisis: Overview and Issues for Congress." *Congressional Research Service,* September 26, 2012. https://fas.org/sgp/crs/row/R42377.pdf.

Nesbit, Jeff. "Donald Trump Supporters Are Using a Nazi Word to Attack Journalists." *TIME,* October 25, 2016. https://time.com/4544562/donald-trump-supporters-lugenpresse/.

"New Pact on Migration and Asylum Package." *European Commission*, September 23, 2020. https://ec.europa.eu/commission/presscorner/detail/en/ip_20_1706

Nienaber, Michael, and Thomas Seythal, "Germany Avoids Record Economic Plunge in 2020 Despite COVID-19 hit." *Reuters,* January 14, 2021. https://www.reuters.com/article/us-germany-economy-gdp/germany-avoids-record-economic-plunge-in-2020-despite-covid-19-hit-idUSKBN29J10T.

Norris, Pippa, and Ronald Inglehart. *Cultural Backlash: Trump, Brexit, and Authoritarian Populism.* New York: Cambridge University Press, 2019.

"Official Provisional Result of the 2013 Bundestag Election." *The Federal Returning Officer,* September 23, 2013. https://www.bundeswahlleiter.de/en/info/

presse/mitteilungen/bundestagswahl-2013/2013-09-23-vorlaeufiges-amtliches-ergebnis-der-bundestagswahl-2013.html.

Oltermann, Phillip. "Germany's AfD Thrown into Turmoil by Former Neo-Nazi's Expulsion." *The Guardian,* May 18, 2020. https://www.theguardian.com/world/2020/may/18/germany-afd-thrown-into-turmoil-by-former-neo-nazi-explusion-andreas-kalbitz

Pappas, Takis S. "Populist Democracies." *Government and Opposition* 49, no. 1 (2014): 18–19.

Park, Jeanne. "Europe's Migration Crisis." *Council on Foreign Relations.* Accessed July 12, 2021. https://www.cfr.org/backgrounder/europes-migration-crisis

"Poll of Polls," *Politico,* https://www.politico.eu/europe-poll-of-polls/.

Porter, Noah. "Like Sands Through an Hourglass, So Are Angela Merkel's Approval Rating." *American Institute for Contemporary German Studies John Hopkins University,* August 12, 2020. https://www.aicgs.org/2020/08/like-sands-through-an-hourglass-so-are-angela-merkels-approval-ratings/

Rensmann, Lars. "The Noisy Counter-Revolution: Understanding the Cultural Conditions and Dynamics of Populist Parties in Europe in the Digital Age." *Politics and Governance* 5, no. 4 (2017): 131.

Riegert, Bernd. "World Refugee Day: Migration Problems Help Populists Prosper in Europe," *Deutsche Welle,* June 19, 2018. https://www.dw.com/en/world-refugee-day-migration-problems-help-populists-prosper-in-europe/a-44263784.

Rooduijn, Matthjis. "The Nucleus of Populism: In Search of the Lowest Common Denominator." *Government and Opposition* 49, no. 4 (2013): 573–99.

Salzborn, Samuel. "Discussion of New Right Elements in German Right-Wing Extremism Today." *German Politics & Society* 34, no. 2 (2016): 36–63.

Schreiber, Manfried, and Yung Ping Chen. "Ideology of the National Democratic Party of Germany." *Journal of Thought* 6, no. 2 (1971): 88–104.

Schumacher, Elizabeth. "German populists AfD Adopt Anti-Islam Manifesto." *Deutsche Welle,* May 1, 2016. https://www.dw.com/en/german-populists-afd-adopt-anti-islam-manifesto/a-19228284.

"Solidarity Cannot be Voluntary,' Portugal Begins Talks on EU Migration Pact." *Reuters,* January 5, 2021. https://www.reuters.com/article/us-portugal-europe-migration/solidarity-cannot-be-voluntary-portugal-begins-talks-on-eu-migration-pact-idUSKBN29A2SE.

Spindler, William. "2015: The Year of Europe's Refugee Crisis." *UNHCR,* December 8, 2015. https://www.unhcr.org/en-us/news/stories/2015/12/56ec1ebde/2015-year-europes-refugee-crisis.html

Statista. "Wie macht Angela Merkel ihre Arbeit als Bundeskanzlerin alles in allem gesehen?" Accessed July 13, 2021. https://de.statista.com/statistik/daten/studie/675140/umfrage/bewertung-der-arbeit-von-angela-merkel-als-bundeskanzlerin/#professional.

Staudenmaier, Rebecca. "AfD's Alice Called German Government 'Pigs' in Racist Email." *Deutsche Welle,* September 20, 2017. https://www.dw.com/en/afds-alice--called-german-government-pigs-in-racist-email/a-40433932

The Alternative for Germany Party. "Programm für die Wahl zum Deutschen Bundestag am 24. September, 2017," 16–20. Accessed April 18, 2021. https://manifesto-project.wzb.eu/.

The Alternative for Germany Party. "Walhprogram Parteitagsbeschluss vom 14.04.2013." Accessed April 18, 2021. https://manifestoproject.wzb.eu//down/originals/41953_2013.pdf.

Vehrkamp, Robert, and Wolfgang Merkel. "Populism Barometer 2020: Populist Attitudes Among Voters and Non-Voters in Germany 2020." *Bertelsmann Stiftung*, 2020. https://www.bertelsmann-stiftung.de/fileadmin/files/BSt/Publikationen/ GrauePublikationen/ZD_Populism_Barometer_2020.pdf.

Weidel, Alice. "Merkel's Lockdown-Forever Halting ist ein offenbarungseid für Offenbarugnseid für unsere Demokratie." *Alternative für Deutschland,* February 9, 2021. https://www.afd.de/alice-weidel-merkels-lockdown-forever-haltung-ist-ein-offenbarungseid-fuer-unsere-demokratie/

3 Decentralizing and Democratizing Identity Narratives through Regional Tourism

A Lesson from Catalonia

Max Ferrer

1 Introduction

The increasing visibility of national and subnational cultural identities on the European continent during the latter half of the twentieth century embodies both a cause and effect of the growing uncertainty surrounding the concept of a united Europe. Spain's autonomous region of Catalonia represents a primary example of such a subversive ideational geography, where industry, government, activists, and civilians have participated in a process of cultural differentiation since Spain's return to democracy in 1978. The growing salience of national and regional identities represents a challenge to those attempting to encourage a European identity. This chapter examines the tension between the dream of a European identity and the growth of regional identities by studying Catalonia's flourishing tourism industry.

Somewhat paradoxically, the increasing strength of national and regional identities in the latter half of the twentieth century is contemporaneous with the deliberate consolidation of European politics, society, and identity. Indeed, this period witnessed the reorganization and consolidation of competing models of social structures, nationalism, and statehood throughout the world's hegemonic powers. With the rise and decline of the Soviet empire, the aggressive spread of American economic empire, and the consolidation of a European community, governments and citizens from different cultures and contexts wrestled with what it meant to be a nation, a state, and an empire. As Europe attempted to rebuild from the geographical and ideational ruins of the mid-twentieth century, not only did national borders and the foundations of international relations shift, but professed values, identities, and historical narratives were renegotiated and reinterpreted. This rupture allowed for unprecedented international cooperation, though it also provided fertile soil for the growth of national and regional identities that have come to challenge the ability of European leaders to promote a cohesive European identity.

The relationships between local, regional, national, and transnational identities are incredibly complex, as reflected by the proliferation of

DOI: 10.4324/9781003182344-4

scholarly debate surrounding European identity in recent years. As we will see, the issue is not that the existence of national and regional identities threatens the existence of a European identity, nor that the tension between different geographical identities originates from antagonistic narratives contained within them. Rather, the challenge facing European leaders is that decentralized power over definition and transmission of national and regional narratives makes it difficult for the European Union (EU) to corral varying identities into a single narrative that may serve the continent as a whole.

In this chapter, I present one such challenge by centering an agent of identity formation that is, at best, an afterthought in European identity literature, and is more often than not overlooked altogether: tourism. In doing so, I aim to make three main points. First, tourism is a powerful didactic tool that is central to the creation and dissemination of national narratives. Second, the tourism industry's decentralization and shift toward regionally specific cultural and heritage attractions further enhances the ability of regional trends and actors to stimulate regional identities. Third, the existence of these regional identities needn't threaten the existence of a broader European one. However, tourism allows smaller regions to retain incredible power in dictating certain characteristics of identity that, while outside of the control of the EU, need to be addressed in any European-wide identity narrative.

In order to examine these points, I take on the case study of the autonomous Spanish region of Catalonia, which is home to one of Europe's most potent regional independence movements. While enjoying little progress toward independence in the realm of politics, the *Catalanisme* movement has found great success in terms of preserving and promoting its cultural uniqueness. One primary avenue of the dissemination of culture has been a booming cultural tourism industry that emerged in the wake of the 1992 Barcelona Olympics Games. While a unique Catalan identity is not necessarily antagonistic to a European one, the particular contours of its national narrative may pose a challenge to those seeking a broader European narrative. Specifically, the region's imperial history is important to its political identity and its ambitions. This is in contrast with the EU, which has come under criticism for not sufficiently recognizing the continent's imperial legacy. This tension begs the question: Will democratization of identity through a growing tourism industry encourage more people to identify with Europe, or will it foster narrative contradictions that make European cohesion all the more unlikely?

2 Nested European Identities

Given its theoretical complexity, one can approach the problem of identity from numerous starting points. When applied to a specific political entity or region like Europe, the potential entryways into creating a sufficient understanding seem to multiply. For this reason, scholarly attempts to understand, categorize, critique, or predict the potential for a European identity has yielded an incredibly saturated field with various approaches but little consensus. The abundance of questions that scholars ask about European identity – What is European identity? Does it exist? Is it important? Who identifies with Europe? Why? How can we measure it? – reveal the numerous approaches one can take toward trying to understand, including the conceptual, existential, political, sociological, methodological, and normative. I will not attempt to establish an exhaustive topography of the myriad problematizations and approaches to identitarian phenomena. Rather than taking a side in the countless debates that arise in each of these approaches, I proceed from a point of near-universal agreement.

Most scholars concur that no matter the strength of a European identity, it is not the only identity to which an individual European might subscribe. Put another way, Europe is not the only geographical or political entity with which a European might identify. A European may identify with their town or village, but this does not preclude them from also maintaining an identity attached to other geographical groupings such as their region, nation, state, or continent.[1] A question of central importance, then, is how these separate identities, or separate identifications, might interact. The most agreed-upon answer to this question can be found in Juan Diaz Medrano and Paula Gutierrez's theory of 'nested identities.' They define their conceptualization in the following terms:

> Nested identities are lower- and higher-order identities such that the latter encompass the former. My identity as a resident in city 'a', is nested in my identity as resident of region 'A' – which includes city 'a' – which is in turn nested in my identity as resident of country 'Alpha', and so on.[2]

The degree to which individuals identify with each unit is both variable and contextual. Crucially, however, the simple existence of lower- and higher-order identities does not threaten the existence or adoption of another. In fact, recent trends in globalization have led to stronger identification with both lower- and higher-order identities. That is, in the face of globalized economics and culture, individuals have turned to various orders of identification as mechanisms of both individual differentiation and inclusion in various groups.[3]

According to Diaz Medrano and Gutierrez, the existence of regional identities does not threaten European identity as a whole. However, national, regional, and local institutions retain significant power over what a European identity can mean. That the existence of local, regional, national, and international identities are not mutually exclusive is of fundamental importance for any possibility of a European identity. That said, this should not be taken to mean that tensions cannot arise between the various orders of identity. Remember, the lower-order identities are nested *inside* the higher-order ones, meaning that identification with one unit can be affected if the narratives associated with another identity are contradictory. Additionally, identification with the same unit might mean different things to different groups of people. Thus, if there is to be a professed and cohesive European-wide identity narrative, it cannot conflict with the narratives of lower-order identity groups. In this regard, a European body such as the EU has its power of identity creation checked by the arbiters of lower-order identities. One primary example of this phenomenon is the manner in which actors within the cultural tourism industry promote distinct national and regional identities.

3 Tourism and Identity

Tourism theorists have long recognized the industry's nationalist potential. Indeed, tourism wields tremendous didactic power by literally writing and promoting the cultural narratives encountered by both locals and visitors. Sociologist Dean MacCannell argues that "tourists take a voyage of discovery on which they attempt 'to discover or reconstruct a cultural heritage or a social identity.'"[4] The more tourism offers specific cultural attractions rather than simply leisure, the more "tourism [creates] new forms of knowledge, defining what 'ought' to be seen, a valorization that [engages] both visual and written texts concerning tourist sites themselves."[5] Tourists flock to these sites in order to consume not only the commodities and luxuries that various destinations have to offer but to gain knowledge about and experience of the locales they are visiting. In essence, tourists consume the places themselves.

In his aptly named book *Consuming Places*, John Urry argues that the economic and didactic potential of tourism is largely dependent on what he pinpoints as the primary tourist function: gaze.[6] This gaze involves looking "individually or collectively upon aspects of a landscape or townscape which are distinctive, which signify an experience which contrasts with everyday experience."[7] Tourist gaze, Urry suggests, is not focused on random cultural objects. Rather,

> An array of tourist professionals...attempt to reproduce ever new objects of the tourist gaze. These objects are located in a complex and changing hierarchy. This depends upon the interplay between, on the one hand, competition between different capitalist and state interests involved in the provision of such objects; and on the other hand, changing class, gender and generational distinctions of taste within the potential population of visitors.[8]

Tourists then participate in the specific ways in which tourist sites are made meaningful, though only inasmuch as they are consumers. The tourist professionals retain most of the power over the specific cultural narratives they produce and have great freedom in doing so, as long as they remain profitable. In her study on Austrian tourism, Jill Steward argues that, as a result of this bilateral process of meaning-making, specific organization and narrative representations of an individual place gain commercial significance with the introduction of tourism.[9] All the while, in the face of increasing competition for tourism dollars, it pays to be distinct.

This process of making distinct and commodifying certain narratives of place and their resulting attractions is not new; in fact, it has been practiced for centuries. As Orvar Lofgren argues in a Swedish context, "national projects were made transnational, imported and transformed into new, unique national settings" as early as the nineteenth century when "nations started to construct their heritage and tourist attractions in contrast and comparison with others."[10] Indeed, the usefulness and profitability of the tourism industry in creating a distinct national identity is a centuries-old tactic.

The ability to control "the authoritative representation of 'ourselves,' of 'our' landscape, traditions, and way of life that was presented in the millions of promotional materials disseminated each year" is what literary scholar James Buzard terms 'autoethnography.'[11] The increased power of autoethnography during the latter half of the twentieth century grew along with the cultural tourism industry throughout Europe, but is particularly identifiable in Catalonia, where domestic political developments created a boom in the creation, presentation, and celebration of Catalan culture. This power of self-definition, motivated to portray cultural uniqueness, yields narratives that are fundamentally guided by the same dynamics that determine local identity.

4 Twentieth-Century Spain and the Importance of Tourism

A brief discussion of twentieth-century Spanish history is necessary to put the discussion of developments in Catalonia's tourism industry into context and to illustrate their significance. Owing to a complex history stretching back over a millennium, Catalonia has remained, in many ways, culturally distinct from the rest of Spain. As recent political developments in the region suggest, this distinction continues to foment conflict between Catalonia and the central Spanish government. Historically, many Spanish monarchs, dictators, and even republican administrations have, to varying degrees of severity, attempted to limit or completely do away with any recognition of Catalan cultural difference and political autonomy. Indeed, the fraught nature of the region's political status is rooted in political developments stretching back to the first time its territories were united in the year 878.

Despite the rich and ancient history of the region, Catalan nationalism is a rather recent phenomenon, with its origins in the cultural *Renaixença*, or renaissance, that took place in the mid-nineteenth century. One of the central developments that influenced the strength and form of modern *Catalanisme* was the fascist regime of General Francisco Franco that held power from 1939 until his death in 1975. Beginning with the defeat of the Republicans during the Spanish Civil War (1936–1939), and continuing throughout the entirety of his regime, Franco sought nothing less than the complete erasure of Catalan culture and the *Catalanisme* movement. In promoting a singular, Castilian Spain, [12] Franco sought to quash any regionalist movements, cultural distinction, and political separatism. In Catalonia, this meant revoking the statute of autonomy won during the Second Republic (1931–1939), the dissolution of almost all political parties, the elimination of the free press and many civic organizations, and, perhaps most significantly, the prohibition of the Catalan language.

Franco was also well aware of the power that tourism had in creating international reputation and identity, and it is no coincidence that Minister of Information and Tourism Manuel Fraga Iribarne launched the 1964 tourism campaign under the slogan 'Spain is Different!'[13] This marketing scheme would not only draw visitors from abroad to Spain but would allow Spanish authorities significant control over the sites and narratives that tourists would encounter. Importantly, while Spain was certainly different from the rest of Europe in many internal respects, Franco sought to present the nation as a unified cultural and political entity.

> Since foreigners and Spaniards alike now related to Spanish culture through the filter of tourism, the industry framed the Spanish nation as an organic, harmonious entity bound by a common identity and shared cultural and geographical treasures, and clearly differentiated the country from others.[14]

In a world where advertising occupied an increasingly central role in knowledge production, tourism, and its capacity for marketing destinations, became a tool with unquestionable narrative strength. In Fraga's view, tourism in Spain was successful precisely because of the unified yet distinctive nature of the Spanish people and state. On the flip side, tourism was "necessary in order to discern, express, and 'defend' that same distinctiveness."[15] This self-referential, and indeed mutually constitutive process, is fundamental to the relationship between tourism and national identity, which grew even stronger in the second half of the twentieth century.

The intense crackdown on unique Catalan culture during Franco's regime also had a destructive effect on the bastions of leftist Catalan institutions, such as civil society organizations and trade unions. Given the success of Franco's repression, the leftist Catalan national movement had been effectively crushed by the dictatorship by the 1960s. In the aftermath of the dictatorship, these organizations enjoyed popular support but lacked cohesive direction or unified strategy, conditions which allowed a more conservative expression of commercial and capitalistic *Catalanisme* to thrive. It was in this environment that Catalans began harnessing the didactic power of tourism for their own political ends. As we can see in Estela Marine-Roig's study of Catalan tourism marketing in European guidebooks during the twentieth century, the tourism infrastructure and relevant advertising of Catalonia shifted from the Franco-inspired, culturally homogenous sun, sand, and sea messaging, to a Catalan-specific cultural tourism.[16]

In the period after Franco's death and Spain's return to democracy in 1978, *Catalanisme* found itself with a new set of tools by which it could construct and promote a national identity and fight for autonomy. The post-Franco shift toward the mass commercialization of Catalan culture was a response to the specific opportunities and limitations presented by Spain's new democratic regime. While democracy and cultural liberalization allowed Catalans the freedom to once again speak their language and practice their regional traditions, the ratification of the 1978 Spanish constitution limited the ways in which Catalan politicians could further the political cause of *Catalanisme*. Significantly, however, this newly free cultural space allowed for the promotion and exportation of a uniquely Catalan cultural identity. This cultural differentiation was encouraged through various means, such as tourism excellence programs, which aimed to provide local governments with the resources to reinvigorate and reorient their civic spaces to accommodate cultural tourism. Through such plans, the Catalan government in partnership with private industry has helped smaller communities revamp tourism industries that had run into issues such as poor infrastructure and tarnished natural resources while focusing "on improving the quality and image of local destinations."[17]

In the midst of drastic political developments during the 1980s and 1990s owing to Spain's democratization,[18] it is important to remember that the tourism industry allowed many Catalans the opportunity to consume their own national identity for the first time. After decades of brutal political repression, Catalans could attend their own cultural festivals, speak their regional language, visit national monuments, and publically embrace their Catalan heritage without fear of retribution. Kevin Walsh argues that the expansion of the heritage industry is a response to the disconnection that many people feel from history and that commercialization represents an opportunity to find roots.[19] The rapid development of Catalan heritage tourism in the 1980s and 1990s supports this theory, as Catalans had been deprived of their language and cultural practices after decades of suppression. As the Catalan heritage industry grew, tourism narratives became a primary creator and transmitter of national memory through specific narratives concerning Catalonia, its relationship to Spain, and Europe more broadly.

When considering the European narratives present in Catalan tourism attractions, it is important to remember Frank Mols, Jolanda Jetten, and S. Alexander Haslam's point that EU identification does not exist in a vacuum, and is, in fact, heavily influenced by regional and national political concerns.[20] Catalan intellectuals Albert Balcells and Salvador Giner argue that in addition to being the source of their oppression, Catalans have historically viewed Castilian Spain as backwards and anti-modern in relation to the wealthy, progressive region of Catalonia.[21] Indeed, Catalonia has often been on the forefront of political and industrial trends in the nineteenth and twentieth centuries, while the rest of Spain developed more slowly and disjointedly.[22] These historical trends have led many Catalanists to believe that the region has more in common with Europe than with the rest of Spain. Moreover, many believe that Castilian Spain is holding Catalonia back from becoming a cultural and economic leader in Europe and throughout the world.[23] As we begin to discuss the specific autoethnographic historical and political narratives present in Catalan tourism attractions, it is of crucial importance to remember that *Catalanisme* has long tried to distance and differentiate itself from the rest of Spain, while making claims to its 'rightful' place as a European leader.

5 Imperial Memory and Catalan Identity

Emerging from a period of what many felt was colonization by Castilian Spain, Catalans presented their region not only as a nation in its own right but one that previously presided over its own empire. Looking forward to Catalonia and Spain's political futures, these narratives put forth an understanding of Catalonia as a modern economic leader that should become the political, economic, and cultural leader within Spain. Achieving domestic hegemony would naturally bring international renown. Such progress would affirm Catalonia's national destiny by bringing it in line with Europe's other leading powers not only through their professed values, but also through their shared history of international domination and economic progress. This measure of success is not just referred to by modern thinkers such as Balcells and Giner, but by their intellectual forbearers from earlier in the twentieth century. Indeed, the Europeanization and modernization programs of prominent politician Enric Prat de la Riba[24] and the outright imperial language of historian Jaume Vicens Vives[25] embrace Catalan and European exceptionalism while centering the need for international economic dominance and cultural hegemony. Rooted in the imperial systems of the time, this narrative of Catalan regional identity associated what it means to be European with having enjoyed imperial power.

On the heels of the *Renaixença*, a mid-nineteenth century romantic movement that reinvigorated Catalan language and culture, the end of the nineteenth century would bring yet another territorial and political shock to Spain and Catalonia. After the various conflicts between Cuba and Spain from 1868 to the Spanish American War in 1898, Spain lost possession of the island. The loss of Cuba and the consequent collapse of the Spanish empire triggered a profound political and ideological crisis. National self-esteem, founded largely on Spain's status as an empire and a first-rate international power, disappeared. The loss of empire provoked similar calamity in Catalonia, given the significance of the island in not just the Catalan economy but the Catalan imagination. During the years in which Cuba was held under Spanish possession, it represented not only an incredibly fruitful economic opportunity for Catalan trade, but for Catalan individuals as well. Often termed 'the Fifth Province of Catalonia,' Cuba was the destination for thousands of Catalan immigrants looking to escape poverty and make a fortune in one of the world's richest colonies before returning home. This pattern of migration gave rise to the myth of the *Indianos* or *Americanos*: adventurous Catalan entrepreneurs who set out for the Caribbean seeking wealth and returned from Cuba with vast fortunes. For Catalans, the separation from Cuba was not only a massive economic loss, but a cultural loss as well, which further provoked animosity toward the ineffective and discriminatory Spanish state. The fall of the Spanish empire left an indelible mark on Catalan memory and identity. Attributing this colonial failure to Castilian Spain, regional Catalanist political parties won power promising regional autonomy and a return to their imperial heights. In the post-Franco period, the tourism industry in Catalonia would codify and amplify this identity narrative to the millions of locals and tourists who would visit regional attractions.

Perhaps the highest-profile example of this didactic power was the 1992 Barcelona Olympic Games. The bid to host the games was put forward by Catalonia's socialist government in 1981, very shortly after the death of Franco and just three years after Spain's return to democracy. The Catalan and Spanish governments supported the bid, albeit to separate and often competing ends. According to John Hargreaves, "the Spanish government saw the Games primarily as a matter of national prestige: it was determined to show that Spain is a fully modernized, mature democracy and member of the European community."[26] Catalan nationalists, however, saw the Games as an opportunity to promote their cause on an international level, further modernize the city of Barcelona, and establish the region as the rightful cultural and economic leader of democratic Spain. What followed was an intense and prolonged mission to 'Catalanize' the Games. This mission was a success not only because Catalan leaders won the battle to put many symbols of Catalan culture directly in front of viewers, but because it provided a strategic template for the future of the *Catalanisme* movement.[27] The 1992 Barcelona Olympic Games showed Catalan leaders that they could further their cause not only through political negotiation but through commercial promotion. This strategy would be adopted by the Catalan government and industry in the years following the Olympics during the massive expansion of the region's tourism infrastructure and economy.

In the decades following the Olympic games, Catalonia transitioned into a global center of cultural tourism. Tourism was a new economic program made possible by international investment before and after the Olympic Games and made exceptionally profitable by the money that tourists from around the world now spend in the region. Harnessing the tourism industry would not only restore Catalonia to its economic dominance within Spain (after Franco turned Madrid into the country's financial capital) but would, crucially, allow Catalonia to present its own cultural and national narrative to the world.

6 Catalan Tourism Attractions

In order to demonstrate the didactic power of tourism and the challenge that it presents to European leaders aiming to stimulate a pan-European identity, I have selected three specific Catalan tourist attractions devoted to the region's transatlantic history created and advertised in the decades following the transition to democracy. As I will include in my discussion of each of these attractions, much of Catalonia's history and national identity is predicated on the region's industrial success and international presence in the eighteenth and nineteenth centuries. These successes were made possible by Catalonia's imperial relationship with Cuba. Each of these attractions refer to this relationship and, in one way or another, address the underlying anxieties pervading Catalan culture surrounding Catalonia's history, its hampered prosperity, subjugation to Spain, and relationship with Europe. In doing so, these tourist attractions bring Catalonia's former imperial qualifications to the fore, intentionally placing this history at the center of the modern conception of what it means to be Catalan.

The annual *Cantada d'Havaneres* in Palafrugell is a popular music festival attended by thousands of Catalans and foreign visitors alike. For one day in early June, festival-goers gather in this coastal town and enjoy performances by the most popular *habanera* groups. *Habanera*, named for Cuba's capital city, became a popular type of music after 1898 and remains a strong signifier of Catalan culture and identity.[28] The themes in lyrics of prominent songs concern love, longing, and loss resulting from the imperial experience. Though popular throughout Spain in the early twentieth century, in the second half of the century *habanera* songs were published far more often in Catalan (as opposed to Castilian Spanish) and came to be identified with Catalan culture. The *Cantada d'Havaneres* was first held in 1966 as a meeting of a group of singers coinciding with the presentation of the book *Calella de Palafrugell i les havaneres*, which was the second collection of *habaneras* published in Catalonia. The success of that first event inspired organizers to set up a more formal gathering the following summer. In the early years, the *Cantada* was hosted by the singing groups themselves and later by the *Amics de Calella* association from 1967 to 1972.[29] The bottom-up nature of this event's inception and its quick success is understandable not only because of the cultural importance of public festivals in Catalan society, but also because it was one of the few times Catalans could publically enjoy a unique cultural signifier of their own in the final few years of the Franco dictatorship.[30] Additionally, while still under the yoke of Franco's repression, *habanera* music evoked nostalgia for a time when the region enjoyed greater autonomy, economic dominance, and imperial power of its own.

In 1973, the *Amics de Calella* held the event in association with the Palafrugell City Council and the Tourism Community of Costa Brava. By 1977, the municipal tourism office of Palafrugell took over the planning and production and remained at the helm until 2005, when the *Institut de Promoció Econòmica de Palafrugell* took over. The *Institut* still runs the event today. Tourism falls under the jurisdiction of such an economic body because it makes up such a large part of the local economy. According to the *Institut*, "Actualment, el turisme és el sector principal de Palafrugell, amb gairebé un 80% de les empreses municipals dedicades al sector dels serveis."[31] ("Currently, tourism is the main sector of Palafrugell, with almost 80% of companies in the municipality dedicated to the service sector.")

Such a progression of civic groups putting on local festivals under government oversight and economic motivation is not uncommon. Jill Steward traces a similar development in alpine tourism in Austria. She claims the main support for the tourism industry came from various local organizations, such as alpine associations, who initially aimed "to promote the love of the mountains, but soon became important vehicles for the development of tourism."[32] In the Catalan case, this development is illustrative not only of the specific progression of this event (from small cultural event to large-scale tourist attraction) during the transition period but also a recognition on the part of Catalan government officials of the profitability of cultural tourism and the subsequent move to restructure the economy to serve the industry.

Today, the event is an explicitly government-organized economic project. It receives funding from the *Generalitat*, the *Diputació de Girona*, and the Girona Tourism Department, as well as private sponsorship funding from La Caixa Bank and the popular beer company Estrella Damm. Additionally, the event is organized in collaboration with various cultural and media organizations such as TV3, *Fundació Ernest Morató*, *Club Vela Calella*, AVAC (*L'Amics de Calella*), *Xarxa de Municipis Indians*, and *Cultura i Identitat Costa Brava Pirineu de Girona*.[33] One of these organizations, *Cultura i Identitat Costa Brava Pirineu de Girona*, is a member of the Costa Brava Girona Tourist Board, which was founded in 1976. According to its mission, it serves as "the meeting point between the various government bodies and the tourism sector in Girona province, focusing its work on three areas: External marketing, Internal marketing, Competitiveness."[34] While the *Cantada* began as a small gathering of local musicians, today its organizers' priorities seem less musical in nature than political.

The *Fira d'Indians* festival in Begur is another summer tourist event that entered the cultural marketplace in the decades following the transition to democracy.[35] First held in 2004, much later than the *Cantada*, the *Fira d'Indians* is a product of the post-1992 tourism boom in Catalonia. The fair was a self-conscious attempt by the local government to attract visitors and promote local culture, with the municipality of Begur responsible for its organization since its inception. The fair itself celebrates

> the strong connection between Cuba and Begur, which dates back to the large numbers of local people who emigrated to the island over the course of the 19th century. On their return to the town, those who had made their fortune in business built showy houses that still adorn the streets of Begur. Known as the "Americans", they aimed to recreate their Cuban lifestyle, while leaving behind a varied cultural legacy. On the first weekend in September, Begur is transformed, recreating a period of history which left a profound influence on our town and on our identity.[36]

This description from the town's tourism authority describes a celebration of Catalan nostalgia for imperial supremacy. Recalling fortunes made overseas, sensuous and exotic Caribbean life, as well as the richness of their own culture, the organizers present an image of a former imperial power. The magnitude of Catalonia's overseas prosperity subverts the reality of the failure of Spanish imperialism by claiming successful imperialism as their own. Catalan intellectuals, such as Albert Balcells and Salvador Giner, claim that such imperial greatness and economic prosperity is not only at the heart of ethnic *Catalanisme* but also a justification for why they should be their own nation today.[37]

It is worth noting that the *Fira d'Indians* is held every year on the first weekend of September. This is not only the height of the region's tourist season, but it also falls the week before *L'onze de Setembre*, Catalonia's day of national celebration. The program from the 2019 festival advertises various DJs and Cuban bands, premieres of new *habanera* songs, academic panels, dancing lessons, theater performances, and workshops on making and selling handicrafts. So, while the festival fulfills the necessity that the tourist experience must be participatory and easily consumed,[38] imperial history and international visibility are associated with the upcoming celebration of Catalan nationalism. In this sense, while tourists are not only consuming Catalan history and the narrative of its imperial glory, they are also consuming Catalan nationalism.

A similar connection is on display in the *Rutas de Indianos* that appear in multiple Costa Brava municipalities. These tourism routes build on the success of other *Indianos*-related events such as the *Cantada d'Havaneres* and *Fira d'Indians*. These routes are managed and promoted by *La Xarxa de Municipis Indians*, which was founded during the tourist season of

2008. Aiming to "investigar, identificar y difundir el patrimonio material e inmaterial de los indianos en Catalunya,"[39] ("...to investigate, identify and disseminate the tangible and intangible heritage of Indianos in Catalonia,") the network consists of 11 participating municipalities that offer tours of the ports, towns, and mansions built and utilized by Catalan *Indianos*. They are funded primarily by the individual townships, but they also receive occasional subsidies from the *Diputacion de Barcelona, Girona* and *Tarragona*, as well as the *Generalitat de Catalunya*.

Whether emphasizing the strategic importance of various ports, describing the Caribbean influence on architecture from the period, or touring the homes of wealthy *Indianos* who built mansions to use upon their return from Cuba, these routes further associate the imperial history of Costa Brava and Catalonia with their modern identity. In cementing the importance of imperialism within modern *Catalanisme*, these attractions are reflective of broader trends in European tourism and identity creation. Indeed, the *Rutas de Indianos* are simultaneously a part, and at the forefront of, a European-wide initiative aimed at reunderstanding and promoting post-colonial heritage. The International Network of Emigrant Towns and European Post-Colonial Heritage, founded and headquartered in Begur, "is defined as an International Association formed by public institutions and social and cultural organisations interested in the preservation and dissemination of historical memory and the culture of emigrants who returned to Europe."[40] This initiative is funded not only by the *Generalitat de Catalunya* but also by the EU via the Cultural Routes and the Council of Europe Program

> Launched by the Council of Europe in 1987, the Cultural Routes demonstrate, by means of a journey through space and time, how the heritage of the different countries and cultures of Europe contributes to a shared and living cultural heritage.[41]

In this sense, the leveraging and centering of colonial history is not solely a Catalan project. Rather, the region is at the forefront of a broader trend in tourism development involving not only civic reorganization, but spatial and temporal re-imagination. This reinterpretation of historical relationships is not only used to prompt a Catalan national identity but is institutionally encouraged by Europe's governing body.

Each of the tourist attractions presents a specific and intentional image of Catalonia that is consumed by the tens of thousands of foreign visitors they attract each year. The image they project inextricably links Catalonia to its imperial past, cementing the ethnic characteristics of economic savvy and international prominence. By doing so, the narratives understand Spanish imperial glory as Catalan rather than Castilian in nature, placing Catalonia in the same league as other former European empires. Two of the examples I presented are specific festivals, which Raj, Griffin, and Morpeth identify not only as "very important motivators of tourism" but also as figuring "prominently in the development and marketing plans and strategies of most cities and destinations."[42] Organizers of these events traffic explicitly in the realm of cultural creation and promotion as visitors seek to gain cultural exposure. While the 1992 Olympics are the most dramatic case study, the examples I have chosen similarly elucidate the ways in which self-conscious nationalism is written not only in Catalan cultural narratives but are foundational to the economic and civic organization of the region.

7 Colonialism, Catalonia, and European Identity

The prominence of Catalonia's former imperial relationship with Cuba in Catalan tourism narratives is no accident. Many Catalans understand the region's former imperial grandeur and continued economic prosperity as defining qualities and, for those with Catalanist sentiments, as justification for its independence. This centering of imperial history is largely out of step with Europe's reckoning – or its lack thereof – with its own colonial past. The atrocities and legacies of European imperialism is, understandably, a difficult topic for the EU and its Member States to adequately address. However, many scholars argue that the EU has failed to sufficiently reckon with this history on both an institutional and discursive level.[43] One important issue is that this independence narrative supports an identity and a movement that challenges the territorial sovereignty of an EU Member State and raises questions about the application of European values of democracy and self-governance. That, however, is not the point I wish to explore. Rather, I want to suggest that if Catalanist identity finds pride in its imperial history, then any European identity that aspires to include Catalanists will necessarily need to accommodate this view of imperial history. This necessarily limits the power and freedom of European leaders in their project of articulating a continental identity.

As a number of scholars have noted, while the EU has gone to great lengths to recognize and reckon with its history of Stalinism and Nazism, it has failed to do so with the legacy of imperialism.[44] The absence of remembrance is particularly interesting given Aline Sierp's claim that:

> Europe's identity and the EU's history have been intrinsically linked to its rule over the rest of the world. As Michelle Pace and Roberto Roccu write: 'Colonialism is silently inscribed in the genes of the European integration project since its origins.'[45]

I argue that it is precisely the fundamental relationship between European identity and colonialism to which Catalan identity speaks. This returns to Mols, Jetten, and Haslam's assertion that identities are not formed in a vacuum. Catalan identity is crafted in response to Catalonia's relationship with Spain and with Europe, among other geographical and political relationships. In this light, we should read *Catalanisme*'s centering of imperial history as not only a reaction to the colonialism fundamental to the 'Europeanness' to which *Catalanisme* aspires, but also a rejection of the legitimacy of Spanish rule over Catalonia. The question remains, though, whether this is a narrative that the rest of Europe could support. While Europe struggles to create a narrative reconciling a colonial past it condemns and an economically dominant future it aspires to, might its lack of control over regional identities cause confusion, if not splintering?

As discussed, tourism is a unique social field given the explicit nature in which it portrays national identity. However, it is unique not just in its presentation of cultural narratives, but also in its audience. Many scholars have suggested that those who interact with other Europeans feel the strongest European identity, but this type of European interaction is often limited to the contexts of business and higher education.[46] Not only do these fields of interaction contain mostly the economically and socially privileged (those who benefit from and are thus more likely to identify with the European project), but they are also largely apolitical. Tourism, however, is an expansion of the European public sphere that is outside the purview of political and economic elites and apolitical niceties. In a similar manner, visiting and learning about other cultures and their associated identities through specially crafted tourism narratives can bring people of different states and nations together. This is, in fact, the explicit hope of many of the EU's tourism campaigns. At the same time, though, tourism can cause disagreement, offense, and outrage – particularly in a region as politically charged and contested as Catalonia. How might other Europeans react to Catalan claims that to be European is to have been an empire?

As European leaders aim to foster a continental identity, it is these types of interactions and potential discursive conflicts that will have to be accommodated. With the proliferation of tourism, not only do more and more Europeans come into contact with each other, but individual regions gain more power over their own identity narratives. This is another example of what Neil Fligstein identifies as scholarship's failure to pay "much attention to the horizontal ties between people and organizations across Europe."[47] In the early days of the EU, it was elites that interacted most with other Europeans, and thus elites were able to define the central tenets of European identity. Today, the forces of globalization, including increased air travel and generalized affluence throughout Europe, have allowed for an increase in affordable tourism opportunities. Consequently, everyday citizens, including those who do not necessarily identify as 'European' in the sense that the EU attempts to promote, will come into contact with different national and regional identity narratives. These developments take place within the context of a global market that incentivizes tourist destinations to be unique in their cultural attractions. Moreover, attractions, and by extension, narratives, are often under the authority of government agencies and corporations. The result is a broad range of identity narratives, the proliferation of which highlights the decentralized and democratized identitarian forces at work. This phenomenon not only challenges our understanding of nested identities by giving greater weight to lower-order ones, but will require leaders to react and adapt when attempting to promote a European identity. At present, European leaders have not recognized the strength and uniqueness of lower-order identities, like Catalan regionalism, whether because they choose to ignore them or simply are unaware of their local embeddedness. Nevertheless, failure to account for these localized identities will not only fail to strengthen a European identity based on universal values, but threatens to undermine the project of a common European identity altogether.

8 Conclusion

In the complex scholarly realm concerning the future of European identities, scholars agree that there exists a multitude of identities and no limit to the amount to which one individual may feel connected to their various identities. The nested nature of these identities means that higher-order identities contain lower-order ones inside them that often respond to local, regional, and national circumstances. As a result, the dynamics of local and regional identity creation can pose major ideological and political challenges to national and supranational identity narratives. Political and cultural developments in Catalonia over the last century have given rise to a particularly salient regional identity that many Europeans encounter through business and education but also tourism. The region's tourism boom exemplifies the global surge of cultural tourism in the latter half of the twentieth century, during which tourism industries and national projects often played a mutually constructive role. While this is just one of the many strategies employed to retain and promote Catalan identity, the tourism industry has provided government and industry a means by which to create cultural narratives that situate Catalan history and its political and ideational relationships in a specific, favorable context. This in turn creates a national identity that is marketed to the world. The Catalan case is but one of many in Europe in which cultural narratives and images are produced and negotiated by both nationalism and tourism, as the two work symbiotically to promote the nation to a global audience.

Catalan tourism narratives highlight the economic and imperial dominance that it enjoyed during its renaissance period in the mid-nineteenth century. Relying largely on pre-1898 nostalgia, Catalan tourism narratives present the case for national legitimacy on the grounds of former imperial grandeur. Events such as the *Cantada d'Havaneres* and the *Rutas Indianos* throughout the Costa Brava locate Catalonia's imperial and international history and economic strength at the center of the modern Catalan identity. In doing so, they respond to historical animosity with what they consider to be a backwards, anti-European Spain. In the Catalan view, Spain has failed to ingratiate itself as one of Europe's leading powers: an interpretation of twentieth-century history that is not far off the mark. Instead, Catalonia, and the tourism narratives that I've reviewed in this chapter, construct a regional identity as well as a broader European one centered on its imperial past. Just as Catalans find Spanish decadence at fault for their loss of empire in 1898, Spain is again at fault for keeping Catalonia from achieving its European destiny today.

While the existence of a Catalan regional identity does not threaten the existence of a broader European one, provocative and controversial identities such as this one highlight the challenges that confront those who aim to promote continental identity narratives. Tourism is a democratizing force when it comes to identity creation, and the industry's trend toward cultural and heritage tourism have further vested individual regions and Member States with narrative power over identity that may conflict with the aims of European leaders. Colonialism is not the only topic over which regional narratives have autoethnographic power, and, as more Europeans experience Europe on a local and personal level, the democratization and proliferation of different identity narratives may prove to sustain a cognitive dissonance that erodes a common European identity, if one existed in the first place.

Notes

1 While this chapter is concerned only with identifications with political geographies, these coexist with countless other group identifications, such as linguistic groups, ethnic groups, sports clubs, civil society organizations, and fraternities.
2 Juan Díez Medrano and Paula Gutiérrez, "Nested Identities: National and European Identity in Spain," *Ethnic and Racial Studies* 24, no. 5 (December 2001), 757, https://doi.org/10.1080/01419870120063963.
3 Medrano and Gutiérrez, "Nested Identities," 759.
4 Shelley Baranowski and Ellen Furlough, eds., *Being Elsewhere: Tourism, Consumer Culture, and Identity in Modern Europe and North America* (Ann Arbor: University of Michigan Press, 2001), 3.
5 Baranowski and Furlough, *Being Elsewhere,* 9.
6 John Urry, *Consuming Places* (New York: Routledge, 1995), 132.
7 Urry. *Consuming Places,* 132.
8 Urry. *Consuming Places,* 133.
9 Baranowski and Furlough, *Being Elsewhere,* 9.
10 Baranowski and Furlough, *Being Elsewhere,* 139.
11 Baranowski and Furlough, *Being Elsewhere,* 300.
12 "Castilian" refers to the cultural and linguistic descendants of the Crown of Castile, first formed in the thirteenth century. The Crown of Castile united the Kingdoms of Castile and León. These two territories make up the majority of what is now modern Spain. However, these territories notably exclude Catalonia. The union of the Crown of Castile and the Crown of Aragon, which included the Catalan territories, in the fifteenth century would lead to the formation of the Monarchy of Spain. There are significant contemporary linguistic and political ramifications of this history. The language that English speakers call "Spanish," Spaniards refer to as *Castellano*, referring to the territory and legacy of Castile. This cultural and linguistic tradition, as opposed to *Catalan*,

the language spoken in Catalonia, was understood and promoted by Franco as the state's unifying language and cultural tradition.

13 Justin Crumbaugh, *Destination Dictatorship: The Spectacle of Spain's Tourist Boom and the Reinvention of Difference* (Albany: SUNY Press, 2009), 59.
14 Crumbaugh, *Destination Dictatorship*, 59.
15 Crumbaugh, *Destination Dictatorship*, 60.
16 Estela Marine-Roig, "The Image and Identity of the Catalan Coast as a Tourist Destination in Twentieth-Century Tourist Guidebooks," *Journal of Tourism and Cultural Change* 9, no. 2 (June 2010): 118–39, http://dx.doi.org/10.1080/14766825.2011.566929.
17 Lorena Beas Secall, "Effects of the Implementation of Tourism Excellence Plans (1992–2006) in Spain. The Case of the Catalan Coast," *Journal of Policy Research in Tourism, Leisure and Events* 4, no. 1 (March 2012): 84–104, https://doi.org/10.1080/19407963.2011.642875.
18 Namely, the liberalization of cultural policy, adoption of neoliberal economic policy, and greater acceptance into the international community.
19 Kevin Walsh, *The Representation of the Past: Museums and Heritage in the Postmodern World* (New York: Routledge, 1992).
20 Frank Mols, Jolanda Jetten, and S. Alexander Haslam, "EU Identification and Endorsement in Context: The Importance of Regional Identity Salience," *Journal of Common Market Studies* 47, no. 3 (2009): 602.
21 See Balcells' *Catalan Nationalism* and Giner's *The Social Structure of Catalonia*.
22 Joseph Harrison, "Introduction: The Historical Background to the Crisis of 1898," in *Spain's 1898 Crisis: Regenerationism, Modernism, Post-Colonialism*, ed. Joseph Harrison (Manchester: Manchester University Press, 2000).
23 Max Ferrer, "Touring Imperial Catalonia: Consuming Nostalgia, Constructing Identity" (MA Thesis, Columbia University, 2021).
24 Enric Prat de la Riba, *La Nacionalitat Catalana* (Barcelona: La Cataluña, 1910).
25 Jaime Vicens Vives, *Noticia de Cataluña* (Barcelona: Ediciones Destino, 1954).
26 John Hargreaves, *Freedom for Catalonia: Catalan Nationalism, Spanish Identity, and the Barcelona Olympic Games* (New York: Cambridge University Press, 2000).
27 See Hargreaves' *Freedom for Catalonia?* and Illas' *Thinking Barcelona* for further discussion on the attempt to "Catalanize" the 1992 Olympic games.
28 For further reading, Galina Bakhtiarova has written extensively on the significance of *habanera* music and Cuba in the Catalan imaginary. See "Empires of the Habanera: Cuba in the Cultural Imaginary of Catalonia," "The Iconography of the Catalan Habanera: Indianos, Mulatas and Postmodern Emblems of Cultural Identity," and "Transatlantic Returns: The Habanera in Catalonia."
29 "HISTORY OF THE CANTADA," *Havanerescalella.Cat* (blog), accessed September 7, 2020, http://www.havanerescalella.cat/en/history-of-the-cantada/.
30 Temma Kaplan, *Red City, Blue Period: Social Movements in Picasso's Barcelona* (Berkeley: University of California Press, 1992).
31 Institut de Promoció Econòmica de Palafrugell, "Turisme," accessed September 7, 2020, https://ipep.cat/ca/turisme.
32 Baranowski and Furlough, *Being Elsewhere*, 114.
33 "MORE INFORMATION," *Havanerescalella.Cat* (blog), accessed September 7, 2020, http://www.havanerescalella.cat/en/more-information/.
34 Patronat de Turisme Costa Brava Pirineu, "About Us," accessed September 7, 2020, https://trade.costabrava.org/en/about-us/.
35 There are similar fairs held in Palafrugell and Sant Feliu de Guixols, though Begur's is the largest and most prominent.
36 Visit Begur, "Fira d'Indians Fair," accessed September 7, 2020, https://visitbegur.cat/en/fira-dindians-fair/.

37 See Balcells' *Catalan Nationalism* and Giner's *The Social Structure of Catalonia.*
38 Razaq Raj, Kevin A. Griffin, and Nigel D. Morpeth, eds., *Cultural Tourism* (Cambridge: CAB International, 2013), 53.
39 Xarxa de Municipis Indians, "Quienes somos," accessed September 7, 2020, https://www.municipisindians.cat/es/la-xarxa/qui-som.
40 International Network of European Postcolonial Heritage and Municipalities, "Project of a Council of Europe Cultural Route," accessed September 7, 2020, https://www.municipisindians.cat/forum/.
41 Council of Europe, "Cultural Routes of the Council of Europe," accessed September 7, 2020, https://www.coe.int/en/web/cultural-routes.
42 Raj, Griffin, and Morpeth, *Cultural Tourism*, 191.
43 See Michell Pace and Roberto Roccu's "Imperial Pasts in the EU's Approach to the Mediterranean" and Aline Sierp in *History, Memory, and Trans-European Identity: Unifying Divisions* (New York: Routledge, 2014), https://doi.org/10.4324/9781315766973.
44 I list these two authoritarian and violent political regimes together not because one can or should attempt to compare the two, but because they are two major moral and political crimes of recent European history to which the EU has dedicated time and resources in order to address. For further discussion on the logical and moral pitfalls of drawing an equivalence between the two, see Susan Neiman's *Learning from the Germans: Confronting Race and the Memory of Evil.*
45 Aline Sierp, *History, Memory, and Trans-European Identity: Unifying Divisions*, 2–3.
46 Neil Fligstein, *Euroclash: The EU, European Identity, and the Future of Europe* (Oxford: Oxford University Press, 2008), 3, http://www.columbia.edu/cgi-bin/cul/resolve?clio14073540.
47 Fligstein, *Euroclash*, 10.

Bibliography

Balcells, Albert. *Catalan Nationalism: Past and Present.* London: Palgrave Macmillan, 1996.

Baranowski, Shelley and Ellen Furlough, ed. *Being Elsewhere: Tourism, Consumer Culture, and Identity in Modern Europe and North America.* Ann Arbor: University of Michigan Press, 2001.

Beas Secall, Lorena. "Effects of the Implementation of Tourism Excellence Plans (1992–2006) in Spain. The Case of the Catalan Coast." *Journal of Policy Research in Tourism, Leisure and Events* 4, no. 1 (March 2012): 84–104. https://doi.org/10.10 80/19407963.2011.642875.

Council of Europe. "Cultural Routes of the Council of Europe." Accessed September 7, 2020. https://www.coe.int/en/web/cultural-routes.

Crumbaugh, Justin. *Destination Dictatorship: The Spectacle of Spain's Tourist Boom and the Reinvention of Difference.* Albany: SUNY Press, 2009.

Ferrer, Max. "Touring Imperial Catalonia: Consuming Nostalgia, Constructing Identity." MA Thesis, Columbia University, 2021.

Fligstein, Neil. *Euroclash: The EU, European Identity, and the Future of Europe.* Oxford: Oxford University Press, 2008. http://www.columbia.edu/cgi-bin/cul/resolve?clio14073540.

Giner, Salvador. *The Social Structure of Catalonia.* Sheffield: Anglo-Catalan Society, 1984.

Hargreaves, John. *Freedom for Catalonia: Catalan Nationalism, Spanish Identity, and the Barcelona Olympic Games.* New York: Cambridge University Press, 2000.

Harrison, Joseph, ed. "Introduction: The Historical Background to the Crisis of 1898." In *Spain's 1898 Crisis: Regenerationism, Modernism, Post-Colonialism*, edited by Joseph Harrison. Manchester: Manchester University Press, 2000.

"History of the Cantada," *Havaneres Calella*. Accessed February 20, 2022. https://www.havanerescalella.cat/en/history-of-the-cantada/.

Institut de Promoció Econòmica de Palafrugell. "Turisme." Accessed September 7, 2020. https://ipep.cat/ca/turisme.

International Network of European Postcolonial Heritage and Municipalities. "Project of a Council of Europe Cultural Route." Accessed September 7, 2020. https://www.municipisindians.cat/forum/.

Kaplan, Temma. *Red City, Blue Period: Social Movements in Picasso's Barcelona*. Berkeley: University of California Press, 1992.

Marine-Roig, Estela. "The Image and Identity of the Catalan Coast as a Tourist Destination in Twentieth-Century Tourist Guidebooks." *Journal of Tourism and Cultural Change* 9, no. 2 (June 2010): 118–39. http://dx.doi.org/10.1080/14766825.2011.566929.

Medrano, Juan Díez, and Paula Gutiérrez. "Nested Identities: National and European Identity in Spain." *Ethnic and Racial Studies* 24, no. 5 (December 2001): 757. https://doi.org/10.1080/01419870120063963.

Mols, Frank, Jolanda Jetten, and S. Alexander Haslam. "EU Identification and Endorsement in Context: The Importance of Regional Identity Salience." *Journal of Common Market Studies* 47, no. 3 (2009): 602.

"More Information," *Havaneres Calella*. Accessed February 20, 2022. https://www.havanerescalella.cat/en/more-information/.

Neiman, Susan. *Learning from the Germans: Confronting Race and the Memory of Evil*. New York: Farrar, Straus and Giroux, 2019.

Patronat de Turisme Costa Brava Pirineu. "About Us." Accessed September 7, 2020. https://trade.costabrava.org/en/about-us/.

Prat de la Riba, Enric. *La Nacionalitat Catalana*. Barcelona: La Cataluña, 1910.

Raj, Razaq, Kevin A. Griffin, and Nigel D. Morpeth, eds. *Cultural Tourism*. Cambridge: CAB International, 2013.

Sierp, Aline. *History, Memory, and Trans-European Identity: Unifying Divisions*. New York: Routledge, 2014. https://doi.org/10.4324/9781315766973.

Urry, John. *Consuming Places*. New York: Routledge, 1995.

Vicens Vives, Jaime. *Noticia de Cataluña*. Barcelona: Ediciones Destino, 1954.

Visit Begur. "Fira d'Indians Fair." Accessed September 7, 2020. https://visitbegur.cat/en/fira-dindians-fair/.

Walsh, Kevin. *The Representation of the Past: Museums and Heritage in the Postmodern World*. New York: Routledge, 1992.

Xarxa de Municipis Indians. "Quienes somos." Accessed September 7, 2020. https://www.municipisindians.cat/es/la-xarxa/qui-som.

4 The Birth of the Maastricht Generation

The Role of Young Hungarians in Defending European Democracy

Floris Maria Rijssenbeek

1 Introduction

"The health and stability of a modern democracy depends not only on the justice of its 'basic structure' but also on the qualities and attitudes of its citizens."[1] Writing in 1994, Will Kymlicka and Wayne Norman predicted one of the key political questions of our time: how to sustain mass support of democratic structures. With concern mounting over Central and Eastern European countries facing a 'democratic recession,' we again are in the midst of a vivid intellectual and public debate on the future of Europe's democratic project.[2] Hungary, once considered a poster child for smooth democratic transition, has increasingly been at the center of this debate. The ruling government, backed by an overwhelming electoral majority, has consistently dismantled democracy in the past decade. Since Viktor Orbán, Hungary's now-long serving prime minister, came to power in 2010, he has systematically eroded the foundations of democracy and the rule of law. The attitudes of Hungarians toward democracy seem to have declined under Orbán's watch, as the stability of democracies depends not only on the resilience of its basic institutions but also on the engagement of its citizens.[3]

It is increasingly argued that for young democratic regimes in the post-Soviet space, 25 years have proven to be insufficient to establish resilient democratic institutions.[4] Because the euphoric expectations of democracy in post-communist Hungary were dispelled as the country moved toward democratic disillusion and disengagement, many Hungarians by 2010 came to be less supportive of democracy than people elsewhere in Europe.[5] This was amplified by the fact that, as Orbán came to power, the Hungarian youth grew increasingly unsupportive of the liberal democratic system and became unwilling to engage in it.[6] What has not yet been examined, however, is how this trend among Hungary's youth (16–29) has evolved since Orbán's rise to authority. As such, this chapter asks the question: How has the Hungarian youth's engagement with democracy developed since 2010?

By drawing on new data from several large-scale surveys on youth engagement with democracy, conducted as democratic backsliding progressed under Orbán's regime, this chapter concludes that young Hungarians in 2020 are increasingly supportive of democracy compared to their 2010 counterparts.[7] Moreover, although they seem to turn away from voting in elections, young Hungarians have gradually turned to alternative ways to engage with democracy and put pressure on the authoritarian regime. Both findings point to an emergent democratic generation, what I deem the 'Maastricht Generation.' This is a group of young, pro-democracy Europeans who have only ever lived in a democratic and free European Union (EU) and who, as they emerge into voting adults, will support the democratic idea of Europe. As the youth picks up the fight for democracy, it is essential to recognize this dynamic while exploring ways forward for democratic resilience in Hungary and beyond. As Habermas notes, "the institutions of constitutional freedom are only worth as much as a population makes of them."[8]

2　Hungary's Three Antidemocratic Waves: The Context of Today's Emergent Democrats

'Friends of civic freedom have to remember what is at stake here: the fate of universal human rights and ultimately, the guarantees of peace.' - Miklós Haraszti (2018).[9]

In order to contextualize and analyze the changing political attitudes of the Hungarian youth during the last decade, a fundamental understanding of the historical and political dynamics in the period leading up to the 2010s is needed. I propose three distinct developmental phases in post-communist Hungarian history. The first is from 1990 to 2004, in which Hungary redefined itself as a promising post-communist state in democratic transition. It was a time of pro-EU sentiment and high hopes for future prosperity. The second period, from 2004 to 2010, was one in which Hungary as a new EU Member State was subject to persistent corruption, economic disillusionment, and rising anti-EU sentiment. The final period, from 2010 to 2020, has been characterized by rising authoritarian sentiments fueled by broader public disillusion with liberal democracy. During this period, Orbán took office as the prime minister and, backed by the overwhelming majority of the Fidesz party, began to implement laws and policies that destroyed the young Hungarian democracy from the inside out.[10]

Understanding the political developments in all three periods helps to illuminate the broader context of Hungary's democratic backslide, the environment in which young Hungarians have come of age as political actors. This, in turn, sheds light on the political attitudes of this emergent generation.

2.1 1990–2004: The Most Promising Democratic Kid on the Block

With the conclusion of the Cold War in 1991, and in the sudden absence of the Union of Soviet Socialist Republics' political control in Central and Eastern Europe (CEE), democracy began to spread throughout the region.[11] Hungary, already one of the most liberal communist countries, was considered a "forerunner of building democracy and market economy" in the region.[12] It became the first CEE country to develop a functioning party system, with a major party both on the left and right of the political spectrum.[13] While every Eastern European country that democratized from 1989 to 1990 had a constitutional or tribunal court, Hungary's was considered even more powerful than those in Western Europe, holding "remarkably broad jurisdiction and extensive authority."[14] This constitutional court functioned as a judicial safeguard for democratic reforms, meant to uphold the rule of law.[15] After all of these democratic components were established, and with support from the West, Hungary held its first democratic elections in April 1990.[16]

During the first free election campaign in 1990, there was a shared belief among the political parties that the most important foreign policy goal was an early Hungarian membership in the EU.[17] EU membership had become a symbol and perquisite of a prosperous and democratic state. Most parties, among them Fidesz, emphasized the economic advantages of EU membership and saw it as the final death knell for the old socialist regime. In that sense, it was seen as a *sine qua non* of modernization.[18] Other parties, like the Christian Democratic People's Party, argued that on top of the economic benefits of EU membership, Hungary had always been an organic part of the West, having been "violently isolated from its natural environment for forty years."[19] Thus, that party's political slogan was not 'the road to Europe,' but rather 'return to Europe.'

While Hungary was tasked to enact substantial institutional reforms to be eligible for accession to the EU,[20] the sentiment in Brussels and Budapest was that Hungary's intention to democratize would suffice for a smooth transition toward democracy and EU membership.[21] Despite significant shortcomings both in Hungary's process of democratization[22] and the EU's application of the Copenhagen criteria,[23] the EU's eventual declaration that Hungary had fulfilled all of the requirements seemingly signaled a bright and prosperous future for Hungary.

2.2 2004–2010: Rising EUphobia and Democratic Disillusionment

Hungary's transition to democracy was not as linear as initially expected. Hungary's accession to the EU took place later than expected and the anticipated economic benefits, notably increased income and welfare, were not met. According to data gathered in 2004, the proportion of Hungarians who thought that EU membership would be advantageous for Hungary peaked in autumn 2002 at 76%, followed by consistent decline afterwards.[24] As "the requirements set and support offered by the Union became clear" after 2002, the proportion of optimists decreased by 18 percentage points by spring of 2004, "when only 58 percent of Hungarian citizens professed to believe that EU membership would be advantageous for the country."[25] As a result, soon after Hungary's accession in 2004, the EUphoria in Hungarian society was replaced by a feeling of disappointment. This sentiment and feeling of missing out on the promised welfare increase was further strengthened following the 2008 financial crisis and the consequent economic crisis. Whereas in 2004, 49% of respondents considered membership a good thing, by 2011 only 32% stated that this was the case. The proportion of those opposing membership rose from 10% to 22% between 2004 and 2011, with a further rise to 23% in 2009 at the peak of the financial-economic crisis.[26]

Moreover, the rather fast transition toward democracy did not pave the way for a non-corrupt and well-functioning government. From 2002 to 2010, when the socialist-liberal party, the Social Democrats MSZP, and the Liberals SZDSZ led the government, corruption soared as the ruling political elite used its contacts to enrich itself. Moreover, the socialists, unified in a semi-reformed version of the communist party, were unable to transform themselves into a genuine social democratic party. At the same time, the Free Democrats, the country's urban liberals, tore itself apart with in-fighting. Consequently, half of the country was neglected and left economically underdeveloped. This opened the door to the rise of far-right nationalist parties like Jobbik and Fidesz.[27]

Consequently, in the 2010 elections, the socialists lost most of their political support while the far-right Jobbik party garnered an astounding 17% of the votes, including 23% of votes cast by Hungarians 18–29 years old. The real victory, however, was enjoyed by the center-right Fidesz party. Orbán, the long-time leader of Fidesz, received more than a two-thirds majority in parliament, which meant a non-coalition government could be formed.[28] The massive electoral support that Fidesz received in the 2010 election was a firm rejection of the Socialist party's austerity policies and an endorsement of Fidesz's promises of tax cuts, job creation, and support for local businesses.[29]

2.3 *2010–2020: Democratic Backslide and Diminishing Rule of Law*

Since the electoral victory of Fidesz in 2010, the Hungarian political and governmental landscape has changed significantly. Orbán built the so-called 'system of national cooperation,' in which the antagonistic dualism between the government and the opposition was replaced by a 'central political field of force' (centralis erőter). Essentially, this allowed Orbán to eliminate political opposition and centralize power in the executive, notably including passing new media laws that restricted media pluralism and established a government-controlled body overseeing Hungary's media environment.[30]

The centralization of power also made it easier for the ruling government to draft and approve a new constitution. This constitution received criticism from the Venice Commission for Democracy through Law of the Council of Europe and other EU institutions like the European Parliament and the European Commission, which subsequently launched infringement proceedings against Hungary for breaches of the principles of democracy and the rule of law.[31] The Venice Commission noted that

> the more policy issues are transferred beyond the scope of simple majority, the less significance will future elections have and the more possibilities a two-third majority have of combining its political preferences and the country's legal order. If not only the fundamental principles but also very specific rules on certain issues will be enacted by means of cardinal laws, the principle of democracy itself is at risk.[32]

These developments have broadly been described as the intensification of the democratic backslide in a country that once was believed to be a European model of democratic transition. The changes made to the constitutional framework were considered signs of deconsolidation of Hungary's liberal democratic institutions and a move to entrench illiberal or partial democracy.[33] Fidesz's complete stranglehold on power across various government bodies allowed it not only to adopt a new and weakened constitution, but at the same time expand the usage of cardinal laws (special acts of parliament) and ensure its power over broad areas of public life. These constitutional changes enabled the governing party to criminalize homelessness, establish the sentence of life imprisonment without parole, and define marriage exclusively as being between a man and a woman.[34] Under Orbán's lead, the party further strengthened the executive power of the government, in part by subordinating the legislative and judicial branches. As such, the government lowered the age of retirement of members of the judiciary from 70 to 62 years which effectively allowed the government to replace about 10% of the judicial body.[35]

The democratic backslide continued after the general elections in 2014, when Fidesz, together with coalition partner Christian Democrats (KDNP), upheld a majority in parliament.[36] At a more rapid pace than before, the government passed laws that undermined the democratic processes of consultation, negotiation, and consensus, and additionally further pursued the dismantling of the rule of law.[37] By doing so, the openly illiberal government manipulated legislative norms, impeded the functioning of judicial institutions, and demolished the separation of powers. Consequently, nearly all independent human rights bodies of the United Nations and the Council of Europe began raising concerns about the state of Hungary's democracy.[38] Support for Orbán catapulted during the refugee crisis of the mid-2010s. In direct opposition to EU policies, the Hungarian government refused to participate in refugee resettlement programs, claiming that such policies would challenge the national character of Hungary. By fanning the flames of xenophobia through anti-refugee rhetoric, Orbán successfully distracted the Hungarian public from issues of endemic corruption.[39] This rhetorical shift not only helped Fidesz remain in power after the 2018 election, it helped it secure a parliamentary majority. At the time, many saw Fidesz's electoral success as a victory for right-wing populism throughout Europe.[40]

Today, Hungary's opposition remains fragmented. Opposition parties increasingly contend with state-imposed obstacles and restrictions that lower their ability to gain power through fair elections. These include unequal access to media, politicized audits, smear campaigns, and a campaign environment skewed by the ruling coalition's mobilization of state resources.[41]

In conclusion, ten years of democratic backsliding has deeply shaken the fundamental tenets of democracy in Hungary. After taking power in the 2010 elections, Orbán's Fidesz party pushed through various constitutional and legal changes that have allowed Orbán to consolidate control over the multiple national independent institutions. More recently, the Fidesz-led government has moved to institute policies that impede the operations of opposition groups, journalists, universities, and nongovernmental organizations (NGOs) whose perspectives it finds unfavorable. Concerningly, the Hungarian population has largely been quiescent to these democratic erosions; national elections have demonstrated that most voters support Fidesz's illiberal policies. There is now only one main hope for the future of Hungarian democracy: the Maastricht Generation. Is Hungary's emergent youth likely to push back against Orbán's illiberalism?

3 Hungary's Emergent Democrats: An Analysis of Hungarian Youth Politics

Although the general political context in Hungary since 2010 has been dominated by Orbán and his Fidesz party, it must still be seen what political orientation Hungary's emergent generation takes. To do so, I focus on two youth cohorts: that of 2011 and that of 2020.

The 2011 youth cohort is the group of young people who were between the ages of 16 and 29 one year after Orbán came to power with a supermajority in parliament. Roughly speaking, most of them were born around the fall of the Iron Curtain, a period of democratic and European euphoria. Many of this cohort were first-time voters in the 2010 elections.

The 2020 youth cohort is the group that was between the ages of 16 and 29 in 2020, ten years after Orbán came to power. Many of the 2020 youth cohort were, in contrast to the 2011 cohort, born just before Hungary's accession to the EU in 2004. In other words, they have only known Hungary as an EU Member State. Moreover, some of the 2020 cohort were first-time voters during the national election in 2018 and/or European election in 2019. Studying the difference in engagement with democracy between these two cohorts may therefore tell us something about how the ongoing democratic backslide has affected the political attitude of Hungarian youth in the last decade.

Both Eastern and Western Europe experienced a populist authoritarian wave from around 2010 onwards, with many studies finding that this wave enjoyed major and increasing support among the Hungarian youth.[42] This resulted in the following hypothesis:

> *H1: The further away a cohort is from the communist era, the less it will support democracy because few members will recall the horrors of communism.*

Through empirical analysis, I will argue that this is not the case and therefore reject the prevailing hypothesis in order to explain the change in engagement with democracy of young Hungarians in the last decade. After rejecting the accepted hypothesis, I introduce and discuss an alternative hypothesis that, in many ways, can be seen as the inverse hypothesis of the original. I label it as an inverse hypothesis because it uses similar dynamics but in the opposite direction. While the 2010 authoritarian wave was fueled by democratic disillusion, the 2020 democratic generation is partially fueled by authoritarian disillusion as Orbán's government not only increasingly fails to live up to its promises but indeed takes away important civic freedoms. Therefore, the alternative hypothesis goes as follows:

> *H2: The more a cohort has grown up under Orbán's regime, the more likely it will support democracy since fewer members will recall the age of democratic disillusionment.*

4   Youth Attitude Toward Democracy, 2010–2020

As there are no extensive studies yet which analyze youth attitudes toward democracy in the context of the recent democratic backslide in Hungary, this section will try to fill this gap. I analyze data from multiple surveys on youth political attitudes in Hungary that were conducted between 2010 and 2020. These surveys include large-scale surveys on youth civic engagement in Hungary conducted by the Active Youth (Aktív Fiatalok) Research Group and surveys conducted by Political Capital in 2017 and 2020.

In order to understand and contextualize how attitudes toward democracy have changed over the course of the last decade, I will focus on data that speak to four questions: (1) What is the youth's preferred system of governance? (2) Is this reflected in the youth's party preferences? (3) How are Hungarian youth's party preferences linked to political concerns? (4) How does the Hungarian youth participate in politics?

4.1 Preferred System of Governance: Democracy

In order to investigate the youth's preferred system of governance, I draw on data that stems from a large-scale survey on youth civic engagement in Hungary conducted by the Active Youth (Aktív Fiatalok) Research Group.

The Active Youth Research Group has conducted four surveys, in 2011, 2013, 2016, and 2019, using the same methodology. Each report surveyed a single social cohort consisting of more than 1,300 respondents, most of whom were students. Students may not necessarily represent the Hungarian youth as they are typically of relatively privileged socioeconomic status and often tend to lean to the liberal spectrum of political thought.[43] Any bias stemming from this premise will not be expected to affect the analysis of this section as I compare preferences for systems of governance over a period of time, in search for general trends or developments in young people's engagement with democracy.

Looking at the data of respondents that answered the question 'what system of political governance has your preference,' some interesting findings can be pointed out. First, a provocative result from the survey in 2011, a year after Orbán took office, is that many Hungarian youth were highly critical of democracy. Less than 40% of the respondents

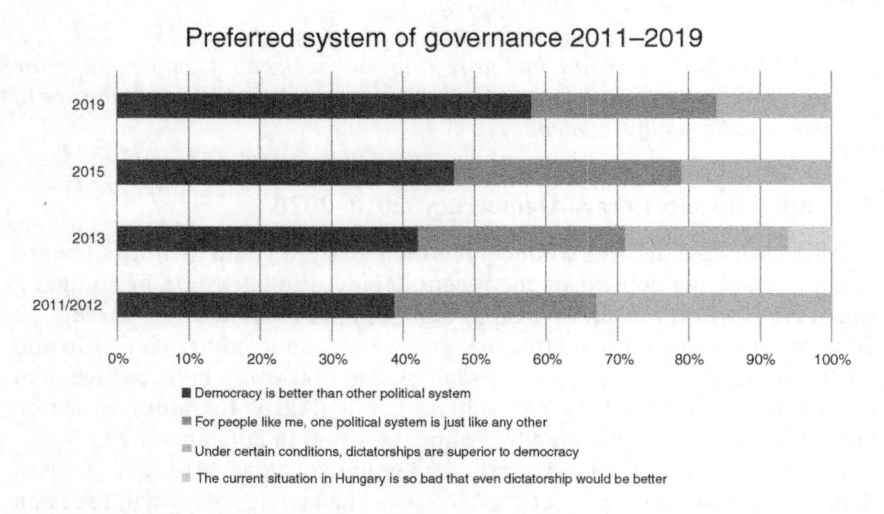

Preferred system of governance 2011–2019

- Democracy is better than other political system
- For people like me, one political system is just like any other
- Under certain conditions, dictatorships are superior to democracy
- The current situation in Hungary is so bad that even dictatorship would be better

Figure 4.1 Youth preference for democracy, 2011–2019.

deemed democracy to be better than other political systems. One third even thought that dictatorship is acceptable under 'certain circumstances.' Moreover, nearly three quarters stated that it is all the same to them what kind of political system they live in. More specifically, the 2011 Active Youth Research Group survey reveals that 78% of the respondents were highly dissatisfied with the operation of democracy, while satisfied respondents made up only 22% of the population.

In 2013, we can observe a small growth of 3% for those who deemed democracy to be better than another political system. But we can also observe the emergence of a group that deemed the current situation in Hungary so bad that even a dictatorship would be better. This might reflect the political turmoil in that year as the new constitutional reforms were implemented to wipe out what was left of opposition forces against the government.[44]

However, a few years into Orbán's semi-authoritarian regime, we already see a larger shift toward a more pro-democratic stance. By April 2015, the youth's commitment to democracy seems to have increased significantly: 47% of them stated that democracy was better than other political systems, and the rate of those who deemed dictatorship an acceptable form of governance decreased by 11% in comparison to 2011. Moreover, the group which deemed the current situation in Hungary so bad that even a dictatorship would be better completely vanished from the picture.

This trend intensified even further as the democratic backslide in Hungary sharpened under Orbán's watch. By 2019, after nearly a decade of consistent democratic backsliding in Hungary, the Hungarian youth seems to have become widespread supporters of democracy: 58% said that democracy is better than any other political system, a 10% increase since 2015. Moreover, the rate of respondents thinking that dictatorship is acceptable under certain circumstances decreased from 21 to 16%. Based on the data from these surveys, one can safely conclude that the surveyed youth cohort in 2020 professes to be more liberal and pro-democratic than its 2011 counterpart.

Findings from yet another recent survey on Hungarian youth's attitude and engagement toward democracy echo the findings from the Active Youth Research Group. The Political Capital Institute conducted two large public opinion polls, in 2017 and 2020, of Hungarian youth aged 16 to 29 to explore the political attitudes and political participation of young people in Hungary. The first survey research data was collected through telephone interviews in 2017 from a sample of 500 citizens of Hungary, ages 16 to 29. This was just before national elections were held in 2018.[45] A key finding of the 2017 survey was that most respondents professed a strong commitment to democracy in general. Of the respondents, 69% agreed with the statement that 'Democracy is the best possible political system.'[46] That number grew by a modest 5% in 2020, when 74% of respondents agreed that democracy is the best possible system of government.[47] While acknowledging these results, it is paramount to note that both percentages are significantly higher than the corresponding percentages found in Active Youth Research Group's survey. This could be due to various reasons. First of all, while the Active Youth Research Group survey offered alternative answers, the Political Capital survey question was answered on an agree–disagree scale which could potentially skew the results. Another reason could be that, while the Active Youth Research Group survey was conducted primarily among students, the Political Capital survey was conducted among a broader population. Therefore, the higher percentages of the Political Capital survey could imply that Hungarian students are, in contrast to common assumptions, in fact less liberal than the general population. Nonetheless, these implications do not harm our general findings, as the trends that are signaled by both surveys point in the same direction: that the Hungarian youth has increasingly come to support democracy since Orbán's rise to power in 2010. In other words, although the percentages are nominally different, both surveys signal the same increasingly pro-democracy trend.

As both surveys demonstrate, the political attitude among Hungary's youth has become more pro-democratic over the last decade. What remains to be understood, however, is whether this trend is true only for the youth cohort or if it reflects a broader political shift in Hungary's general population. In other words, is this trend unique to the youth? Gerő and Szabó analyzed similar themes among the adult population over 18 years between 2015 and 2018. They found that Hungarian society's commitment to democracy in general increased by 8% (from 48% to 56%) between 2015 and 2018.[48] Thus, it seems that the data measured in the youth surveys are in accordance with the dynamics taking place in the broader Hungarian society regarding its commitment to democracy. However, it is important to note that Gerő and Szabó observed polarizing trends in terms of perceptions of democracy and dictatorship. On the one hand, they measured a strong increase in the proportion of people in support of democracy. On the other hand, the proportion of Hungarians who think of dictatorship as acceptable in certain circumstances also increased, albeit to a lesser extent.[49] This is rather remarkable because, among the youth cohorts, we observed a stark decrease in the proportion of respondents who think of dictatorship as acceptable in certain circumstances. This means that, while the increased support for democracy is a general population trend, the starkly decreased support for authoritarian alternatives seems to be a youth-specific trend. In that sense the youth seems to be more liberal than its counterparts in the general population.

In conclusion, the data of both surveys reveal two provocative insights. First, a positive attitude toward democracy among the young in Hungary has emerged significantly over the past decade. Although this seems to correspond with the trend in the general population, it has been markedly stronger among the youth, with preference for democracy increasing by nearly 20% since 2010. Second, we observed a youth-specific trend

Political party preferences

Parties	Dec 2011 – Jan 2012	Mar – Apr 2013	Apr 2015	Feb 2019
Momentum Mozgalom	-	-	-	16
Fidesz	15	16	12	16
Jobbik	19	17	20	14
MKKP	-	-	2	13
LMP	18	8	14	9
MSZP-P	5	3	3	3
DK	3	1	2	2
Egyutt, PM	-	14	4	-
Other answer	1	2	5	1
Would definitely not go	9	6	9	3
Undecided	25	24	19	10
Abstain	5	9	13	13

Data: Active Youth 2011/2012, 2013, 2015 and 2019. In percent of the total sample population.

Figure 4.2 Youth political party preferences, 2011–2019.

regarding strongly decreasing levels of preference for authoritarian alternatives, with pro-authoritarian sentiment among the young cohort decreasing by almost 17% in the last decade. This is especially noteworthy as it seems that the more Orbán's regime has tried to tear down democracy and replace it with an authoritarian alternative, the more the youth seem to disfavor dictatorship.

4.2 Political Party Preference: Increasingly Liberal and Democratic

The increasing support of the youth for liberal democratic governance can also be found when studying the data on political party preferences. This data stems from the same four surveys by Active Youth Research Group. Although this data does indicate a growing support for more liberal democratic parties from 2011 to 2019, this growth seems to be less linear in comparison to findings of the previous section.

At the turn of 2011/2012, the largest and third-largest voter groups sided with far-right parties, which held skeptical views regarding democracy. Nineteen percent of respondents identified themselves as Jobbik voters and 15% as Fidesz-KDNP voters. By 2013, we do not see significant changes except that the LMP (the Hungarian Greens) lost many votes to the newly emerging centrist social–liberal Együtt party. This was the result of the ongoing internal conflict within the Greens.[50]

In 2015, one can observe a surge of growing support for the far-right party Jobbik, indicating a further shift in political attitude among the youth toward more authoritarian and right-wing politics. Recalling the findings from the earlier historical exposition, this likely echoes the rising general concern in Hungary on security issues following the migration crisis of 2015. It comes as no surprise, then, that Jobbik, and to a lesser extent Fidesz, enjoyed widespread support, as they were the ones advocating for strict anti-migrant laws.

But just as Jobbik and Fidesz seemed to be at their strongest, a new anti-Orbán party emerged. The *Magyar Kétfarkú Kutya Párt* (MKKP), the Two-tailed Dog Party, was originally founded as a joke political party in 2006; it did not register as an official party until 2014. Its main features are strong anti-Orbán campaigns and humorous anti-anti-migration campaigns. Moreover, the party offers a protest alternative to those who are increasingly disillusioned with Hungarian politics. Despite its anti-Orbán stance, MKKP enjoyed only marginal support from the youth in 2015.

By 2019, however, we can observe several interesting changes. Most importantly, Jobbik's support ceased growing. Although the Jobbik and Fidesz parties still received support from the youth, the data reveals that the newly established progressive-leaning party *Momentum Mozgalom* (Momentum Movement) was the most popular political party among respondents in 2019. Momentum was expected to receive 16% of the votes of the total sample population by 2019. Considering that Momentum did not manage to get into parliament during the 2018 elections, this increase in potential voter share among the youth is especially noteworthy, not least because Momentum is considered to be the only party in opposition that represents young people with a liberal democratic and pro-European stance. Furthermore, the 2019 data shows that support for MKKP grew from 2% to 13%. This indicates that an increasing number of young Hungarians support an anti-Orbán protest party.

In conclusion, while the support for right-wing authoritarian parties like Jobbik and Fidesz seems to enjoy relatively constant support from 2011 to 2013, we see a spike in support of the Jobbik party in 2015. This anomaly can be linked to the migration crisis that intensified societal concerns of security. By 2019, however, we see an uptake of fresh political views by young Hungarians. The Fidesz and Jobbik parties, while still enjoying major support, were flanked by two newcomers: Momentum, a pro-democratic liberal party, and MKKP, an anti-Orbán protest party. Thus, the data on political party preference shows that, since the intensification of Hungary's democratic backslide beginning in 2015, the youth has increasingly supported parties that oppose Fidesz in favor of parties that are more liberal, democratic, and antiauthoritarian.

4.3 Political Concerns: Corruption and Democratic Decline

Now that we have established that the Hungarian youth, and especially the 2020 cohort, seems to support democracy over dictatorship and more liberal parties over authoritarian parties, the question remains if this dynamic is reflected in and can be linked to their most pressing political concerns. In order to answer this question, I will again call upon the data that has been produced by Political Capital surveys in 2017 and 2020.

Most strikingly, the democratic decline and the rise of authoritarianism became a major concern for Hungarian youth, with a 15% increase in expressed concern from 2017 to 2020. This could explain the dramatic increase of support for the antiauthoritarian and anti-Orbán MKKP as well as for Momentum. As Orbán continuously tried to tear down the pillars of democracy in Hungary over the past ten years, the youth in 2020 became more concerned with the decline of democracy. This finding alone is quite telling. But the survey results reveal that not only are young Hungarians more and more concerned over growing authoritarianism, they have become more supportive of left-leaning and progressive issues.

The issues that are often used by the right and far-right authoritarian parties, like Fidesz and Jobbik, to mobilize their electorate are increasingly less on top of the agenda of the youth in 2020 as compared to 2017. For example, concerns over terrorism and immigration have decreased by more than 10%. This clearly signals a decline of concerns on security issues among the youth by 2020. The concerns over migration and terrorism decreased more than a dozen percentage points. To understand this stark change in issue priorities, we can look to two explanations. It could be that, for the 2020 cohort, immigration and terrorism are of lesser concern than they were for the 2017 cohort, with other issues having become more pressing. This would imply in general that the youth in 2020 has become less concerned with issues addressed by right-wing parties. It could also be, however, that the increasingly strict anti-migrant laws that have been implemented since 2015 have addressed some of the concerns the youth experienced with migrants and terrorism. If the latter were the case, it would be expected that the support for anti-migration parties would have grown or remained constant. This was true in the case of the ruling Fidesz party, which experienced an increase of 4% in its electoral fortunes. However, one can actually observe

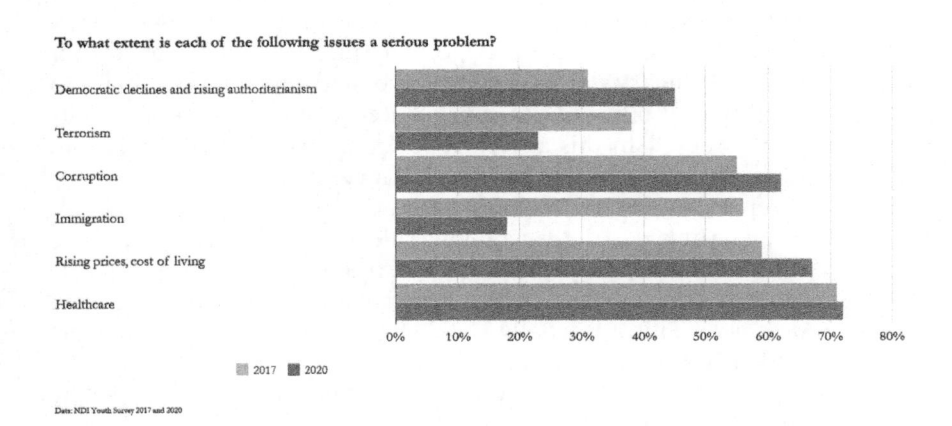

Figure 4.3 Political concerns among Hungary's youth, 2017–2020.

a decline of support by 6% for the mainly anti-migration Jobbik party. This was offset by a more than 11% increase in support for the anti-anti-migration MKKP party, suggesting that Hungary's youth became less anti-migration in 2020 than it was in 2017.

Moreover, we see that issues central to left and liberal party platforms have increasingly become the main policy areas of concern for Hungary's youth voters. One can observe either steady or growing concerns over corruption, increased cost of living, and healthcare. Starting with the latter, it seems that concerns over healthcare did not really change but simply have persisted over time. A crucially necessary reform of the healthcare structure and system has awaited Hungary since the transition from the communist era. Despite the long-standing importance of healthcare reforms, little to no concrete action has been taken to date. This has proven to be a serious oversight of the Orbán government, as he had the opportunity to effect change given Fidesz's parliamentary majority, time in power, and financial resources. Thus, neither Hungary's early democratic parties nor its more recent illiberal parties have been able to satisfy this important policy grievance. The data thus indicates that, in 2020, Hungary's youth continue to wish for healthcare reform and have become disillusioned with the ability for an authoritarian government to provide the necessary reforms.

Another set of issues which are often prioritized by left and liberal parties are rising prices, increased cost of living, and corruption.[51] In order to contextualize the increase of concerns over corruption, the latest report on the Corruption Perceptions Index (CPI) of 2019 called 'Corruption, Economic Performance and the Rule of Law in Hungary' offers valuable insights.[52] By 2019, Hungary's resistance to corruption scored 44 on a scale of 0 to 100. This score is formed on the assessment of experts and businessmen interviewed in the surveys forming the basis of the CPI. Compared to the previous surveys of the last decade, this is the lowest score.[53] The CPI report found that Hungary is among the few EU Member States still seriously affected by corruption. Furthermore, despite sustained growth over the past decade, Hungary's gross domestic product per capita continues to lag far behind that of other EU Member States, due at least in part to its growing kleptocracy.[54] In this aspect, it is not surprising that the youth's concerns on corruption and rising prices had increased by 2020.

The CPI report, in line with other studies, even suggests that persistent corruption can be linked to the decade-long rule of Orbán's government. The CPI report stated that the majority of the institutions which are responsible for exercising control over the government have been in a defunct state in the past decade. This is partially the case because of the erosion of the rule of law that has occurred under Orbán's watch. This resulted in state institutions that maintain a certain interest in not just promoting the public good, but also in favoring the governing party's actors by keeping them in power and facilitating their accumulation of wealth. In this context, the rising concerns over corruption and authoritarianism by the youth can be linked. This in turn offers yet another explanation for the marked increase of support for the antiauthoritarian and anti-Orbán party, the MKKP, as well as for Momentum.

In conclusion, one can observe a decrease in right-wing political concerns over security issues, including terrorism and migration. On the other hand, one does see an increase in political concerns surrounding corruption, cost of living, and rising authoritarianism and declining democracy. These are issues that in recent years have only been addressed by Hungary's liberal democratic and left parties. Thus, the voter preference data signals that, by 2020, young Hungarians have become disillusioned with the ruling authoritarian regime and the issues it represents; instead, the youth now longs for liberal democracy.

4.4 Political Participation: Increasingly Unconventional

Now that we have established that the 2020 youth cohort seems to want democracy, prefers democratic parties, and is increasingly concerned with the decline of liberal democracy, the question arises whether they are demonstrating democratic support through voting and other forms of political participation. To speak to this question, I once again draw on the data that has been produced by Political Capital in 2017 and 2020. These surveys include polls exploring the political participation of young people in Hungary in a wide range of forms of engagement.

There are several interesting findings when comparing the sort and frequency of political participation in 2017 to 2020. First of all, when looking at institutional ways of participation, such as voting in national and local elections, the engagement rate in 2017 was as high as 76 and 82%, respectively. In 2020, this rate dropped considerably on both accounts by more than 10%. This data signals that the 2020 cohort is considerably less

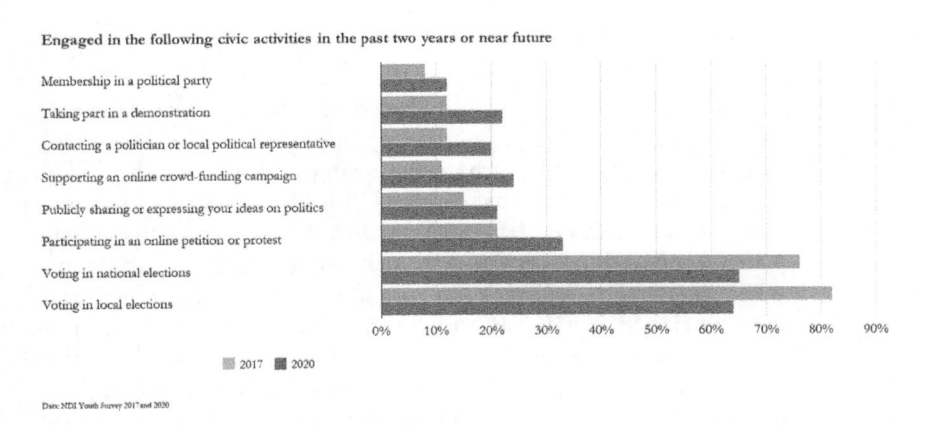

Figure 4.4 Methods of Hungarian youth political participation, 2017–2020.

willing to participate in politics when it comes to using their right to vote in elections. At first glance, therefore, the data seems to indicate that the Hungarian youth is increasingly less willing to participate in democracy.

However, when looking at all other ways of political participation, mostly noninstitutional, the data shows a nearly consistent increase by ten percentage points across all remaining forms of political engagement. By 2020, the youth seems to be more engaged with political parties, more in touch with politicians, and more willing to express their ideas on politics in public. The accounts that show the highest increase rates are participating in a protest or demonstration and supporting a crowdfund campaign. This comes as no surprise as Hungary has indeed experienced an increased number of big protests and demonstrations in recent years. Among the most noteworthy ones were the protest against the law that forced the Central European University out of the country and the so-called 'slave law,' in which Orbán's government introduced an amendment to a law that increases the number of overtime hours employees can be asked to work without additional pay.[55] The amendment allows companies to ask their staff to work up to 400 extra hours per year of overtime.[56] Both protests mobilized tens of thousands of Hungarians in Budapest in 2018 and 2019. Both protests were very heavily anti-Orbán, with a large part of the protest population made up of young Hungarians.

Thus, while the youth cohort votes less frequently in 2020 than before, one can observe an increased engagement with democracy in nearly all other accounts. This is particularly true in the case of noninstitutional ways of political participation like protesting and demonstrating. In this sense, young Hungarians are not, in fact, politically indifferent or inactive but simply participate in democratic politics increasingly through non-electoral means. This should come as little surprise given increasing electioneering and Orbán's step-by-step dismantling of traditional democratic structures.

****

In conclusion, the findings discussed above are quite striking and telling with regards to youth attitudes toward democracy in the context of Hungary's recent democratic backslide. As Orbán increasingly tore down the pillars of democracy in Hungary in the past decade (2010–2020), we observed four pro-democratic trends among Hungary's youth: they increasingly favor democracy and disfavor dictatorship; they increasingly support parties that oppose the Fidesz party, namely parties that are more liberal, democratic, and antiauthoritarian like MKKP and Momentum; there has been a simultaneous decrease in salience for far-right security issues like migration and terrorism and an increase in salience for political concerns such as corruption, increased cost of living, rising authoritarianism, and the decline of democracy, resulting in Hungary's youth rejecting authoritarianism and longing instead for liberal democracy; finally, while youth participation in local and national elections decreased in recent years, their overall political participation has increased. This is especially the case for noninstitutional forms like protests and demonstrations.

5 Testing the Prevailing Hypothesis: Youth Disillusionment with Democracy

Now that we understand the empirical trends of Hungary's youth engagement with democracy, we can probe whether the prevailing hypothesis is true, namely whether the further a cohort is from communism, the less likely it is to support democracy. In order to test this hypothesis, I will first discuss the theoretical mechanism underpinning this dynamic before evaluating if the data matches the theory.

5.1 The 'Growing Democracy Disillusion' Thesis

To understand the suggested dynamic behind this hypothesis, it is necessary to briefly revisit the political context of 2010 and the theories that have emerged since. Both Eastern and Western Europe were dealing with a populist authoritarian wave from around 2010 onwards, and it seemed that this wave enjoyed increasing support among the Hungarian youth.[57] Several studies revealed that far-right and authoritarian parties were overrepresented among the youth in Hungary in the mid-2010s.[58]

Erin Marie Saltman was among the few scholars who attempted to theorize this dynamic. She argued that the explanation should be found in the formative years in which the political socialization of the 2010 youth cohort took place.[59] Due to the context in which the 2010 cohort came to age, it developed a certain political attitude, referred to as the 'cohort effect.'[60] In this view, there are differences between cohorts because of the different political conditions in which they come of age.[61] As a result, cohorts may differ from one another in their attitudes due to differences in the social and political environment prevailing during their formative years.[62] Based on this cohort effect, the hypothesis was built that the further away a cohort is from communism, the less it will support democracy because fewer people will remember what it was like to exist in a nondemocratic state.

The 2010 cohort was, roughly speaking, born around the fall of the Iron Curtain, a period of democratic and European euphoria. The Hungarian population still very clearly remembered the terrors of communism and longed for freedom, believing that the transition to democracy would also contribute to the prosperity and growing welfare of Hungary. Through the early 2000s, though, this euphoria and trust in democracy transformed into disillusionment as neither EU membership nor the democratic transition provided what was expected of it. Indeed, Hungary was not the only one to experience this dynamic. In most post-communist societies, euphoric expectations were replaced with a mixture of realism and cynicism during the last three decades. Moreover, dissatisfaction with growing corruption has been widespread and has caused additional distrust in democratic processes and institutions.[63] As a result, young cohorts were expected to grow increasingly dismissive of multiparty electoral systems and the liberal democratic system writ large.[64]

Saltman found supporting evidence for this hypothesis. She found that young generations in Hungary indeed seemed to be more prone to authoritarian right-wing political sentiment, hinting at the strong youth base for the Fidesz and Jobbik parties as Orbán gained control of the Hungarian government in 2010.[65] Moreover, in line with other studies, Saltman found low levels of democratic participation among Hungarian youth. Compared with other post-communist countries, adherence to the principles of human rights, international networking, and participation in political organizations are particularly low in Hungary.[66] Although there were some organizations directed at youth involvement in democratic civil society, their memberships remain relatively small compared to the overall Hungarian population.[67] Furthermore, scholars argue that although civic participation is generally measured as a positive indicator of a healthy democracy, most active civic movements in Hungary are not cultivators of liberal democratic values.[68] These findings contribute to the general belief that the youth is growing more politically indifferent and inactive. Various authors have shown that young Hungarian voters were less likely to vote in 2010 than in any prior free election, to be a member of a political party, or to take part in traditional forms of politics in general.[69] The same was found to be true for other methods of noninstitutional political participation (e.g. crowdfunding an online campaign or taking part in a demonstration).[70] Since 2010, only very few Hungarian-specific studies have looked at youth political participation.[71] But the above-discussed conclusions of other studies forecast a rather negative picture of the youth political involvement in democracy in Hungary.

5.2 The 'Growing Democracy Disillusion' Thesis Rejected

The expected dynamic of engagement with democracy based on this hypothesis would play out as follows in relation to the four different dynamics hypothesized in this chapter: (1) One would expect the preferred system of governance to increasingly be some alternative to democracy, including illiberalism and authoritarianism. The percentage of respondents who think that 'democracy is the best system of governance' would be expected to decrease; (2) Youth party preference would increasingly favor parties which advocate for a more authoritarian approach; (3) The political concerns of Hungary's youth would increasingly center on law and order and other issues that are addressed by authoritarian parties; and (4) There would be a decrease in the overall democratic participation rate.

When we look at the data in the previous section, we indeed see that illiberal parties, such as Fidesz and Jobbik, enjoyed major support among the youth in 2011. From 2011 to 2013, this support for right-wing authoritarian parties was quite stable, with even some modest growth. Moreover, we saw a spike in support of the Jobbik party in 2015 in the context of the migration crisis. As a result, the illiberal regime alterations supported by the youth represented a threat to Hungary's unconsolidated democracy and exemplified a challenge prevalent across European politics.[72] At this point, the 'growing democracy disillusionment' thesis would still hold.

However, the 2019 data tells a rather different story. The Fidesz and Jobbik parties, while still enjoying major support within Hungarian society, have been flanked by two newcomers: Momentum and MKKP. These parties, which are both liberal democratic and anti-Orbán, gain much of their support from young voters, meaning that by 2019 Hungary's youth cohort, in contradistinction to that of 2011, favors democracy over dictatorship. In short, while the 2019 cohort is further away from the communist experience, instead of being disillusioned with democracy, they are tired of the ruling authoritarian regime and long for liberal democracy more than their 2011 counterpart. We can therefore safely reject the growing 'democracy disillusion' thesis.

6 The Maastricht Generation Hypothesis: Growing Youth Democratic Sentiment

Now that we have rejected the prevailing hypothesis, what explains this reverted change toward democracy and liberalism? I suggest an inverted hypothesis that the more a cohort has grown up under Orbán's regime, the more likely it will be to support democracy since fewer members will recall the era of democratic disillusionment.

6.1 The Maastricht Generation Thesis

The Maastricht Generation theory uses a similar logic to the democratic disillusionment thesis, except that the causal dynamic is reversed. Before 2010, Hungarians were so tired of the poor performances of the newly born democracy, in terms of economy, governance, and corruption, that they were willing to tolerate a stricter, less democratic regime in exchange for better governmental performance. When Fidesz came to power, Europe was hit hard by the global economic crisis and struggled to support itself, let alone less developed economies like Hungary's. In this context, Orbán promised an alternative path to welfare, one independent of the stringent restrictions imposed by the EU and International Monetary Fund (IMF).

As it turned out, however, Orbán failed to deliver on his promise. Consequently, those willing to tolerate illiberalism in exchange for better governmental performance became disillusioned with Orbán's authoritarian promise. In other words, the period of democratic disillusionment was replaced by a growing sense of authoritarian disillusionment. As a result, subsequent voter cohorts after 2010 became more supportive of democracy as the authoritarian ruling regime failed to live up to its promises.

The 2019 youth cohort was, in contrast to the 2011 cohort, born just before Hungary's accession to the EU in 2004. In other words, they have not known a Hungary that is apart from the EU. Moreover, the expectations of democracy were already tempered by the time this cohort came to age, meaning that the political socialization of the youth cohort of 2019 was already less heavily influenced by the post-communist disillusion in comparison to its 2011 counterpart.[73] Furthermore, the formative years of adolescence of the 2019 cohort coincided with the years in which the democratic backslide of Hungary intensified. This suggests that democratic backsliding heavily impacted youth political socialization to an extent that it experienced a trend in the complete opposite direction with regards to its 2011 cohort counterpart. Whereas the 2011 cohort, filled with liberal democracy disillusionment, welcomed more authoritarian regimes, the 2019 cohort, filled with illiberal authoritarian disillusionment, now increasingly longs for more liberal democracy. Liberal democracy is a fundamental cornerstone of the Maastricht Treaty that should make sure that all Members States of the EU adhere to the values of democracy and freedom.[74]

6.2 The Maastricht Generation Thesis Supported

If indeed more young people desire democracy, then the youth should be expected to be active in democratic practices. For this hypothesis to be true, we should expect the following results in relation to the four dynamics posited in this chapter: (1) One would expect the preferred system of governance to be democracy. The percentage of respondents that think that 'democracy is the best system of governance' would be expected to increase; (2) Party preference would increasingly be for those who advocate for a liberal and democratic approach; (3) The political concerns of the youth cohort would focus on liberal and democratic issues that are addressed by liberal democratic parties; and (4) We would see an increase in the overall rate of democratic participation.

The data demonstrates that a positive attitude toward democracy among the youth in Hungary has emerged over the past decade. Although this seems to correspond with the trend in the general population, we can observe increased levels of youth preference for democracy of almost 20%.[75] We also observed more youth-specific trends regarding strongly decreasing levels of preference for authoritarian alternatives by almost 17% in the last decade.[76] These two factors together give reason to believe that the more

Orbán's regime tears down democracy and replaces it with an authoritarian alternative, the more the youth seems to disfavor dictatorship.

One can observe this dynamic concretely when looking at party preferences. The 2020 youth cohort seems to increasingly support parties that oppose the current illiberal authoritarian government. Rather than casting their votes for the right-wing Fidesz and Jobbik parties, by 2019, Hungarian youth increasingly voted for progressive and anti-Orbán parties like Momentum and MKKP. The data on political party preference shows that since the intensification of Hungary's democratic backslide beginning 2015, the youth has increasingly supported parties that oppose the Fidesz party.

Additionally, the youth expressed growing concerns over corruption and rising authoritarianism. Corruption and state-capture has expanded dramatically under Orbán's watch, despite his campaign promises prior to 2010 that he would curb corruption and modernize the country.[77] For the 2020 youth cohort, this failure to reverse trends of corruption has translated into growing illiberal authoritarian disillusionment – the more Orbán fails to deliver on his illiberal promises, the more Hungary's youth turn toward alternative governance systems.

Perhaps most importantly, Hungary's current youth cohort is not just more democratic than its older counterparts, they also engage in politics through a greater number of vectors. Although there are few traditional democratic means left untarnished by Orbán's government, young Hungarians are increasingly reaching for alternative, noninstitutional means to make their voices heard rather than simply becoming indifferent or inactive. This is a key finding, as most research on Hungarian civic engagement to-date narrowly defines the notion of youth political engagement and thus underestimates the scope and strength of youth political activity.[78] Hungary's youth does not vote in droves not because they do not care about voting, but because the restrictive nature of the current regime prevents them from engaging in a truly democratic manner. As several recent studies have noted, younger citizens do not necessarily engage less in political affairs, but simply use new forms of participation to engage in the political debate.[79] This is especially the case when young voters are disillusioned with the traditional mechanisms of politics.[80]

Traditional politics in Hungary have failed to produce democratic results, instead allowing a regime that has slowly but persistently undermined democracy. Hungary's electoral system was one of the most vigorously targeted democratic institutions. Freedom House, an independent institution that evaluates the strength of democratic institutions around the world, has consistently pointed this out in its yearly reports. Although Hungary's last parliamentary elections in 2018 were free, they were far from fair, according to Freedom House observers. Prior to these elections, the State Audit Office, which was controlled by Orbán's party, fined many opposition parties on baseless accusations. The fines impacted the competing parties' ability to become frontrunners in the ballot box. Moreover, Orbán's government abused state resources, including state media, for electioneering purposes.[81]

These dynamics surely added to the growing belief among the young that formal political structures are not fit to properly address their concerns.[82] To put it less mildly, Hungary's youth have been forced, given the intensifying authoritarian circumstances, to make their voices heard differently.[83]

7 Conclusion

> *'The youth has been at the forefront of political changes in the post-communist arena.' - Bunce and Wolchik.*[84]

Following the May 2019 European Parliament elections, David Sassoli, President of the European Parliament, acknowledged that "the very significant boost in voter turnout in May's European elections shows that people, especially the younger generation, value their democratic rights and believe that the European Union is stronger when acting in unison to address their concerns."[85] This chapter has picked up on Sassoli's argument and investigated the attitudes of Hungary's young Europeans toward the EU. In doing so, this chapter challenged the persistent narrative that the EU is experiencing a widespread legitimacy crisis.

Although the EU currently faces one of its most unstable periods in its history, with destabilization and disintegrative efforts led largely by Viktor Orbán's Hungary, I contend that the Hungarian case discussed in this chapter is actually cause for hope for the European project. The emergence of a pro-democratic Hungarian youth generation, what I call the Maastricht Generation, signals a broader movement across Europe. As young Europeans, who have only ever known a unified Europe, come to political adulthood, they will increasingly push for more democracy and more unity across the continent.

The shifting political sentiments among Hungary's youth by 2020 paint a different future from the Europessimism of pundits decrying the rise of illiberal authoritarians like Orbán. Rather, it suggests a brighter and pro-democratic European future. In fact, the Hungarian youth seems to be a nascent democratic generation that might just hold the key to redefine democracy in Hungary from the inside out. After 2010, Hungary's youth was written off as being antidemocratic because they were increasingly tolerant of Hungary's growing illiberalism and were considered unwilling to engage in democratic practices while Orbán came to power. But over the course of the 2010s, the growing illiberal trend among Hungary's youth was wholly reversed. By 2020, the Hungarian youth had become progressively more willing to participate in and engage with democracy and the EU. The Hungarian authoritarian regime since 2010 did not only fail to live up to its promises in terms of economic performance but also started to dismantle civic freedoms and drifted away from the values the EU holds dear. This unleashed a new wave of democratic support among the Hungarian youth and an increased preference for liberal democratic parties, even though this trend is not mirrored by high voter turnout. This is not, however, due to indifference, as young citizens in Hungary, disillusioned with traditional politics because of rampant corruption and electioneering, tend to turn to noninstitutional forms of political participation.[86]

The case of the young democratic Hungarians is even more striking when we place it in the wider European context. If we can observe these dynamics of changing political sentiments among the youth in one of the most illiberal and anti-European Member States, it could also signal a wider European dynamic. If similar trends can be observed in other countries as well, then Europe is likely to experience a boost in EU-optimism in the near future. In other words, it could indicate the flowering of the wider European pro-democratic generation I refer to as the Maastricht Generation. This generation, born in the debris of the Berlin Wall and Europe's triumphal victory in the Cold War, grew up amidst unprecedented levels of European integration unleashed by the Treaty of Maastricht. Only now emerging onto the political scene in Europe, the Maastricht Generation will defend and fight for the existence of the EU and push for an ever closer Union, as it has only ever known Europe to be an integrated community. Traditionally, young generations are associated with low political participation and voter turnout. This is not true of the Maastricht Generation. Rather, it is a young polity that knows how to organize itself, particularly using today's digital methods of social communication, and is increasingly exercising its political voice. By relying on the voices of Europe's youth in Hungary, this chapter demonstrates that the EU is likely to emerge stronger as the Maastricht Generation awakens.

Notes

1 Will Kymlicka and Wayne Norman, "Return of the Citizen: A Survey of Recent Work on Citizenship Theory," *Ethics* 104, no. 2 (1994): 352–81.
2 Grigore Pop-Eleches and Joshua A. Tucker, "Communist Legacies and Left-Authoritarianism," *Comparative Political Studies* 53, no. 12 (2020): 1861–89.
3 Hyeong-Ki Kwon, "Associations, Civic Norms, and Democracy: Revisiting the Italian Case." *Theory and Society* 33, no. 2 (2004): 136.
4 Michael Zeller, "Shifting Political Dynamics and Democratic Disillusionment in Hungary's Political Youth." *The Eurasian Era* 1, no. 1, (2016): 3–11.
5 Julia Weiss, "What is Youth Political Participation? Literature Review on Youth Political Participation and Political Attitudes." *Frontiers in Political Science* 2 (2020): 1; Ben Berger, "Political Theory, Political Science and the End of Civic Engagement." *Perspectives on Politics* 7, no. 2 (2009): 335–50.
6 Zeller, "Shifting Political Dynamics," 3–11.
7 While social and psychological studies define 'youth' by life stages, there is debate on whether to separate individuals in generational terms or define them as a specific cohort. Defining a 'cohort' refers to a group of people born in a specific time range. I choose to refer to youth as a cohort since I am looking at a specific age group.

8 Jürgen Habermas, *Citizenship and National Identity: Some Reflections on the Future of Europe* (Praxis International, 1992), 7.
9 Miklos Haraszti, "Countering Illiberal Usurpations of Democracy" in *Resisting Ill Democracies in Europe*, (Croatia: Center for Peace Studies, 2017), 6–7.
10 Michael Zeller, "Shifting Political Dynamics," 3–11.
11 Samuel P. Huntington, "Democracy's Third Wave," *Journal of Democracy* 2, no. 2 (1991): 16.
12 Dorottya Szikra, "Democracy and Welfare in Hard Times: The Social Policy of the Orbán Government in Hungary between 2010 and 2014," *Journal of European Social Policy* 24, no. 5 (2014): 487.
13 Vesselin Dimitrov, Klaus H. Goetz, and Hellmut Wollmann, *Governing After Communism: Institutions and Policymaking* (Rowman & Littlefield, 2006), 49–50.
14 John W. Schiemann, "Explaining Hungary's Powerful Constitutional Court: A Bargaining Approach," *European Journal of Sociology/Archives Européennes de Sociologie* 42, no. 2 (2001): 357.
15 Ibidem.
16 John R. Hibbing and Samuel C. Patterson. "A Democratic Legislature in the Making: The Historic Hungarian Elections of 1990." *Comparative Political Studies* 24, no. 4 (1992): 430–54.
17 Tibor Navracsics, *A Missing Debate?: Hungary and the European Union* (Sussex European Institute, 1997), 12.
18 Ibidem.
19 Ibidem, 13.
20 Eline De Ridder, "Democratic Conditionality in the Eastern Enlargement: Ambitious Window Dressing," *European Foreign Affairs Review* 16, no. 5 (2011): 604–5.
21 Dimitry Kochenov, "Behind the Copenhagen Façade. The Meaning and Structure of the Copenhagen Political Criterion of Democracy and the Rule of Law," *European Integration Online Papers* 8, no. 10 (2004): 19–20.
22 See, for example, the EU Commission's progress report for Hungary of 13 November 2001.
23 Tanja Marktler, "The Power of the Copenhagen Criteria," *Croatian Yearbook of European Law & Policy* 2, no. 1 (2006): 343–63.
24 Anna Molnár, "Economic Crisis and Euroscepticism: A Comparative Study of the Hungarian and Italian Case (1990–2013)," *Politics in Central Europe* 12, no. 3 (2016): 70.
25 Eurobarometer. Public Opinion in the Candidate Countries, National Report, Executive summary, Hungary, 2004.
26 Eurobarometer. Public Opinion in the Candidate Countries, National Report, Executive summary, Hungary, 2011.
27 Interestingly, Fidesz, Orbán's party, was initially a left-leaning protest movement. It was not until the 2000s that Orbán, the original leader of Fidesz, steered his party far to the right. See Peter Wilkin, *Hungary's Crisis of Democracy: The Road to Serfdom* (Lexington Books, 2016): 101.
28 Anna Molnár, "Economic Crisis", 70.
29 Ibid, 70.
30 European Parliament, European Parliament resolution of 10 March 2011 on media law in Hungary. See: https://www.europarl.europa.eu/doceo/document/TA-7-2011-0094_EN.html
31 András Laszlo Pap and Anna Śledzińska-Simon, "The Rise of Illiberal Democracy and the Remedies of Multi-Level Constitutionalism," *Hungarian Journal of Legal Studies*, 60, no. 1 (2019): 69.

32 European Commission for Democracy through Law (Venice Commission), Opinion on Act CCVI of 2011: On the Right to Freedom of Conscience and Religion and the Legal Status of Churches, Denominations and Religious Communities of Hungary (CDL-AD(2012)004) (Adopted by the Venice Commission at its 90th Plenary Session, Venice, 16–17 March 2012); European Commission for Democracy through Law (Venice Commission), Opinion on the Fourth Amendment to the Fundamental Law of Hungary (CDL-AD(2013)012) (Adopted by the Venice Commission at its 95th Plenary Session, Venice, 14–15 June 2013); European Commission for Democracy through Law (Venice Commission), Opinion on the New Constitution of Hungary (CDL-AD(2011)016) (Adopted by the Venice Commission at its 87th Plenary Session (Venice, 17–18 June 2011).

33 Gábor Halmai, "The Rise and Fall of Constitutionalism in Hungary," in *Constitutional Acceleration Within the European Union and Beyond* (Routledge, 2017), 215–31.

34 Ibidem.

35 Kim Lane Scheppele, "What Can the European Commission do When Member States Violate Basic Principles of the European Union? The Case for Systemic Infringement Actions," *Assises de la Justice* (2013): 4.

36 John S. Ahlquist, Nahomi Ichino, Jason Wittenberg, and Daniel Ziblatt, "How do Voters Perceive Changes to the Rules of the Game? Evidence from the 2014 Hungarian Elections," *Journal of Comparative Economics* 46, no. 4 (2018): 906–19.

37 Miklos Haraszti, "Countering Illiberal Usurpations of Democracy," in *Resisting Ill Democracies in Europe* (2017), 14.

38 Attila Ágh, "The Decline of Democracy in East-Central Europe: Hungary as the Worst-Case Scenario," *Problems of Post-Communism* 63, no. 5–6 (2016): 277–87.

39 Theresa Gessler, Gergő Tóth, and Johannes Wachs, "No country for asylum seekers? How short-term exposure to refugees influences attitudes and voting behavior in Hungary." *Political Behavior* (2021): 9.

40 Lilia Ilikova and Andrey Tushev, "Right-Wing Populism in Central Europe: Hungarian Case (Fidesz, Jobbik)," *Utopía y Praxis Latinoamericana* 25, no. 12 (2020): 325–32.

41 Freedom House, "Freedom of the Press 2017-Hungary," (2017).

42 Zeller, "Shifting Political Dynamics", 3–11.

43 Andrea Szabo, *Political Integration of Hungarian Students* (Prague: Heinrich Böll Stiftung, 2019): 103–13.

44 Pap and Śledzińska-Simon, "The Rise of Illiberal Democracy", 69.

45 "Youth Attitudes of Politics and Democracy: Hungary," *National Democratic Institute* (blog), https://www.ndi.org/publications/youth-attitudes-politics-and-democracy-hungary.

46 Ibidem.

47 This time survey data was collected through face-to-face interviews in 2020 from a sample of 750 citizens of Hungary. Ages varied from 16 to 29. This was one year after the European election held in 2019 and amidst the global pandemic. The margin of error is ±3.6%.

48 Gerő Márton and Szabó Andrea, *A magyar társadalom és a politika, 2019: A magyar társadalom politikai gondolkodásmódja, politikai integráltsága és részvétele* (Budapest: Social Sciences Research Center of the Hungarian Academy of Sciences, 2019).

49 Ibidem, 12.

50 Szabo, "Political Integration of Hungarian Students."

51 Corruption is an issue that is neither really left or right. This is an issue that is commonly addressed by both sides.

52 Kristof Tamas Szombati, "Protesting the "Slave Law" in Hungary: The Erosion of Illiberal Hegemony?" *Corruption Perceptions Index* (Transparency International, 2020), 4.

53 In 2019, the score was 44 (*Corruption Perceptions Index,* Transparency International, 2019); in 2018, the score was 46 (*Corruption Perceptions Index,* Transparency International, 2018); in 2017, the score was 45 (*Corruption Perceptions Index,* Transparency International, 2017); in 2016, the score was 48 (*Corruption Perceptions Index,* Transparency International, 2016); in 2015, the score was 51 (*Corruption Perceptions Index,* Transparency International, 2015).

54 In the period between 2012 and 2018, the GDP per capita grew from EUR 10,050 to EUR 13,690. *Corruption Perceptions Index* (Transparency International, 2019), 4.

55 Zsolt Enyedi, "Democratic Backsliding and Academic Freedom in Hungary," *Perspectives on Politics* 16, no. 4 (2018): 1067–74.

56 Kristof Tamas Szombati, "Protesting the "Slave Law" in Hungary: The Erosion of Illiberal Hegemony?" (2018).

57 Zeller, "Shifting Political Dynamics," 3–11.

58 See Cas Mudde, *Youth and the Extreme Right* (Amsterdam: International Debate Education Association, 2014) and Wouter Van der Brug, Meindert Fennema, Sarah De Lange, and Inger Baller, *Radical Right Parties: Their Voters and Their Electoral Competitors* (Abingdon: Routledge, 2012).

59 Erin Marie Saltman, "Turning Right: A Case Study on Contemporary Political Socialization of the Hungarian Youth" (PhD diss., University College London, 2014).

60 Kenneth Ka-Lok Chan, "Strands of Conservatism in Post-Communist Democracies," *ECPR Joint Sessions of Workshops* 4 (1999).

61 Kent M. Jennings and Laura Stoker, "Generational Change, Life Cycle Processes, ad Social Capital." Presented at Citizenship on Trial: Interdisciplinary Perspectives on the Political Socialization of Adolescents (Montreal, Canada: McGill University, 2002).

62 Duane F. Alwin and Jon A. Krosnick. "Aging, Cohorts, and the Stability of Sociopolitical Orientations over the Life Span," *American Journal of Sociology* 97, no. 1 (1991): 169–95.

63 Simeon Djankov, Elena Nikolova, and Jan Zilinsky. "The Happiness Gap in Eastern Europe," *Journal of Comparative Economics* 44, no. 1 (2016): 108–24.

64 Saltman, "Turning right: A case study on contemporary Political Socialization of the Hungarian youth."

65 Ibidem.

66 Aida Savicka, "Volunteer Work: Our Way Back to Civil Society? Specifics of Volunteering in a Post Communist Milieu," in *Political Transformation and Changing Identities in Central and Eastern Europe*, eds. Andrew Blasko and Diana Janušauskienė (Washington, DC: The Council for Research in Values and Philosophy, 2008).

67 András Keil, "European Values and Youth in Hungary: Mobility, Tolerance, Post-Materialist Values and Participation of Hungarian Youth in a Comparative Perspective," Paper presented at the *UACES 41st Annual Conference* (Cambridge, 5–7 September 2011).

68 Ibidem.

69 Saltman, "Turning Right: A Case Study on Contemporary Political Socialization of the Hungarian youth."

70 Ibidem.

71 Mária Vásárhelyi, "A huszonévesek és Trianon'," *Élet És Irodalom*, June 3, 2011.
72 Zeller, "Shifting Political Dynamics," 3–11.
73 Ibidem.
74 Justin Gibbins, "The Maastricht Treaty," in *Britain, Europe and National Identity*. (London: Palgrave Macmillan, 2014), 80–126.
75 Szabo, "Political Integration of Hungarian Students."
76 "Youth Attitudes of Politics and Democracy: Hungary."
77 Zoltán Ádám, "Explaining orbán: A Political Transaction Cost Theory of Authoritarian Populism," *Problems of Post-Communism* 66, no. 6 (2019): 385–401.
78 Rys Farthing, "The Politics of Youthful Antipolitics: Representing the 'Issue' of Youth Participation in Politics," *Journal of Youth Studies* 13, no. 2 (2010): 181–95
79 Therese O'Toole, Michael Lister, Dave Marsh, Su Jones, and Alex McDonagh, "Tuning Out or Left Out? Participation and Non-Participation Among Young People." *Contemporary politics* 9, no. 1 (2003): 45–61.
80 Ibidem.
81 Freedom House, "Freedom of Globe-2019-Hungary," 2019.
82 Dominic Wring, Matt Henn, and Mark Weinstein, "Young People and Contemporary Politics: Committed Scepticism or Engaged Cynicism?" *British Elections & Parties Review* 9, no. 1 (1999): 200–16.
83 Magdelina Kitanova, "Youth Political Participation in the EU: Evidence from a Cross-National Analysis," *Journal of Youth Studies* 23, no. 7 (2020): 819–36.
84 Hyeong-Ki Kwon, "Associations, Civic Norms, and Democracy: Revisiting the Italian Case." *Theory and Society* 33, no. 2 (2004): 136.
85 See full speech by David Sassoli: https://www.europarl.europa.eu/news/en/press-room/20190923IPR61602/2019-european-elections-record-turnout-driven-by-young-people.
86 Magdelina Kitanova, "Youth Political Participation in the EU: Evidence from a Cross-National Analysis," *Journal of Youth Studies* 23, no. 7 (2020): 819–36.

Bibliography

Ádám, Zoltán. "Explaining orbán: A Political Transaction Cost Theory of Authoritarian Populism." *Problems of Post-Communism* 66, no. 6 (2019): 385–401.
Ágh, Attila. "The Decline of Democracy in East-Central Europe: Hungary as the Worst-Case Scenario." *Problems of Post-Communism* 63, no. 5–6 (2016): 277–87.
Ahlquist, John S., Nahomi Ichino, Jason Wittenberg, and Daniel Ziblatt. "How Do Voters Perceive Changes to the Rules of the Game? Evidence from the 2014 Hungarian Elections." *Journal of Comparative Economics* 46, no. 4 (2018): 906–19.
Alwin, Duane F., and Jon A. Krosnick. "Aging, Cohorts, and the Stability of Sociopolitical Orientations over the Lifespan." *American Journal of Sociology* 97, no. 1 (1991): 169–95.
Berger, Ben. "Political Theory, Political Science and the End of Civic Engagement." *Perspectives on Politics* 7, no. 2 (2009): 335–50.
De Ridder, Eline. "Democratic Conditionality in the Eastern Enlargement: Ambitious Window Dressing." *European Foreign Affairs Review* 16, no. 5 (2011): 604–05.
Dimitrov, Vesselin, Klaus H. Goetz, and Hellmut Wollmann. *Governing After Communism: Institutions and Policymaking*. Lanham: Rowman & Littlefield, 2006.
Djankov, Simeon, Elena Nikolova, and Jan Zilinsky. "The Happiness Gap in Eastern Europe." *Journal of Comparative Economics* 44, no. 1 (2016): 108–24.

Enyedi, Zsolt. "Democratic Backsliding and Academic Freedom in Hungary." *Perspectives on Politics* 16, no. 4 (2018): 1067–74.

Eurobarometer. Public Opinion in the Candidate Countries. Executive Summary. National Report. Hungary, 2004.

Eurobarometer. Public Opinion in the Candidate Countries. Executive Summary. National Report. Hungary, 2011.

European Commission for Democracy through Law (Venice Commission), Opinion on Act CCVI of 2011: On the Right to Freedom of Conscience and Religion and the Legal Status of Churches, Denominations and Religious Communities of Hungary (CDL-AD(2012)004) (Adopted by the Venice Commission at its 90th Plenary Session, Venice, 16–17 March 2012).

European Commission for Democracy through Law (Venice Commission), Opinion on the Fourth Amendment to the Fundamental Law of Hungary (CDL-AD(2013)012) (Adopted by the Venice Commission at its 95th Plenary Session, Venice, 14–15 June 2013).

European Commission for Democracy through Law (Venice Commission), Opinion on the New Constitution of Hungary (CDL-AD(2011)016) (Adopted by the Venice Commission at its 87th Plenary Session (Venice, 17–18 June 2011).

European Parliament Resolution of 10 March 2011 on media law in Hungary. https://www.europarl.europa.eu/doceo/document/TA-7-2011-0094_EN.html.

Farthing, Rys. "The Politics of Youthful Antipolitics: Representing the 'Issue' of Youth Participation in Politics." *Journal of Youth Studies* 13, no. 2 (2018): 181–95.

Freedom House. "Freedom of the Press 2017-Hungary." 2017.

Freedom House. "Freedom of Globe-2019-Hungary." 2019.

Gessler, Theresa, Gergő Tóth, and Johannes Wachs. "No Country for Asylum Seekers? How Short-Term Exposure to Refugees Influences Attitudes and Voting Behavior in Hungary." *Political Behavior* 9 (2021). https://link.springer.com/content/pdf/10.1007/s11109-021-09682-1.pdf.

Gibbins, Justin. *Britain, Europe and National Identity.* London: Palgrave Macmillan, 2014.

Habermas, Jürgen. "Citizenship and National Identity: Some Reflections on the Future of Europe." *Praxis International* 12, no. 1 (1992): 1–19.

Halmai, Gábor. "The Rise and Fall of Constitutionalism in Hungary." In Paul Blokker (ed.), *Constitutional Acceleration Within the European Union and Beyond,* 215–31. New York: Routledge, 2017.

Haraszti, Miklos. "Foreward – Countering Illiberal Usurpations of Democracy." In *Resisting Ill Democracies in Europe,* 6–7. Croatia: Center for Peace Studies, 2017.

Hibbing, John R., and Samuel C. Patterson. "A Democratic Legislature in the Making: The Historic Hungarian Elections of 1990." *Comparative Political Studies* 24, no. 4 (1992): 430–54.

Huntington, Samuel P. "Democracy's Third Wave." *Journal of Democracy* 2, no. 2 (1991): 16.

Ilikova, Lilia, and Andrey Tushev. "Right-Wing Populism in Central Europe: Hungarian Case (Fidesz, Jobbik)." *Utopía y Praxis Latinoamericana* 25, no. 12 (2020): 325–32.

Jennings, Kent M., and Laura Stoker. "Generational Change, Life Cycle Processes, ad Social Capital." Presented at Citizenship on Trial: Interdisciplinary Perspectives on the Political Socialization of Adolescents. Montreal, Canada: McGill University, 2002.

Keil, András. "European Values and Youth in Hungary: Mobility, Tolerance, Post-Materialist Values and Participation of Hungarian Youth in a Comparative Perspective." Paper Presented at the *UACES 41st Annual Conference*. Cambridge, 5–7 September 2011.

Ka-Lok Chan, Kenneth. "Strands of Conservatism in Post-Communist Democracies." *ECPR Joint Sessions of Workshops* 4 (1999).

Kitanova, Magdelina. "Youth Political Participation in the EU: Evidence From a Cross-National Analysis," *Journal of Youth Studies* 23, no. 7 (2020): 819–36.

Kochenov, Dimitry. "Behind the Copenhagen Façade. The Meaning and Structure of the Copenhagen Political Criterion of Democracy and the Rule of Law." *European Integration Online Papers* 8, no. 10 (2004): 19–20.

Kwon, Hyeong-Ki. "Associations, Civic Norms, and Democracy: Revisiting the Italian Case." *Theory and Society* 33, no. 2 (2004): 136.

Kymlicka, Will, and Wayne Norman. "Return of the Citizen: A Survey of Recent Work on Citizenship Theory." *Ethics* 104, no. 2 (1994): 352–81.

Marktler, Tanja. "The Power of the Copenhagen Criteria." *Croatian Yearbook of European Law & Policy* 2, no. 1 (2006): 343–63.

Márton, Gerő, and Szabó Andrea. *A magyar társadalom és a politika, 2019: A magyar társadalom politikai gondolkodásmódja, politikai integráltsága és részvétele*. Budapest: Social Sciences Research Center of the Hungarian Academy of Sciences, 2019.

Molnár, Anna. "Economic Crisis and Euroscepticism: A Comparative Study of the Hungarian and Italian Case (1990–2013)." *Politics in Central Europe* 12, no. 3 (2016): 70.

Mudde, Cas. *Youth and the Extreme Right*. Amsterdam: International Debate Education Association, 2014.

Navracsics, Tibor. *A Missing Debate?: Hungary and the European Union*. Sussex: Sussex European Institute, 1997.

O'Toole, Therese, Michael Lister, Dave Marsh, Su Jones, and Alex McDonagh. "Tuning Out or Left Out? Participation and Non-Participation Among Young People." *Contemporary Politics* 9, no. 1 (2003): 45–61.

Pap, András Laszlo and Anna Śledzińska-Simon. "The Rise of Illiberal Democracy and the Remedies of Multi-Level Constitutionalism." *Hungarian Journal of Legal Studies* 60, no. 1 (2019): 65–85.

Pop-Eleches, Grigore, and Joshua A. Tucker. "Communist Legacies and Left-Authoritarianism." *Comparative Political Studies* 53, no. 12 (2020): 1861–89.

Saltman, Erin Marie. "Turning Right: A Case Study on Contemporary Political Socialization of the Hungarian Youth." PhD diss., University College London, 2014.

Savicka, Aida. "Volunteer Work: Our Way Back to Civil Society? Specifics of Volunteering in a Post Communist Milieu." In *Political Transformation and Changing Identities in Central and Eastern Europe*, edited by Andrew Blasko and Diana Janušauskienė. Washington, DC: The Council for Research in Values and Philosophy. 2008, 281–324.

Scheppele, Kim Lane. "What Can the European Commission do When Member States Violate Basic Principles of the European Union? The Case for Systemic Infringement Actions." *Assises de la Justice* 4, 2013.

Schiemann, John W. "Explaining Hungary's Powerful Constitutional Court: A Bargaining Approach." *European Journal of Sociology/Archives Européennes de Sociologie* 42, no. 2 (2001): 357.

Szabo, Andrea. *Political Integration of Hungarian Students.* Prague: Heinrich Böll Stiftung, 2019.

Szikra, Dorottya. "Democracy and Welfare in Hard Times: The Social Policy of the Orbán Government in Hungary Between 2010 and 2014." *Journal of European Social Policy* 24, no. 5 (2014): 487.

Szombati, Kristof Tamas. "Protesting the "Slave Law" in Hungary: The Erosion of Illiberal Hegemony?" *LeftEast*, 9 January 2019, https://lefteast.org/protesting-the-slave-law-in-hungary-the-erosion-of-illiberal-hegemony/.

Corruption Perceptions Index. Transparency International, 2020.

Corruption Perceptions Index. Transparency International, 2019.

Corruption Perceptions Index. Transparency International, 2018.

Corruption Perceptions Index. Transparency International, 2017.

Corruption Perceptions Index. Transparency International, 2016.

Corruption Perceptions Index. Transparency International, 2015.

Van der Brug, Wouter, Meindert Fennema, Sarah De Lange, and Inger Baller. *Radical Right Parties: Their Voters and Their Electoral Competitors.* Abingdon: Routledge, 2012.

Vásárhelyi, Mária. "A huszonévesek és Trianon'," *Élet És Irodalom*, 2011.

Weiss, Julia. "What is Youth Political Participation? Literature Review on Youth Political Participation and Political Attitudes." *Frontiers in Political Science* 2 (2020): 1

Wilkin, Peter. *Hungary's Crisis of Democracy: The Road to Serfdom.* Lanham: Lexington Books, 2016.

Wring, Dominic, Matt Henn, and Mark Weinstein. "Young People and Contemporary Politics: Committed Scepticism or Engaged Cynicism?" *British Elections & Parties Review* 9, no. 1 (1999): 200–16.

"Youth Attitudes on Politics and Democracy: Hungary." National Democratic Institute, NDI Survey of Young People in Central Europe, July 2020.

Zeller, Michael. "Shifting Political Dynamics and Democratic Disillusionment in Hungary's Political Youth." *The Eurasian Era* 1, no. 1 (2016): 3–11.

5 Who's Afraid of the Big Bad Wolf? RT's Reporting on the European Union in Central and Eastern Europe

Emma Flaherty

1 Introduction

Brussels cries 'conspiracy' over Hungary's ads showing smiling Soros behind EU immigration agenda.[1] This is but one headline among many that appeared on RT.com in the run-up to the European Parliament elections in May 2019. The European Union (EU) has challenged Russia's geopolitical strategy since the 1990s when former Soviet bloc countries began to join the Union, pivoting away from Russia's sphere of influence. The shift to the west of ten countries in Central and Eastern Europe[2] (CEE) damaged Russia's ability to call itself a great power and established the CEE region as an important geopolitical theater for Russia. In the years since these countries' pivot toward the EU and Western Europe, many CEE states have begun to revive their relationships with Russia.[3]

When tensions began to emerge between Western EU members and several Member States in CEE, an opportunity arose for Russia to utilize its soft power tools, such as the news organization RT, to stress the differences between East and West. One method through which RT attempts to do this is by framing and exacerbating internal EU tensions over EU policies and European identity. This study looks at six of these key elements[4] that are also points of friction with Russia, such as competing views on security and energy policies that have been the subject of popular debate.[5] These efforts have amplified the fault lines in the EU–Russia relationship that emerged after Russia's illegal annexation of Crimea in 2014 and are part of Russia's larger attempts to bring the CEE region back within its sphere of influence through both hybrid and soft power means. The use of Russian soft power instruments to amplify divisions in countries that are already experiencing political discord has received widespread attention in areas like the United States and the United Kingdom, but the failure to study how these methods are utilized in CEE presents an ongoing challenge to EU cohesion.[6] Until Russia's methods of swaying audiences within CEE is clearly understood, it will be difficult for the EU to craft a compelling counternarrative that helps restore belief in the European project.

DOI: 10.4324/9781003182344-6

Based on analysis conducted on RT articles, this chapter offers three main conclusions: first, RT's coverage of the EU is overwhelmingly negative, aligning with the Russian Federation's official attitude toward the institution; second, CEE countries with a favorable political and/or economic relationship with Russia tend to be covered by RT with more positive sentiment than those countries with neutral or antagonistic relations with Moscow; third, and most important for future efforts to combat Russian disinformation campaigns, Russia and its affiliated international media alter their messaging toward countries based on their perception of the CEE countries' likelihood to return to Moscow's sphere of influence.

2 Another Tool in Putin's Toolbox: Russia's Use of Media within Its Foreign Policy Strategy

The Kremlin-funded news organization Russia Today, now known as RT, has been the focus of concern for many Western scholars.[7] In the midst of the uproar around Russian disinformation efforts after the US presidential election in 2016, there have been many claims about RT but a lack of data about the news organization's reporting techniques.[8] This research is motivated by Russia's long-standing use of international broadcasting as a key part of its soft power strategy. After the collapse of the Soviet Union, the foreign policy of the Russian Federation has focused on restoring Russia's status as a great power on the global stage.[9] Russia uses a wide range of tools in pursuit of its goal of great power status, ranging from attempts to leverage control of the energy sources European countries rely on to the utilization of "Russian mass media and communication tools."[10]

The biggest shift in Russian foreign policy since the Soviet era[11] has been in the types of actors the country supports. Most scholars agree that Russia seeks to "exacerbate divides and create an echo chamber of Kremlin support" by backing actors across the ideological spectrum.[12] Russia is able to adapt its message to appeal to a wide variety of actors ranging from left-wing parties that dislike the United States' dominance on the global stage to anti-EU, far right parties.

2.1 'Question More:' RT's Role as a Government-Sponsored News Outlet

Russia began developing its international broadcasting tools in the early 2000s, motivated by what it perceived as an opportunity to challenge US dominance in global media.[13] As a subset of its public diplomacy that seeks to "build up dialogue among civilisations, achieve consensus and ensure understanding among peoples," [14] Russia launched the news organization RT in 2005.[15] The news organization began with a 24/7 English-language cable broadcast and has now expanded to include online news, YouTube videos, and television content in six languages.[16] In their study of how Russian news filters through Western media, Gordon Ramsay and Sam Robertshaw found that RT and Sputnik, another Russian-funded news organization, are used as source materials for Western outlets, particularly on topics such as national security where information in these articles may feature Russian officials.[17] Since 2012, RT has gained international prestige by shifting its mission to focus more on news stories that are overlooked by mainstream Western media, such as the Occupy Movements.[18] This shift and the changing media landscape that pressures news outlets to produce stories quickly and cheaply, leading them to rely on foreign officials pushing state propaganda as sources, enable English-language news from RT.com to be quoted in news produced by mainstream Western sources, where it reaches a significantly larger volume of readers.[19] As these stances then appear to originate from trusted sources, people are more inclined to believe RT's message than they may have been if reading it directly on RT.com.[20] Following Russia's annexation of Crimea in 2014, many analysts concurred that a major feature of contemporary Russian foreign policy has been to sow disinformation through its state-funded news organizations, as exemplified by the deliberate misrepresentation of Russian activities in Ukraine.[21] In an interview with the Russian newspaper *Kommersant*, RT Editor-in-Chief Margarita Simonyan described the network as fulfilling a similar role as Russia's defense ministry.[22] Simonyan framed RT as a vital tool for Russia to utilize "in a critical moment [as] we'll already have grown our audience, which is used to come [sic] to us for the other side of the truth, and of course we'll make use of that."[23] The appearance of RT in the US intelligence community's official report on Russian meddling in the 2016 US presidential election as well as the EU's increased funding of its disinformation task force indicates that Western countries are increasingly concerned about the disintegrative role that RT plays in their domestic politics.[24]

Previous investigations and studies on Russia's use of soft power tools have shown that the country commonly uses these resources to widen divisions in foreign countries.[25] This factor and the current state of Russia–EU relations, which according to the Russian Ambassador to the EU have "stabilized at an abnormally low level"[26] after the EU leveled sanctions against Russia in the wake of Russia's illegal annexation of Crimea in 2014, have informed the following three hypotheses. (H1) The amount of negative sentiment in RT's reporting of a country will increase based on how antagonistic the country's bilateral relationship with Russia is; (H2) EU coverage topics that reflect current or potential areas of cooperation between CEE countries and Russia, such as economics, will be covered more positively than topics where the two sides share very little common ground; (H3) Countries that try to keep the EU from warming toward Russia will have a larger percentage of negative EU coverage; however, all EU coverage will be negative due to the ongoing tense relationship between Russia and the EU.

3 Measuring RT's Influence in CEE

In order to systematically classify each CEE country's relationship with Russia, this chapter utilizes the classification method developed by Mark Leonard and Nicu Popescu, with updates[27] to reflect shifts in the geopolitical landscape since their study was published in 2007.[28] This method utilized five country groupings: Trojan Horses, Strategic Partners, Friendly Pragmatists, Frosty Pragmatists, and New Cold Warriors.[29] Trojan Horses[30] value a positive relationship with Russia and are willing to undermine EU policies in order to protect this bilateral relationship. Strategic Partners[31] "enjoy a 'special relationship' with Russia which occasionally undermines common EU policies."[32] Friendly Pragmatists[33] also value a positive relationship with Russia and will prioritize business interests over political ones, though they do tend to support EU policies regarding Russia.[34] Though Frosty Pragmatists[35] also value business relationships with Russia, they will speak out when Russia violates human rights or international norms.[36] New Cold Warriors[37] have "an overtly hostile relationship with Moscow" and are willing to act within the EU to prevent the institution from improving ties with Russia.[38]

There are currently no Trojan Horses within the CEE region; even those that may disagree with the EU on some of its policies toward Russia, such as energy, are unwilling to veto EU sanctions against Russia in the wake of the 2014 illegal annexation of Crimea.[39]

Hungary is a Strategic Partner as its prime minister, Viktor Orbán, has repeatedly spoken out against EU sanctions on Russia. Hungary has a close energy relationship with Russia as illustrated by the signing of a contract with the Russian nuclear company Rosatom to build nuclear reactors in Hungary[40] in early 2018.[41] Orbán also worked with Russia on Hungary's Ukraine policy, which claims Hungary has a right to a part of Western Ukraine.[42] After Ukraine passed a law banning access to education in minority languages, such as Hungarian, Hungary blocked the reapproval of the NATO-Ukraine Commission and communicated its willingness to restrict the EU's talks with Ukraine on further integration until the education law is repealed.[43] Hungary has also implemented legislation requiring that nongovernmental organizations (NGOs) receiving foreign funds past a certain threshold must register with the government;[44] experts view this legislation as directly inspired by Russia's law targeting foreign-funded NGOs.[45]

Three CEE countries are Friendly Pragmatists: the Czech Republic, Bulgaria, and Slovenia. Czech Prime Minister Andrej Babiš has spoken favorably of Russia's annexation of Crimea while also decrying EU sanctions on Russia.[46] Current Czech President Miloš Zeman has argued that the conflict in Ukraine is a civil war, not a Russian invasion.[47] Additionally, the Czech government has devoted attention to preserving its economic ties with Russia in the wake of EU sanctions.[48] When the United States and many EU Member States expelled Russian diplomats in 2018 after the chemical attack against a former member of Russian intelligence, Sergei Skripal, and his daughter, Bulgaria and Slovenia took no action.[49] Additionally, neither Bulgaria nor Slovenia joined other CEE leaders in speaking out against the construction of the Nord Stream 2 pipeline that will transport gas from Russia to Germany.[50]

Estonia and Slovakia are the two Frosty Pragmatists. In 2019, Estonian President Kersti Kaljulaid met with Russian president Vladimir Putin, which was the first meeting between the countries' two leaders since 1991.[51] Russia has historically been one of Estonia's top trading partners, though the amount of trade has declined since the EU placed sanctions on Russia in 2014.[52] President Kaljulaid's meeting with Putin in 2019 was perceived as a thaw in the Estonia–Russia bilateral relationship and a shift, albeit not a large one, away from Estonia's prior hard-liner stance toward Russia. Slovakia has a strong trade and energy relationship with Russia, though the country has joined other CEE countries in criticizing the Nord Stream 2 pipeline.[53] Since 2017, trade between Russia and Slovakia has increased along with the number of Russian tourists visiting Slovakia.[54]

The New Cold Warriors category is the most populous within the CEE countries as Latvia, Lithuania, Poland, and Romania all meet the definition of this classification. In addition to refusing to recognize Russia's annexation of Crimea, Latvia passed a law that declared the Soviet Union's deportation of Crimean Tatars in 1944 was a genocide; though it seems small, efforts to acknowledge historical wrongdoings by the Soviet Union typically lead to Russian ire and indicate that Latvia is trying to support Ukraine through the limited policy options it has.[55] Lithuania criticized Estonia's warming relations with Russia after Estonia's president met with Putin, which highlights the degree of difference in how the two countries view bilateral Russian relations.[56] Poland has a long history of tense relations with Russia that dates back to at least the Second World War.[57] In recent years, Poland has been a vocal critic of the Nord Stream 2 pipeline and has been cautious of the EU's desire to normalize relations with Russia.[58] Romania has worked to uphold the EU's sanctions against Russia even when doing so provokes Russia, such as when Romania refused to allow Russian weapons purchased by Serbia to travel through its territory. All of the New Cold Warrior countries have spoken out against the construction of the Nord Stream 2 pipeline and have followed the example set by the EU on topics such as the response to the Skripal poisoning.[59]

A summary of the country classifications is illustrated in the below table.

Table 5.1 Summary of CEE Country Classifications

New Cold Warriors	Frosty Pragmatists	Friendly Pragmatists	Strategic Partners	Trojan Horses
Latvia	Estonia	Bulgaria	Hungary	None
Lithuania	Slovakia	Czech Republic		
Poland		Slovenia		
Romania				

3.1 Quantifying RT's Reporting on CEE through Data Analysis

In order to empirically assess whether RT utilizes different issue framing when covering CEE, the EU, and areas of friction between the EU and Russia, this study applies sentiment analysis on articles collected from RT.com. Negative reporting on CEE countries and/or EU coverage topics provides an opportunity for RT to highlight the differences between Eastern and Western EU Member States while stressing that the countries that left Russia's sphere of influence are not doing well. These factors led to the general hypothesis that sentiment within RT articles will largely reflect the quality of a country's bilateral relationship with Russia and the potential to cooperate on some issues. This study analyzed six topics of EU coverage that have been the main points of contention between Russia and the EU: values, economics, world order, security, energy, and democracy. The data sample consisted of 211 news articles published on RT.com from 1 February 2019 through 31 July 2019. This time period included the European Parliament elections, held 23–26 May 2019, as well as the nomination process for the new European Commissioner, which began on 2 July 2019. The European Parliament election was perceived by many as an informal referendum on the Union itself and thus provided a unique opportunity for RT to report on these topics of contention.[60]

The articles in this data sample were selected by searching RT.com for each of the ten CEE countries: Bulgaria, the Czech Republic, Estonia, Hungary, Latvia, Lithuania, Poland, Romania, Slovakia, and Slovenia. Any article that was not an op-ed, contained a reference to at least one of these countries, and was published from 1 February 2019 through 31 July 2019 was saved. Op-eds were excluded as they may contain viewpoints that are not endorsed by RT that could impact the findings. Articles that appeared more than once during the sampling process were only included once.

After the articles were collected, they were analyzed in the qualitative software NVivo 12 where codes for the CEE countries, EU coverage topics, month the article was published, and/or EU institutions were applied to sentences that contained these codes within the articles.[61] This allowed for the filtering out of all content within the articles that did not pertain to a CEE country and thus was not relevant to this study. The inclusion of a code for the month the article was published allowed for the analysis of sentiment in EU coverage over time, with particular focus on how the Union was covered in the months prior to the European Parliament elections in May 2019. Next, the sentence-level excerpts were exported to the mixed methods data software[62] Dedoose, which allowed for a preliminary analysis of trends within the data, such as code co-occurrences, that was not supported by NVivo 12. At this stage, the sentence-level excerpts were then exported from Dedoose and analyzed with the software R in order to conduct the sentiment analysis.

The first step of the sentiment analysis process was to transform the sentence-level excerpts from RT.com into individual words[63] as sentiment analysis occurred at the word level.

Sentiment analysis was performed on these individual words using the lexicon developed by Bing Liu and his collaborators, referred to as the 'bing' lexicon.[64] This lexicon contains approximately 6,800 English words that have been categorized as positive or negative and classifies sentiment at the level of single words, rather than sentences.[65] For example, 'precisely' has a positive sentiment and 'warned' has a negative sentiment. If words from the 'bing' lexicon appear in the data sample, they are then given the corresponding 'sentiment' along with all of their codes from the previous stage of analysis.

The six EU coverage topics utilized in this study refer to points of contention in the EU–Russia relationship. They were selected due to their presence within EU messaging about itself and the role the Union plays within the international system. The definitions for these coverage topics were informed by statements made by the EU on these topics as well as a preliminary survey of the RT articles within the data sample. These elements are defined as follows:

- *Values* – pertaining to stated or implied values such as LGBT rights, access to abortions, and other individual freedoms
- *Economics* – pertaining to the economy through references to trade, fiscal policy, workers, etc.
- *World order* – describing a view of the international system, such as realpolitik or liberalism
- *Security* – describing matters of security and safety possibly through the identification of threats (e.g. terrorists) or references to defense (e.g. Permanent Structured Cooperation [PESCO])
- *Energy* – pertaining to natural resources, suppliers, and other related entities (e.g. Gazprom, Nord Stream 2)
- *Democracy* – a stated or implied discussion of elements of a democratic government

3.2 Assessing RT's Coverage of Central and Eastern Europe

After the coded segments were analyzed using the 'bing' lexicon, 712 words were identified as a match to the lexicon and given either a positive or negative classification. The overall sentiment of the data sample was primarily negative, with 63.34% of the words having a negative classification. Within the country groupings, the New Cold Warriors received the most negative coverage (67.71%). Descending from most negatively covered country grouping, the rest were covered as follows: Strategic Partners (64.08% negative), Frosty Pragmatists (55.00% negative), and Friendly Pragmatists (53.25% negative). These findings were unexpected as the Strategic Partners, which have the most positive bilateral relationships with Russia, were covered more negatively than the Frosty Pragmatists and Friendly Pragmatists, which had better relationships with Russia than the New Cold Warriors but are still not incredibly favorable. This finding may be influenced by the higher percentage of EU coverage within the Strategic Partners sample when compared to other country groupings. As the EU was covered largely negatively by RT, its added presence in the Strategic Partners group may have overinflated the amount of negative sentiment used by RT in its articles about this group.

The majority of stories involving at least one code within the EU category was also negative with 61.54% of instances using negative words. Only three out of ten countries had primarily positive coverage: the Czech Republic (75.00%), Slovenia (66.67%), and Slovakia (57.89%). Notably, these countries also appeared less frequently in the data sample as a whole. In contrast, the two most frequently covered countries within the data sample, Poland and Hungary, ranked within the top five countries that were covered most negatively by RT. Poland was reported on most out of the ten CEE countries and had 69.97% of stories containing negative sentiment. Hungary had the next largest number of stories and was fourth-most negative (64.08%). Though neither country was the most negative within the sample as a whole, the large number of stories in RT on these two countries signifies their importance within CEE as well as to Russia. Poland and Hungary are both facing Article 7 proceedings in the EU for democratic deficiencies that resulted from reforms made by the Law and Justice (PiS) and Fidesz governments, respectively.[66] Highlighting the actions these countries have taken to anger the EU furthers Russia's goals of exacerbating existing tensions within the EU.

Among the EU coverage topics that represented six points of contention between Russia and the EU, the coverage topic with the highest percentage of negative coverage across all CEE countries was security with 71.76% of stories containing negative words. Two EU topics had balanced coverage: economics and world order. The finding that economics coverage was relatively balanced and appeared to fluctuate in positivity depending on the state of the country grouping's relationship with Russia supports the second

Table 5.2 Sentiment Across EU Coverage Topic and Country

EU Coverage Topic	Sentiment	Bulgaria	Czech Republic	Estonia	Hungary	Latvia	Lithuania	Poland	Romania	Slovakia
Democracy										
	Negative	--	--	--	50.00%	--	--	33.33%	60.00%	--
	Positive	--	--	--	50.00%	--	--	66.67%	40.00%	--
Economics										
	Negative	--	--	25.00%	35.71%	50.00%	33.33%	52.63%	50.00%	--
	Positive	100%	100%	75.00%	64.83%	50.00%	66.67%	47.37%	50.00%	--
Energy										
	Negative	50.00%	--	--	--	--	100%	66.67%	--	--
	Positive	50.00%	--	--	--	--	--	33.33%	--	--
Values										
	Negative	100%	100%	--	65.12%	36.36%	--	78.26%	--	100%
	Positive	--	--	--	34.88%	63.64%	--	21.74%	--	--
Security										
	Negative	73.68%	33.33%	100%	60.00%	59.09%	100%	79.55%	80.00%	100%
	Positive	26.32%	66.67%	--	40.00%	40.91%	--	21.45%	20.00%	--
World Order										
	Positive	--	--	--	50.00%	--	--	50.00%	--	--
	Negative	--	--	--	50.00%	--	--	50.00%	--	--

hypothesis that Russia seeks to highlight areas of current cooperation with CEE countries. The full trend in this data is shown in the table above. The world order finding is somewhat less significant due to the small size of the data sample, which suggests that RT instead chooses to focus on topics of contention that are easier to quantify to its readers, such as security and values. Slovenia was omitted from the table above as it was the only country in the sample that had no instances of any EU coverage topic. The lack of EU coverage topics in the Slovenia sample is most likely explained by the fact this country had the smallest number of articles by a significant amount.

3.2.1   Putting the Pieces Together: Discussion of Framing within the RT Articles

As described above, there were three hypotheses for this study. H1 predicted that negative sentiment in RT articles would be tied to the degree of negativity in that country's bilateral relationship with Russia. It was partially supported by the data. The New Cold Warriors group, which has the most hostile relationships with Russia, was covered the most negatively out of all country groupings (67.71%), which aligned with the predicted data trend. However, the overall shift in negativity did not completely follow the trend predicted in H1. The Frosty Pragmatists and Friendly Pragmatists reflect the expected behavior, where the Frosty Pragmatists are slightly more positive than the New Cold Warriors and the Friendly Pragmatists have slightly more positive coverage than the Frosty Pragmatists; the Strategic Partners group is a notable outlier. Hungary is the only member of the Strategic Partners group and is currently grappling with the EU on topics like judicial reform and migrant quotas.[67] Hungary is also the country that had the largest number of stories within the sample that included an EU code (29.13% of all Hungary stories). As the EU was covered in a largely negative fashion by RT and appeared predominantly in news articles pertaining to Hungary, this may explain why Hungary was covered more negatively than expected.

The downward trend of negative sentiment for the Frosty Pragmatists and Friendly Pragmatists suggests that there is a shift in RT reporting to cover countries that are closer to Russia's sphere of influence more positively.[68] As these countries generally cooperate with Russia on key issues like economics, it is in RT's interest to report on them positively with the possible intent of encouraging additional collaboration with Russia. In contrast, the New Cold Warriors are highly unlikely to cooperate with Russia on any topic and as such, there is little hope that positive RT reporting would help bring these countries back into Russia's sphere of influence. This supports the idea that Russia has decided the New Cold Warriors are not likely to return to its sphere of influence and, as a result, has instead chosen to sow internal discord and exacerbate tensions with the EU.

The second hypothesis predicted that the EU coverage topics reflecting potential areas of cooperation between CEE and Russia would be covered

Sentiment Across Country Classifications

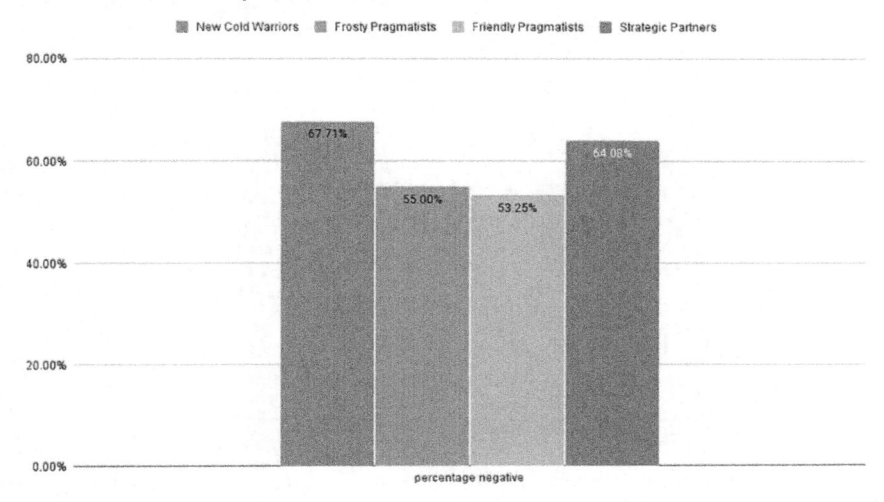

Figure 5.1 Illustrating the trend of negative sentiment in RT articles across the country groupings.

more positively than those that are more contested; it was also partially supported by the data. As seen in Figure 5.1, there were three EU coverage topics that were reported on in all of the country groupings: economics, values, and security. Of these three, economics was the most likely to receive some positive coverage as many of the CEE countries rely on positive economic relationships with Russia, which has led many CEE leaders to publicly complain about EU sanctions on Russia.[69] The sentiment trends in the economics coverage reflects that this reporting appears somewhat impacted by a country's bilateral relationship with Russia. The New Cold Warriors had nearly balanced economic coverage (48.98% positive) and all other groupings had primarily positive economic coverage though the most positively covered grouping was the Friendly Pragmatists and not the Strategic Partners. For coverage topics where cooperation is highly unlikely, such as security, the sentiment used by RT was primarily negative yet it did change slightly across the country groupings. Though the Friendly Pragmatists and Strategic Partners are not willing to work with Russia on security issues outside of EU and NATO frameworks, their security coverage was slightly more positive than those in other country groupings (see Figure 5.2 below).[70] These countries may be perceived as more uncertain in their stance about whether Russia is a threat to the region, which could encourage RT to cover security in a slightly less negative way. As security, and particularly NATO membership, continues to be a point of contention between Russia and all of the CEE countries, it is not surprising that this was the most negatively

Percentage of Positive Sentiment Across Country Groupings

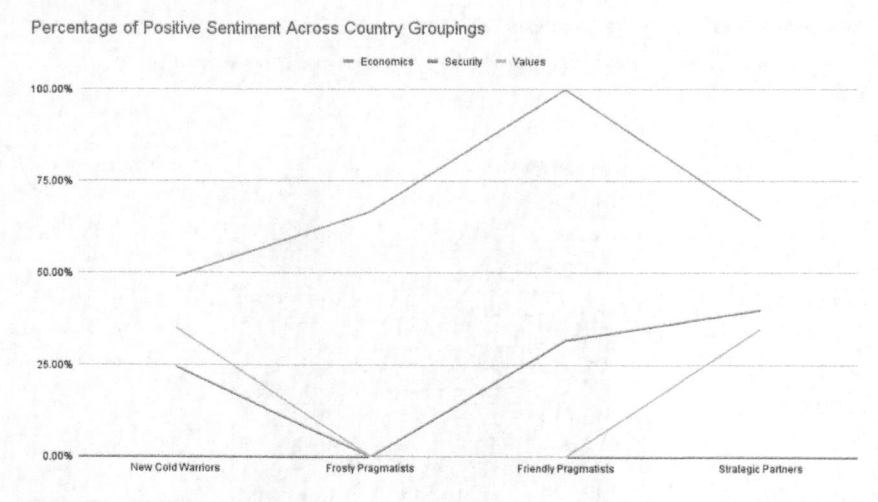

Figure 5.2 Showing the trend in positive sentiment across the country groupings for economics, security, and values EU coverage topics. The measures of no percentage reflect 100% negative sentiment.

covered EU coverage topic. After Russia's annexation of Crimea in 2014, NATO began a concerted effort to bolster its defenses in Member States along Russia's periphery.[71] These actions have provoked a strong Russian response that has not stabilized the security tensions between Russia and NATO.[72]

The third hypothesis predicted that the New Cold Warriors would have a larger percentage of negative EU coverage than the other groups, with the presumption that all EU coverage would be primarily negative. This hypothesis was not supported by the data. The Friendly Pragmatists had the largest percentage of negative EU coverage (100%) followed by the Strategic Partners (56.67%). The New Cold Warriors grouping ranked third with 51.72% negative coverage, while the Frosty Pragmatists did not have any news stories that contained an EU code. The overwhelmingly negative sentiment for the Friendly Pragmatists may be due to the relatively small number of stories about these countries that also contained the EU. The preponderance of Strategic Partners news stories with the EU aligns with the suggestion raised above that this category's coverage was more negative than expected due to the amount of EU stories compared to other groups. The quantity of news articles also indicates that the issue of the EU and Hungary is an important one to RT, particularly during the run-up to the European Parliament elections held in late May 2019. This news content may have attempted to encourage those in other areas of the EU to perceive Hungary as a country that is different from the rest of the Union.

3.2.2 RT Framing within the Country Classifications

The New Cold Warriors group was the largest within the data sample with four CEE countries. All four of these countries had security as their most common EU coverage topic. The coverage for the New Cold Warrior countries was over 50% negative with a cumulative total for the group of 67.71% negative instances. There was a large disparity within the group in terms of the number of stories published. Poland was the most reported-on country both in the data sample as a whole and within this subset. Due possibly to its larger number of stories, Poland was the only country within this group that had reporting on each of the six EU coverage topics. Two of the coverage topics were outliers of the overall negative reporting on Poland; democracy was primarily positive (66.67%) and world order was balanced (split evenly at 50%). The current Polish government has been the subject of a lot of criticism by the EU due to the eroding state of democracy in the country, which makes the primarily positive coverage of democracy surprising.[73] This framing choice may be explained by the fact that Poland's attempts to target rule of law and an independent judiciary within the country reflect changes that align with Russia's approach to democracy.[74] Another New Cold Warrior, Romania, had a majority of negative coverage for democracy (60.00%). Romania's democracy coverage also tends to include references to other countries within Russia's sphere of influence, such as Moldova, that may be the primary driver for the negative coverage. In these instances, RT may be trying to signal to other former Soviet Union countries that pivoting further away from Russia, such as through attempts to join the EU, would produce negative results.

When compared to the data sample as a whole, the New Cold Warriors category contained the two countries with the highest percentages of negative coverage: Romania (73.08%) and Poland (67.97%). The New Cold Warriors group was the only group that had a majority of negative coverage on the EU coverage topic 'economy' (51.02%). This reflects the fact that the New Cold Warriors are least likely out of all groupings to place economic concerns before criticizing Russia.

The Frosty Pragmatists, Estonia and Slovakia, were two of the countries in the more positive half of the data sample, though the combined sentiment for the group was 55.00% negative. Slovakia's coverage was primarily positive (54.17%). While Estonia's coverage was over 50% negative, it did have a lower percentage of negative stories than members of the New Cold Warriors group. Estonia's most frequently used EU topic was security, which aligns with the trend of the data sample as a whole. The most common EU coverage topic for Slovakia was values (100% negative) followed by security, which was also entirely negative.

Slovakia's limited coverage on values focused on the topic of migrants. The negative coverage on values reflects that Slovakia has joined other CEE countries in taking a stand against EU policies on migration. The fact that this action was labeled as 'negative' in sentiment analysis appears to be caused by the words used within the reporting rather than Russia's actual stance toward Slovakia's actions, as one would expect Russia would endorse CEE countries refusing to follow EU policies as this helps sow divisions within countries like Slovakia. Slovakia had no coded excerpts that contained any of the codes included in the EU category, which may have contributed to its positive trend of coverage as instances of the EU tended to be negative.

The Friendly Pragmatists were the most positively covered grouping within the data sample (46.75% positive). This result deviates from H1, which expected the Strategic Partners to have the most positive coverage as they have the closest bilateral relationships with Russia. This category also contained the largest outlier among the CEE countries: the Czech Republic (75.00% positive). Slovenia was the second-most positive country within the overall data sample (66.67%) while Bulgaria was in the more negative half of the sample with 63.64% of stories containing negative sentiments. As the countries in the Friendly Pragmatists group have relatively favorable relationships with Russia, this group appears to support the assumption that they would be covered more positively in a potential attempt to bring them closer to Russia; the Friendly Pragmatists were the group with the largest percentage of positive sentiment in their articles: 46.75%. This finding suggests that Russia may attempt to cover countries with relatively positive bilateral relationships positively with the hopes of encouraging further cooperation on key policy issues.

The three Friendly Pragmatist countries also varied significantly in terms of the number of mentions within the RT articles. Slovenia was the country reported on least frequently; it was mentioned in only 3.79% of the total news stories. Both the Czech Republic and Slovenia had primarily positive sentiment within their news articles, but as each appeared in such a small percentage of the overall data sample, it is challenging to identify whether their positive coverage is due to their status as Friendly Pragmatists or is skewed by the sample size. The Czech Republic was the most positively reported CEE country within the sample, which aligns with their status as a country that vocally supports many of Russia's important issues, such as the annexation of Crimea. In contrast, Bulgaria's negative coverage is more in line with the New Cold Warriors group, though the country has a more positive relationship with Russia than members of that group. The most covered EU topic for Bulgaria was security, which was overwhelmingly negative (73.68%). Coverage of Bulgaria and energy was small yet balanced between positive and negative. During the time period included in this study, Russia was attempting to convince Bulgaria to sign on to the TurkStream 2 pipeline that would transport natural gas from Russia to Western Europe;[75] it would thus harm Russian interests to cover energy in Bulgaria with the same degree of negativity as other EU coverage topics within the Bulgaria sample, such as security and values. This reporting trend also aligns with the findings for the second hypothesis: that RT shifts its reporting on topics of cooperation to be more positive in the hopes of encouraging these efforts to continue. This finding is significant as it suggests that news stories reported by RT reflect the degree of cooperation and goodwill in a country's bilateral relationship with Russia.

Hungary was the only Strategic Partner within the CEE sample. Hungary appeared the second-most frequently within the data sample, appearing in 13.48% of the final sample, second only to Poland's 32.16%. Hungary also ranked third in terms of most-negative coverage (64.08%). Unlike many of the other CEE countries, however, Hungary's most common EU coverage topic was values, not security. Though values also featured prominently in the Poland sample, Hungary had nearly 50% more instances of values with 65.12% negative coverage. In addition to being the most frequently discussed EU topic within Hungary stories, values was also the EU coverage topic reported on most negatively within the Hungary portion of the data. Stories involving Hungary and values tend to draw attention to the tension between Hungary's Prime Minister, Viktor Orbán, and the EU such as the below quote from an RT article that uses loaded language to describe several ongoing conflicts between Hungary and the EU:

> Budapest and Brussels have been at daggers drawn for some time, particularly over immigration issues, but also in relation to the Hungarian government's alleged "attacks" on billionaire regime-change financier George Soros.[76]

The news articles in this category primarily focus on the ongoing tension over immigration policies between Hungary and the EU, particularly the EU's effort "to impose pro-immigration policies" on the Member States.[77] In light of the relationship between Hungary and the EU, especially since Orbán came to power, this news topic is an easy way for RT to suggest that Hungary does not belong in the EU. Stories of this nature conveniently overlook the fact that, despite the friction between Budapest and Brussels, Hungary has continued to follow the EU's sanctions against Russia even as Orbán makes statements decrying them.[78] Hungary also had balanced coverage on the EU coverage topic of democracy, which was surprising as the other country engaged in democratic backsliding within the EU, Poland, received primarily negative reporting about democracy. These stories tend to focus on Orbán's attempts to lead his party, Fidesz, to victory in the European Parliament elections, which are mostly covered positively, and the EU's perception of Fidesz, which is generally covered negatively.

3.2.3 Trends in RT's Reporting on the EU

An analysis of RT's sentiment within EU coverage sought to identify whether there was additional nuance to Russia's perception of the Union beyond merely the low quality of relations between the two entities. Additionally, an analysis of the EU within CEE countries allows for the identification of whether some countries receive more negative EU news than others and thus should be the focus of competing messaging from the EU. In order to measure the sentiment of the EU within RT articles, this study coded for the institution as a whole, for branches of the EU, and for notable EU politicians.[79] Due to the small size of the data sample after sentiment analysis, trends within the EU coverage were analyzed both on an overall level, which looked at all of the EU codes together, as well as on the individual code level. Within the EU sample as a whole, the coverage was principally negative (62.37%). The amount of EU coverage peaked in February and May with 67 stories in both months; the amount of negative sentiment was also identical for these months (62.69%). The amount of EU stories in February appears to be primarily due to the ongoing debate about EU sanctions against Russia, a renewed interest in the debate about whether the EU will increase its focus on security, and the topic of the proposed Nord Stream 2 pipeline.

The increased coverage in May is likely due to the European Parliament elections that occurred later in the month. In the run-up to voting, RT stories focused on divisive issues within the EU such as immigration, the institution's inability to curtail the erosion of democracy in Poland, and the number of regulations created by the EU. There were also numerous articles published in May that challenged the view that Russia was attempting to meddle in European elections, instead blaming organizations affiliated with George Soros for trying to undermine democracy.[80]

June was the month with the highest percentage of negative coverage (66.67%), though this may be due to the fact that this was also the month with the smallest number of EU stories published by RT.com. Many experts viewed the European Parliament elections as a referendum on populist parties within Europe and expected that these parties would perform well in the elections; in the wake of an election with higher voter turnout than previous years and an overall strong showing by pro-EU parties, RT may have increased its percentage of negative EU stories in June to target the shifting narrative that the EU was capable of weathering the crises it was facing.[81]

After sentiment analysis was conducted, the EU code and a CEE country appeared together in 8.70% of the data. This small sample was close to balanced (56.46% negative), particularly when compared to other subsets of the EU data. Five out of ten CEE countries contained at least one story that also included the EU: Bulgaria, Hungary, Lithuania, Poland, and Romania. As shown in Figure 5.4, Bulgaria, Lithuania, and Romania had completely negative sentiment. Bulgaria's presence in this group is surprising as the other two countries are members of the New Cold Warriors, which received largely negative coverage across all codes due to their negative relationship with Russia, while Bulgaria is a Friendly Pragmatist. This negative coverage of the EU in Bulgaria may be due to the fact that despite working toward a positive economic relationship with Russia, Bulgaria

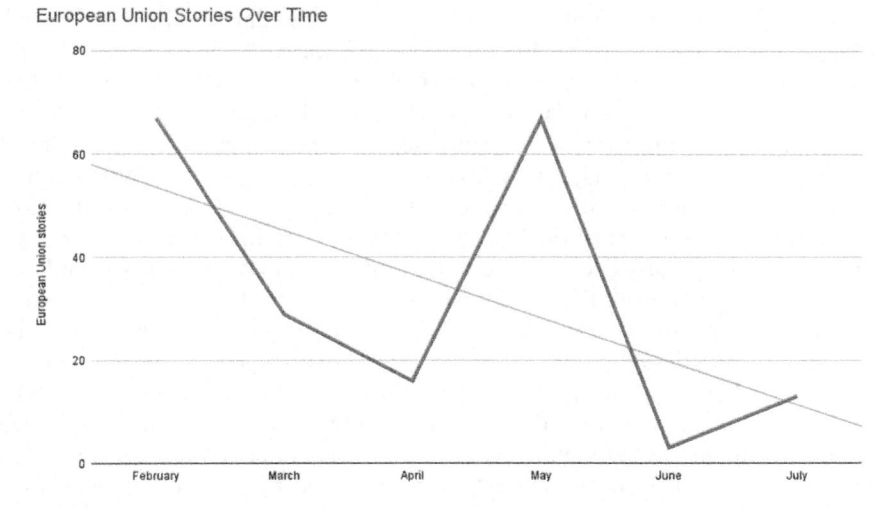

Figure 5.3 Showing the trend in aggregated European Union stories over time. The European Parliament elections occurred in May 2019.

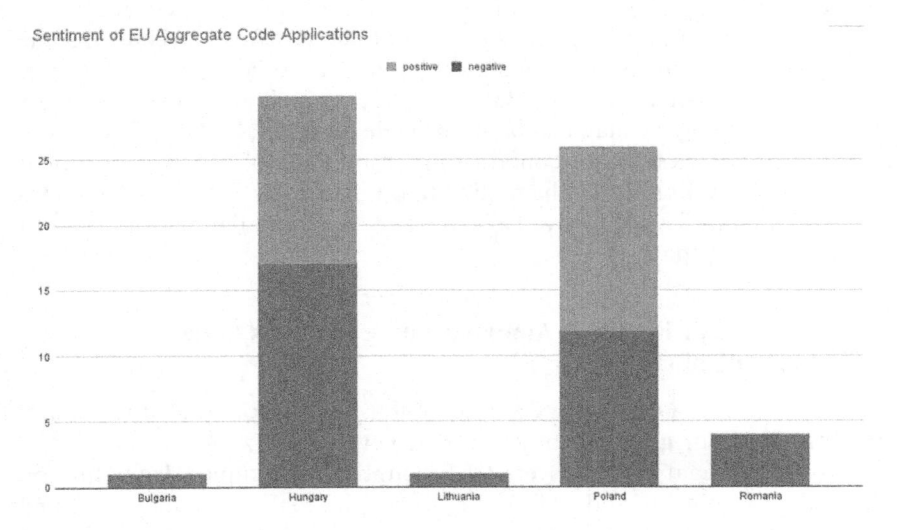

Figure 5.4 Showing the sentiment trends for all co-occurrences of a CEE country and the aggregated European Union code. Only CEE countries that had instances of an EU code application are shown.

continues to support EU sanctions against Russia and views the EU as more likely to help Bulgaria develop than Russia.[82]

The surprising finding within this subset of the data was that Poland had an overall positive percentage of EU news coverage (53.86%), particularly as

Poland was the CEE country with the second-most negative sentiment when all codes were included. The EU and Poland have had a tense relationship since the conservative Law and Justice (PiS) Party returned to power in 2015 and began implementing reforms that have eroded judicial independence.[83] The European Commission implemented Article 7 proceedings against Poland in December 2017,[84] which is one of the EU's most serious means of censuring Member States that do not comply with EU values outlined in Article 2 of the Treaty on European Union.[85] If implemented in their entirety, Article 7 proceedings allow the EU to suspend some of a Member State's rights, including the ability to vote on EU matters.[86] Poland poses a seemingly contradictory case for RT; the country is arguably the most hostile toward Russia within the EU yet has been a vocal critic of major EU policies, such as migrant quotas, and was facing EU procedures that could strip its voting rights within the bloc during the time period represented in the data sample.[87] One would expect to see the same trend in Hungary's EU coverage, as it similarly faced Article 7 proceedings due to the violation of EU values.[88] Surprisingly, however, Hungary's EU coverage was 56.66% negative. Hungary's coverage may be more negative than Poland's as it was the only CEE country to contain references to Jean-Claude Juncker, who was the most negatively covered EU entity. Poland's positive coverage may indicate some degree of implicit support for Poland's efforts to challenge the EU; however, this does not explain why Hungary did not also have primarily positive coverage. A larger data sample that included more stories for Poland and Hungary may be able to provide additional answers as to why these two countries do not contain similar amounts of negative sentiment when the EU is discussed. The finding that Poland was the only CEE country with a majority of positive EU coverage does not align with the rest of the trends in the data.

4 A Question of Framing: Applying These Findings to the European Union

Through an analysis of news articles published by RT, this study found that the Russian government-sponsored news organization changes how positively or negatively it covers CEE countries and topics depending on Russia's geopolitical and soft power strategic goals. The data revealed four key findings that will be essential in combating Russian disinformation campaigns in the future. First, CEE countries with favorable political and/or economic bilateral relations with Russia are generally covered more positively by RT than countries with neutral or antagonistic relationships with Moscow. The notable outlier in this trend was Hungary; despite having a strong relationship with Russia, Hungary was covered predominantly negatively in RT news stories. In the Hungarian case, most of the negative coverage revolved around EU values, with RT stories attempting to present those values as being at odds with Hungary's national values. Second, the Hungary example indicates that RT tailors its messaging based on the political realities in a country with particular emphasis placed on challenging the strength of a shared European identity. Third, in the case of specific issue topics, RT covers issues of bilateral cooperation more positively than issues of contention. For example, energy partnerships and bilateral trade are presented in positive language as opposed to security issues, which revolve around NATO and Russia's ongoing war in Ukraine. In this sense, RT focuses on developing a positive narrative around issues that it, and the Russian government, sees as being more inclined toward cooperation and compromise. Fourth, the positive or negative nature of RT's news stories does not necessarily correspond directly with the nature of Russia's bilateral relationship with a country. Although it was expected that countries with poor bilateral relations with Moscow would be covered most negatively, this was not in fact the case. This suggests that RT prioritizes strategic narratives around specific issues and values as part of Russia's broader soft power strategy rather than adhering strictly to geopolitical fault lines.

CEE is a critical geopolitical theater for both the EU and Russia. As tensions between Western and Eastern EU Member States continue to grow, the CEE countries provide an arena for Russia to utilize its existing soft power strategies, such as news outlets like RT, to attempt to exacerbate existing differences with the goal of furthering its own political goals. Without a comprehensive, data-based understanding of how RT is framing its coverage, which provides insight into the goals Russia hopes to achieve, the EU cannot effectively counter this messaging in the CEE region. The EU should take a page from Russia's playbook and alter its messaging based on the country it is attempting to reach. The core values of the EU remain constant but the issues that matter most to each Member State and its citizenry will vary so the EU should shift its strategy to reflect this. This could be done through a targeted messaging strategy that seeks to highlight how a country benefits from its EU membership, such as through a focus on energy or the free movement of people, depending on the concerns of that particular Member State. A more carefully crafted EU messaging strategy that considers the different domestic political landscapes of each country would be better equipped to counter RT's framing of news stories that seek to further Russian policy goals. Russian disinformation and EU cohesion will be two significant challenges facing the union in the next decade; working to counter Russian-sponsored news in CEE using a data-driven approach is a solid start to tackling these issues and laying the groundwork for a more united EU in the 2020s.

Notes

1 "Brussels Cries 'Conspiracy' over Hungary's Ads Showing Smiling Soros behind EU Immigration Agenda," *RT*, February 20, 2019, https://www.rt.com/news/451876-hungary-soros-juncker-immigration/.

2 The ten countries are Bulgaria, the Czech Republic, Estonia, Hungary, Latvia, Lithuania, Poland, Romania, Slovakia, and Slovenia.
3 Mitchell A. Orenstein, *The Lands in Between: Russia vs. the West and the New Politics of Hybrid War* (New York: Oxford University Press, 2019).
4 The six EU elements investigated in this study are democracy, economics, energy, values, security, and world order. The definitions of these elements are discussed in detail within the Measuring RT's Influence within CEE section of this chapter.
5 Stefan Lehne, "Europe's East-West Divide: Myth or Reality?," *Carnegie Europe* (blog), April 11, 2019, https://carnegieeurope.eu/2019/04/11/europe-s-east-west-divide-myth-or-reality-pub-78847.
6 Committee on Foreign Relations United States Senate, *Putin's Asymmetric Assault on Democracy in Russia and Europe: Implications for U.S. National Security: A Minority Staff Report, 115th Cong., 2nd sess., Jan. 10 2018, S. Prt. 115–121,* https://www.foreign.senate.gov/imo/media/doc/FinalRR.pdf; Milan Šuplata and Milan Nič, *Russia's Information War in Central Europe: New Trends and Counter-*Measures (GLOBSEC Policy Institute, n.d.), https://www.kremlinwatch.eu/userfiles/russia-s-information-war-in-central-europe_15273208769101.pdf.
7 Marcel H. van Herpen, *Putin's Propaganda Machine: Soft Power and Russian Foreign Policy* (Lanham: Rowman & Littlefield, 2016).
8 Steven Erlanger, "Russia's RT Network: Is It More BBC or K.G.B.?," *The New York Times*, March 8, 2017, https://www.nytimes.com/2017/03/08/world/europe/russias-rt-network-is-it-more-bbc-or-kgb.html.
9 Angela Stent, *Putin's World: Russia Against the West and with the Rest* (New York: Twelve, 2019).
10 The Ministry of Foreign Affairs of the Russian Federation, *Foreign Policy Concept of the Russian Federation: Approved by President of the Russian Federation Vladimir Putin on November 30, 2016.* The Ministry of Foreign Affairs of the Russian Federation, 2016, https://www.mid.ru/en/foreign_policy/official_documents/-/asset_publisher/CptICkB6BZ29/content/id/2542248. See also Peter Pomerantsev, "Yes, Russia Matters: Putin's Guerilla Strategy".
11 During the Soviet era, the USSR supported leftist groups. See Peter Pomerantsev and Michael Weiss, "The Menace of Unreality: How the Kremlin Weaponizes Information, Culture and Money," *The Interpreter*, November 22, 2014, http://www.interpretermag.com/the-menace-of-unreality-how-the-kremlin-weaponizes-information-culture-and-money/.http://www.interpretermag.com/the-menace-of-unreality-how-the-kremlin-weaponizes-information-culture-and-money/Pomerantsev and Weiss.
12 *Ibid.*
13 Ilya Yablokov, "Conspiracy Theories as a Russian Public Diplomacy Tool: The Case of Russia Today (RT)," *Politics* 35, no. 3–4 (November, 2015): 301–15, https://doi.org/10.1111/1467-9256.12097.
14 The Ministry of Foreign Affairs of the Russian Federation, *Foreign Policy Concept of the Russian Federation.*
15 TV-Novosti, "About RT," *RT International*, accessed April 21, 2020, https://www.rt.com/about-us/; Gary D. Rawnsley, "To Know Us Is to Love Us: Public Diplomacy and International Broadcasting in Contemporary Russia and China," *Politics* 35, no. 3–4 (November, 2015): 273–86, https://doi.org/10.1111/1467-9256.12104.
16 *Ibid.* The six languages RT provides news in are English, German, Russian, French, Spanish, and Arabic.
17 Gordon Ramsay and Sam Robertshaw. "Weaponising News: RT, Sputnik and Targeted Disinformation." King's College London: Centre for the Study of

Media, Communication & Power, 2018. https://www.kcl.ac.uk/policy-institute/research-analysis/weaponising-news.

18 Andrew E. Kramer, "Russian Cable Station Plays to U.S.," *The New York Times*, August 22, 2010, https://www.nytimes.com/2010/08/23/business/media/23russiatoday.html; RT, "RT's Occupy Wall Street Coverage Brings Second Emmy Nomination," *PR Newswire*, August 23, 2012, https://www.prnewswire.com/news-releases/rts-occupy-wall-street-coverage-brings-second-emmy-nomination-167234015.html.

19 Kohei Watanabe, "The Spread of the Kremlin's Narratives by a Western News Agency During the Ukraine Crisis," *The Journal of International Communication* 23, no. 1 (2017): 138–58; Ramsay and Robertshaw, "Weaponising News."

20 Ramsay and Robertshaw, "Weaponising News."

21 Maria Snegovaya, *Putin's Information Warfare in Ukraine: Soviet Origins of Russia's Hybrid Warfare*, (Washington, D.C.: Institute for the Study of War, September 2015).

22 Digital Forensic Research Lab, "Question That: RT's Military Mission," *Medium*, November 23, 2018, https://medium.com/dfrlab/question-that-rts-military-mission-4c4bd9f72c88. As the initial text of the Simonyan interview is in Russian, I referenced the material partially translated by Digital Forensic Research Lab.

23 *Ibid.*

24 Office of the Director of National Intelligence. "Assessing Russian Activities and Intentions in Recent US Elections," Intelligence Community Assessment, January 6, 2017; "Questions and Answers About the East StratCom Task Force - European External Action Service," accessed November 14, 2019, https://eeas.europa.eu/headquarters/headquarters-homepage/2116/-questions-and-answers-about-the-east-stratcom-task-force_en.

25 Orenstein, *The Lands in between*.

26 "Interview by Permanent Representative of Russia to the EU Ambassador Vladimir Chizhov for 'Die Welt,'" *Permanent Mission of the Russian Federation to the EU* (blog), April 17, 2020, https://russiaeu.ru/en/novosti/interview-permanent-representative-russia-eu-ambassador-vladimir-chizhov-die-welt.

27 As the state of relations between many countries and Russia has changed in the wake of Russia's illegal annexation of Crimea in 2014, many countries no longer belonged in the category initially chosen by Leonard and Popescu. The original classifications appear in footnotes for each classification type defined below.

28 Mark Leonard and Nicu Popescu, "A Power Audit of EU-Russia Relations," *European Council on Foreign Relations* (blog), November 2, 2007, https://www.ecfr.eu/publications/summary/a_power_audit_of_eu_russia_relations.

29 *Ibid.*

30 No CEE countries were originally classified as Trojan Horses.

31 No CEE countries were originally classified as Strategic Partners.

32 Leonard and Popescu, "A Power Audit of EU-Russia Relations," 2.

33 Leonard and Popescu originally classified Bulgaria, Hungary, Slovakia, and Slovenia as Friendly Pragmatists.

34 Leonard and Popescu, "A Power Audit of EU-Russia Relations."

35 Leonard and Popescu originally classified the Czech Republic, Estonia, Latvia, and Romania as Frosty Pragmatists.

36 Leonard and Popescu, "A Power Audit of EU-Russia Relations."

37 Leonard and Popescu originally classified Poland and Lithuania as New Cold Warriors.

38 Leonard and Popescu, "A Power Audit of EU-Russia Relations," 2.

39 Marine Strauss, "EU Extends Economic Sanctions against Russia for Six Months," *Reuters*, December 19, 2019, https://www.reuters.com/article/us-russia-eu-sanctions-idUSKBN1YN1RD.

40 This decision was viewed by some critics as a Russian attempt to increase its control over energy supplies within the EU, particularly as the project was largely financed with Russian investments. See Neil Buckley and Andrew Byrne, "EU Approves Hungary's Russian-Financed Nuclear Station," *Financial Times*, March 6, 2017, https://www.ft.com/content/0478d38a-028a-11e7-ace0-1ce02ef0def9 for more information.

41 Dimitar Bechev, "Central and Eastern Europe's Pushback against Sanctions on Russia," *Atlantic Council* (blog), October 11, 2017, https://www.atlanticcouncil.org/blogs/new-atlanticist/central-and-eastern-europe-s-pushback-against-sanctions-on-russia/.

42 Orenstein, *The Lands in Between*.

43 Creede Newton, "'High Treason': Hungary, Ukraine in Dispute over Language Laws," *Al Jazeera*, October 5, 2018, https://www.aljazeera.com/news/2018/10/5/high-treason-hungary-ukraine-in-dispute-over-language-laws.

44 AFP and Reuters, "Hungary NGO Law Breaches Basic Rights, Top EU Court Rules," *Deutsche Welle*, June 18, 2020, https://p.dw.com/p/3dxnI.

45 Kenneth Roth, "Hungary's Democracy Crisis Demands a European Response," *Human Rights Watch* (blog), September 26, 2019, https://www.hrw.org/news/2019/09/26/hungarys-democracy-crisis-demands-european-response.

46 Rick Lyman, "In Czech Election, a New Threat to European Unity," *The New York Times*, October 17, 2017, https://www.nytimes.com/2017/10/17/world/europe/czech-republic-andrej-babis.html.

47 Jakub Groszkowski, Mateusz Gniazdowski, and Andrzej Sadecki, "A Visegrad Cacophony over the Conflict between Russia and Ukraine," *OSW Centre for Eastern Studies* (blog), September 10, 2014, https://www.osw.waw.pl/en/publikacje/analyses/2014-09-10/a-visegrad-cacophony-over-conflict-between-russia-and-ukraine.

48 *Ibid.*

49 Julian Borger, Patrick Wintour, and Heather Stewart, "Western Allies Expel Scores of Russian Diplomats over Skripal Attack," *The Guardian*, March 27, 2018, https://www.theguardian.com/uk-news/2018/mar/26/four-eu-states-set-to-expel-russian-diplomats-over-skripal-attack.

50 Andrius Sytas, "EU Leaders Sign Letter Objecting to Nord Stream-2 Gas Link," *Reuters*, March 16, 2016, https://www.reuters.com/article/uk-eu-energy-nordstream-idUKKCN0WI1YV.

51 Kristi Raik, "Same, but Different: Estonian and Russian Presidents Held a Historic Meeting," *International Centre for Defence and Security* (blog), April 23, 2019, https://icds.ee/same-but-different-estonian-and-russian-presidents-held-a-historical-meeting/.

52 Derek E. Mix, *Estonia, Latvia, and Lithuania: Background and U.S.-Baltic Relations* (Congressional Research Service, 2020); Raik, "Same, but Different."

53 Nefeli Tzanetakou, "Energy Brings Russia and Slovakia Closer - What It Means for Europe," *Independent Balkan News Agency*, October 12, 2018, https://balkaneu.com/energy-brings-russia-and-slovakia-closer-what-it-means-for-europe/; Sytas, "EU Leaders Sign Letter."

54 Nefeli Tzanetakou, "Energy Brings Russia and Slovakia Closer."

55 RFE/RL, "Latvian Lawmakers Label 1944 Deportation of Crimean Tatars An Act of Genocide," *RadioFreeEurope/RadioLiberty*, May 10, 2019, https://www.rferl.org/a/latvian-lawmakers-label-1944-deportation-of-crimean-tatars-as-act-of-genocide/29933467.html.

56 BNS, "Following Moscow Visit, Lithuania Calls on Estonia to Coordinate Actions," *Eesti Rahvusringhääling*, April 20, 2019, https://news.err.ee/932022/following-moscow-visit-lithuania-calls-on-estonia-to-coordinate-actions.

57 Timothy Snyder, *Bloodlands: Europe Between Hitler and Stalin* (New York: Basic Books, 2010).

58 Anne Applebaum, "Putin's Big Lie," *The Atlantic*, January 5, 2020, https://www.theatlantic.com/ideas/archive/2020/01/putin-blames-poland-world-war-ii/604426/; Joanna Plucinska, "Poland Sees Limited Room for Russia Diplomacy, Despite Macron Overtures," *Reuters*, December 13, 2019, https://www.reuters.com/article/us-poland-russia-macron/poland-sees-limited-room-for-russia-diplomacy-despite-macron-overtures-idUSKBN1YH1YA.

59 Sytas, "EU Leaders Sign Letter"; Borger, Wintour, and Stewart, "Western Allies Expel Scores of Russian Diplomats over Skripal Attack."

60 Susi Dennison and Pawel Zerka, "The 2019 European Election: How Anti-Europeans Plan to Wreck Europe and What Can Be Done to Stop It," *European Council on Foreign Relations* (blog), February 2019, https://www.ecfr.eu/specials/scorecard/the_2019_European_election.

61 The full list of codes is available in appendix A.

62 This software allows for both qualitative analysis, such as measuring the amount of code applications within the data sample, and quantitative analysis where codes can be given descriptive "weights" and then analyzed. This study utilized the qualitative aspects of Dedoose but conducted further analysis in this software as its analysis options were more robust than NVivo 12.

63 Before sentiment analysis was conducted on the segments coded in NVivo12, five words were removed from the lexicon that had the potential to reflect an inaccurate sentiment: "champion," "win," "fans," "trump," and "gymnast."

64 This lexicon is available at Bing's website: https://www.cs.uic.edu/~liub/FBS/sentiment-analysis.html.

65 Bing Liu and Minqing Hu, "Opinion Mining, Sentiment Analysis, and Opinion Spam Detection: Feature-Based Opinion Mining and Summarization (or Aspect-Based Sentiment Analysis and Summarization)," 2004, https://www.cs.uic.edu/~liub/FBS/sentiment-analysis.html.

66 "Rule of Law in Poland and Hungary Has Worsened," *European Parliament News*, January 16, 2020, https://www.europarl.europa.eu/news/en/press-room/20200109IPR69907/rule-of-law-in-poland-and-hungary-has-worsened.

67 Jonas Ekblom, "Poland, Hungary Broke EU Laws by Refusing to Host Migrants: Court Adviser," *Reuters*, October 31, 2019, https://www.reuters.com/article/us-europe-migration-court-idUSKBN1XA1S5; Kriszta Kovács and Kim Lane Scheppele, "The Fragility of an Independent Judiciary: Lessons from Hungary and Poland–and the EU," *Communist and Post-Communist Studies* 51, no. 3 (September 2018): 189–200.

68 The full distribution of sentiment across EU coverage topic and country grouping can be found in the table on page 40.

69 Bechev, "Central and Eastern Europe's Pushback"

70 Tomasz Pradzynski, "Central Eastern Europe: United by Regional Security," *The German Marshall Fund of the United States* (blog), October 12, 2017, https://www.gmfus.org/news/central-eastern-europe-united-regional-security; Jakub Janda, Ilyas Sharibzhanov, Elena Terzi, Markéta Krejči, and Jakub Fiser, "How Do European Democracies React to Russian Aggression?," Kremlin Watch Report (European Values, April 22, 2017), https://www.europeanvalues.cz/wp-content/uploads/2020/09/How-do-European-democracies-react-to-Russian-aggression-1.pdf.

71 Eugene Rumer, "Russia and the Security of Europe" *Carnegie Endowment for International Peace* (blog), June 30, 2016, https://carnegieendowment.org/2016/06/30/russia-and-security-of-europe-pub-63990.

72 Rumer, "Russia and the Security of Europe."
73 "Rule of Law in Poland and Hungary Has Worsened | News | European Parliament."
74 Alena V. Ledeneva, *How Russia Really Works: The Informal Practices That Shaped Post-Soviet Politics and Business* (Ithaca: Cornell University Press, 2006).
75 Peter Cholakov, "Russia's Proposed TurkStream 2 Pipeline Sparks Bulgaria, EU Energy Worries," *DW*, February 28, 2019, https://www.dw.com/en/russias-proposed-turkstream-2-pipeline-sparks-bulgaria-eu-energy-worries/a-47726458.
76 "The Fidesz Party Was NOT Suspended, 'We Suspended Ourselves' - Hungarian FM to RT," *RT*, March 22, 2019, https://www.rt.com/news/454523-fidesz-suspended-itself-szijjarto/.
77 "Breakup of EU 'can't Be Ruled out' if Brussels Tries to Enforce pro-Immigration Policies - Orban," *RT*, March 7, 2019, https://www.rt.com/news/453272-breakup-of-eu-cant-be-ruled-out/.
78 Michael Peel, Henry Foy, and Valerie Hopkins, "Orban-Putin Talks Compound Disquiet Over Hungary's Russia Ties," *Financial Times*, October 30, 2019, https://www.ft.com/content/9a1988e4-f8ff-11e9-a354-36acbbb0d9b6.
79 For a full list of EU codes, refer to Appendix A.
80 Such as "With European Parliament elections looming, the establishment parties and mainstream media are reaching for the playbook of US Democrats and hyping the specter of 'Russia' to drive voters away from the rising tide of populism" from Nebojsa Malic, "EU Establishment Cries 'Russia!' in Desperate Bid to Defeat Critics," *RT*, May 20, 2019.
81 Erik Brattberg, "Making Sense of the European Parliament Election Results," *Carnegie Endowment for International Peace* (blog), May 28, 2019, https://carnegieendowment.org/2019/05/28/making-sense-of-european-parliament-election-results-pub-79221.
82 Janda et al., "How Do European Democracies React"
83 Robert Csehi and Edit Zgut, "'We Won't Let Brussels Dictate Us': Eurosceptic Populism in Hungary and Poland," *European Politics and Society* 0, no. 0 (January 27, 2020): 1–16, https://doi.org/10.1080/23745118.2020.1717064.
84 European Commission, "Rule of Law: European Commission Acts to Defend Judicial Independence in Poland," *European Commission*, December 20, 2017, https://ec.europa.eu/commission/presscorner/detail/en/IP_17_5367.
85 Kovács and Scheppele, "The Fragility of an Independent Judiciary, EU" 189–200.
86 Official Journal of the EU, "Consolidated Version of the Treaty on EU," 2012, https://eur-lex.europa.eu/resource.html?uri=cellar:2bf140bf-a3f8-4ab2-b506-fd71826e6da6.0023.02/DOC_1&format=PDF.
87 Applebaum, "Putin's Big Lie"; Ekblom, "Poland, Hungary Broke EU Laws by Refusing to Host Migrants"; Kovács and Scheppele, "The Fragility of an Independent Judiciary, EU" 189–200.
88 Rebecca Staudenmaier, "EU Parliament Votes to Trigger Article 7 Sanctions Procedure against Hungary," *DW*, September 12, 2019, https://www.dw.com/en/eu-parliament-votes-to-trigger-article-7-sanctions-procedure-against-hungary/a-45459720.

Bibliography

AFP and Reuters. "Hungary NGO Law Breaches Basic Rights, Top EU Court Rules." *Deutsche Welle*, June 18, 2020. https://p.dw.com/p/3dxnI.

Applebaum, Anne. "Putin's Big Lie." *The Atlantic*, January 5, 2020. https://www.theatlantic.com/ideas/archive/2020/01/putin-blames-poland-world-war-ii/604426/

Bechev, Dimitar. "Central and Eastern Europe's Pushback Against Sanctions on Russia." *Atlantic Council* (blog), October 11, 2017. https://www.atlanticcouncil.org/blogs/new-atlanticist/central-and-eastern-europe-s-pushback-against-sanctions-on-russia/.

BNS. "Following Moscow Visit, Lithuania Calls on Estonia to Coordinate Actions." *Eesti Rahvusringhääling*, April 20, 2019. https://news.err.ee/932022/following-moscow-visit-lithuania-calls-on-estonia-to-coordinate-actions.

Borger, Julian, Patrick Wintour, and Heather Stewart. "Western Allies Expel Scores of Russian Diplomats over Skripal Attack." *The Guardian*, March 27, 2018. https://www.theguardian.com/uk-news/2018/mar/26/four-eu-states-set-to-expel-russian-diplomats-over-skripal-attack.

Brattberg, Erik. "Making Sense of the European Parliament Election Results." *Carnegie Endowment for International Peace* (blog), May 28, 2019. https://carnegieendowment.org/2019/05/28/making-sense-of-european-parliament-election-results-pub-79221.

"Breakup of EU 'Can't Be Ruled Out' if Brussels Tries to Enforce Pro-Immigration Policies – Orban." *RT*, March 7, 2019. https://www.rt.com/news/453272-breakup-of-eu-cant-be-ruled-out/.

"Brussels Cries 'Conspiracy' Over Hungary's Ads Showing Smiling Soros Behind EU Immigration Agenda." *RT*, February 20, 2019. https://www.rt.com/news/451876-hungary-soros-juncker-immigration/.

Buckley, Neil, and Andrew Byrne. "EU Approves Hungary's Russian-Financed Nuclear Station." *Financial Times*, March 6, 2017. https://www.ft.com/content/0478d38a-028a-11e7-ace0-1ce02ef0def9 for more information.

Cholakov, Peter. "Russia's Proposed TurkStream 2 Pipeline Sparks Bulgaria, EU Energy Worries." *DW*, February 28, 2019. https://www.dw.com/en/russias-proposed-turkstream-2-pipeline-sparks-bulgaria-eu-energy-worries/a-47726458.

Committee on Foreign Relations United States Senate. *Putin's Asymmetric Assault on Democracy in Russia and Europe: Implications for U.S. National Security: A Minority Staff Report, 115th Cong., 2nd sess.* January 10, 2018. https://www.foreign.senate.gov/imo/media/doc/FinalRR.pdf

Csehi, Robert, and Edit Zgut. "'We Won't Let Brussels Dictate Us': Eurosceptic Populism in Hungary and Poland." *European Politics and Society* 22, no. 1 (January 2020):53–68. https://doi.org/10.1080/23745118.2020.1717064.

Dennison, Susi, and Pawel Zerka. "The 2019 European Election: How Anti-Europeans Plan to Wreck Europe and What Can Be Done to Stop It." *European Council on Foreign Relations* (blog), February 2019. https://www.ecfr.eu/specials/scorecard/the_2019_European_election.

Digital Forensic Research Lab. "Question That: RT's Military Mission." *Medium*, November 23, 2018. https://medium.com/dfrlab/question-that-rts-military-mission-4c4bd9f72c88.

Ekblom, Jonas. "Poland, Hungary Broke EU Laws by Refusing to Host Migrants: Court Adviser." *Reuters*, October 31, 2019. https://www.reuters.com/article/us-europe-migration-court-idUSKBN1XA1S5

Erlanger, Stevan. "Russia's RT Network: Is It More BBC or K.G.B.?" *The New York Times*, March 8, 2017. https://www.nytimes.com/2017/03/08/world/europe/russias-rt-network-is-it-more-bbc-or-kgb.html.

European Commission. "Rule of Law: European Commission Acts to Defend Judicial Independence in Poland." *European Commission*, December 20, 2017. https://ec.europa.eu/commission/presscorner/detail/en/IP_17_5367.

Groszkowski, Jakub, Mateusz Gniazdowski, and Andrzej Sadecki. "A Visegrad Cacophony Over the Conflict Between Russia and Ukraine." *OSW Centre for Eastern Studies* (blog), September 10, 2014. https://www.osw.waw.pl/en/publikacje/analyses/2014-09-10/a-visegrad-cacophony-over-conflict-between-russia-and-ukraine.

"Interview by Permanent Representative of Russia to the EU Ambassador Vladimir Chizhov for 'Die Welt.'" *Permanent Mission of the Russian Federation to the EU* (blog), April 17, 2020. https://russiaeu.ru/en/novosti/interview-permanent-representative-russia-eu-ambassador-vladimir-chizhov-die-welt.

Janda, Jakub, Ilyas Sharibzhanov, Elena Terzi, Markéta Krejči, and Jakub Fiser. "How Do European Democracies React to Russian Aggression?" in *Kremlin Watch Report*. European Values, April 22, 2017. https://www.europeanvalues.cz/wp-content/uploads/2020/09/How-do-European-democracies-react-to-Russian-aggression-1.pdf.

Kovács, Kriszta, and Kim Lane Scheppele. "The Fragility of an Independent Judiciary: Lessons From Hungary and Poland–and the EU." *Communist and Post-Communist Studies* 51, no. 3 (September 2018): 189–200.

Kramer, Andrew E. "Russian Cable Station Plays to U.S." *The New York Times*, August 22, 2010. https://www.nytimes.com/2010/08/23/business/media/23russiatoday.html

Ledeneva, Alena V. *How Russia Really Works: The Informal Practices That Shaped Post-Soviet Politics and Business*. Ithaca: Cornell University Press, 2006.

Lehne, Stefan. "Europe's East-West Divide: Myth or Reality?" *Carnegie Europe*, April 11, 2019. https://carnegieeurope.eu/2019/04/11/europe-s-east-west-divide-myth-or-reality-pub-78847.

Leonard, Mark, and Nicu Popescu. "A Power Audit of EU-Russia Relations." *European Council on Foreign Relations* (blog), November 2, 2007. https://www.ecfr.eu/publications/summary/a_power_audit_of_eu_russia_relations.

Liu, Bing, and Minqing Hu. "Opinion Mining, Sentiment Analysis, and Opinion Spam Detection: Feature-Based Opinion Mining and Summarization (or Aspect-Based Sentiment Analysis and Summarization)." 2004. https://www.cs.uic.edu/~liub/FBS/sentiment-analysis.html.

Lyman, Rick. "In Czech Election, a New Threat to European Unity." *The New York Times*, October 17, 2017. https://www.nytimes.com/2017/10/17/world/europe/czech-republic-andrej-babis.html.

Malic, Nebojsa. "EU Establishment Cries 'Russia!' in Desperate Bid to Defeat Critics." *RT*, May 20, 2019.

Mix, Derek E. *Estonia, Latvia, and Lithuania: Background and U.S.-Baltic Relations*. Washington, DC: Congressional Research Service, January 2, 2020.

Newton, Creede. "'High Treason': Hungary, Ukraine in Dispute Over Language Laws." *Al Jazeera*, October 5, 2018. https://www.aljazeera.com/news/2018/10/5/high-treason-hungary-ukraine-in-dispute-over-language-laws.

Office of the Director of National Intelligence. "Assessing Russian Activities and Intentions in Recent US Elections." Intelligence Community Assessment. January 6, 2017.

Official Journal of the EU. "Consolidated Version of the Treaty on EU." 2012. https://eur-lex.europa.eu/resource.html?uri=cellar:2bf140bf-a3f8-4ab2-b506-fd71826e6da6.0023.02/DOC_1&format=PDF.

Orenstein, Mitchell A. *The Lands in Between: Russia vs. the West and the New Politics of Hybrid War.* New York: Oxford University Press, 2019.

Peel, Michael, Henry Foy, and Valerie Hopkins, "Orban-Putin Talks Compound Disquiet Over Hungary's Russia Ties." *Financial Times,* October 30, 2019. https://www.ft.com/content/9a1988e4-f8ff-11e9-a354-36acbbb0d9b6.

Plucinska, Joanna. "Poland Sees Limited Room for Russia Diplomacy, Despite Macron Overtures." *Reuters,* December 13, 2019. https://www.reuters.com/article/us-poland-russia-macron/poland-sees-limited-room-for-russia-diplomacy-despite-macron-overtures-idUSKBN1YH1YA.

Pomerantsev, Peter, and Michael Weiss. "The Menace of Unreality: How the Kremlin Weaponizes Information, Culture and Money." *The Interpreter,* November 22, 2014. http://www.interpretermag.com/the-menace-of-unreality-how-the-kremlin-weaponizes-information-culture-and-money/.http://www.interpretermag.com/the-menace-of-unreality-how-the-kremlin-weaponizes-information-culture-and-money/Pomerantsev and Weiss.

Pomerantsev, Peter. "Yes, Russia Matters: Putin's Guerilla Strategy." *World Affairs* 177, no. 3 (October 2014): 16–23.

Pradzynski, Tomasz. "Central Eastern Europe: United by Regional Security." *The German Marshall Fund of the United States* (blog), October 12, 2017. https://www.gmfus.org/news/central-eastern-europe-united-regional-security

"Questions and Answers About the East StratCom Task Force - European External Action Service." Accessed November 14, 2019. https://eeas.europa.eu/headquarters/headquarters-homepage/2116/-questions-and-answers-about-the-east-stratcom-task-force_en.

Radio Free Europe and Radio Liberty. "Latvian Lawmakers Label 1944 Deportation of Crimean Tatars An Act Of Genocide." *RadioFreeEurope/RadioLiberty,* May 10, 2019. https://www.rferl.org/a/latvian-lawmakers-label-1944-deportation-of-crimean-tatars-as-act-of-genocide/29933467.html.

Raik, Kristi. "Same, But Different: Estonian and Russian Presidents Held a Historic Meeting." *International Centre for Defence and Security* (blog), April 23, 2019. https://icds.ee/same-but-different-estonian-and-russian-presidents-held-a-historical-meeting/.

Ramsay, Gordon, and Sam Robertshaw. "Weaponising News: RT, Sputnik and Targeted Disinformation." *King's College London: Centre for the Study of Media, Communication & Power,* 2018. https://www.kcl.ac.uk/policy-institute/research-analysis/weaponising-news.

Rawnsley, Gary D. "To Know Us Is to Love Us: Public Diplomacy and International Broadcasting in Contemporary Russia and China." *Politics* 35, no. 3–4 (November 2015): 273–86. https://doi.org/10.1111/1467-9256.12104.

Roth, Kenneth. "Hungary's Democracy Crisis Demands a European Response." *Human Rights Watch* (blog), September 26, 2019. https://www.hrw.org/news/2019/09/26/hungarys-democracy-crisis-demands-european-response.

RT. "RT's Occupy Wall Street Coverage Brings Second Emmy Nomination." *PR Newswire,* August 23, 2012. https://www.prnewswire.com/news-releases/rts-occupy-wall-street-coverage-brings-second-emmy-nomination-167234015.html

"Rule of Law in Poland and Hungary Has Worsened." *European Parliament News*, January 16, 2020. https://www.europarl.europa.eu/news/en/press-room/20200109IPR69907/rule-of-law-in-poland-and-hungary-has-worsened.

Rumer, Eugene. "Russia and the Security of Europe." *Carnegie Endowment for International Peace* (blog), June 30, 2016. https://carnegieendowment.org/2016/06/30/russia-and-security-of-europe-pub-63990.

Snegovaya, Maria. *Putin's Information Warfare in Ukraine: Soviet Origins of Russia's Hybrid Warfare*. Washington, D.C.: Institute for the Study of War, September 2015.

Snyder, Timothy. *Bloodlands: Europe Between Hitler and Stalin*. New York: Basic Books, 2010.

Staudenmaier, Rebecca. "EU Parliament Votes to Trigger Article 7 Sanctions Procedure Against Hungary." *DW*, September 12, 2019. https://www.dw.com/en/eu-parliament-votes-to-trigger-article-7-sanctions-procedure-against-hungary/a-45459720.

Stent, Angela. *Putin's World: Russia Against the West and with the Rest*. New York: Twelve, 2019.

Strauss, Marine. "EU Extends Economic Sanctions Against Russia for Six Months." *Reuters*, December 19, 2019. https://www.reuters.com/article/us-russia-eu-sanctions-idUSKBN1YN1RD.

Šuplata, Milan, and Milan Nič. *Russia's Information War in Central Europe: New Trends and Counter-Measures*. GLOBSEC Policy Institute. https://www.kremlinwatch.eu/userfiles/russia-s-information-war-in-central-europe_15273208769101.pdf.

Sytas, Andrius. "EU Leaders Sign Letter Objecting to Nord Stream-2 Gas Link." *Reuters*, March 16, 2016. https://www.reuters.com/article/uk-eu-energy-nordstream-idUKKCN0WI1YV.

"The Fidesz Party Was NOT Suspended, 'We Suspended Ourselves' - Hungarian FM to RT." *RT*, March 22, 2019. https://www.rt.com/news/454523-fidesz-suspended-itself-szijjarto/.

The Ministry of Foreign Affairs of the Russian Federation. *Foreign Policy Concept of the Russian Federation: Approved by President of the Russian Federation Vladimir Putin on November 30, 2016*. Moscow: The Ministry of Foreign Affairs of the Russian Federation, 2016. https://www.mid.ru/en/foreign_policy/official_documents/-/asset_publisher/CptICkB6BZ29/content/id/2542248.

TV-Novosti. "About RT." *RT International*, accessed April 21, 2020. https://www.rt.com/about-us/

Tzanetakou, Nefeli. "Energy Brings Russia and Slovakia Closer - What It Means for Europe." *Independent Balkan News Agency*, October 12, 2018. https://balkaneu.com/energy-brings-russia-and-slovakia-closer-what-it-means-for-europe/

van Herpen, Marcel H. *Putin's Propaganda Machine: Soft Power and Russian Foreign Policy*. Lanham: Rowman & Littlefield, 2016.

Watanabe, Kohei. "The Spread of the Kremlin's Narratives by a Western News Agency During the Ukraine Crisis." *The Journal of International Communication* 23, no. 1 (2017): 138–58.

Yablokov, Ilya. "Conspiracy Theories as a Russian Public Diplomacy Tool: The Case of Russia Today (RT)." *Politics* 35, no. 3–4 (November, 2015): 301–15. https://doi.org/10.1111/1467-9256.12097.

6 The New *Ostpolitik*

Nord Stream 2 and the Politics of German–Russian Gas Relations

Ruben L. Tjon-A-Meeuw

1 Introduction

The bilateral relationship between Germany and Russia has markedly deteriorated over the past few years.[1] Germany has repeatedly backed the imposition of sanctions on Moscow in response to the Kremlin's illegal annexation of Crimea and its invasion of Eastern Ukraine. Yet, one area that has been strangely unaffected by the escalating tensions is the energy relationship between the two countries. In fact, both sides have supported the construction of a new pipeline, Nord Stream 2, which has the potential to significantly increase the volume of natural gas transported from Russia directly to Germany.

This project has engendered vigorous pushback from Germany's international partners, with criticism centered around two main issues. First, the European Union's (EU's) Central and Eastern European (CEE) Member States[2] as well as Ukraine are nearly unanimous in their rejection of the new pipeline, alleging that it would deprive them of valuable transit fees, increase their gas prices, and jeopardize their energy security. Second, the United States and other North Atlantic Treaty Organization (NATO) allies have berated Berlin for ostensibly increasing its dependence on Russian gas supplies with Nord Stream 2, making it easier for the Kremlin to utilize this leverage over Germany in the pursuit of its geopolitical goals. Despite these criticisms, the German government has been steadfast in its support of the Nord Stream 2 project, raising two key questions: first, why has the German government continued to support this contested pipeline project despite consistent and widespread international condemnation? Second, what precisely are the energy security implications of the new pipeline for both Germany and the EU's CEE Member States?

Regarding the first key question, Berlin's insistence that the project is purely driven by economic factors is somewhat undermined by the obvious political elements and limited financial benefits. I thus contend that geopolitical considerations heavily factor into the German position. With respect to the second question, I argue that the adverse financial and security consequences stemming from Nord Stream 2 would not be as severe as often

DOI: 10.4324/9781003182344-7

claimed. Due to the interdependence created by pipeline exchanges, significant investment in liquified natural gas (LNG) infrastructure, reverse-flow and gas storage capabilities, as well as a changing regulatory and market environment, the likelihood and probable impact of politically motivated supply interruptions are limited, especially in Germany itself. More serious negative consequences would arise for certain CEE countries, but even these can be mitigated by the further integration of the European gas market as well as the continued investment in LNG infrastructure and storage capacity that we are currently witnessing.

The somewhat circumscribed potential impact of Nord Stream 2 begs the question why it has generated so much vitriol and pushback. One answer relates to the manner in which the pipeline affects issues surrounding European integration. Solidarity between Member States is viewed as something close to an article of faith in German politics. Berlin often invokes European integration when justifying policy proposals related to matters such as migration and fiscal policy. It is thus perhaps no surprise that other EU Member States disapprove when they perceive Germany, arguably the continent's leading power, to be acting in a way that benefits its parochial interests at the expense of wider European ones. This is exacerbated by the fact that the controversy pertains to a matter as geopolitically sensitive and internally divisive as the EU's relationship with Moscow. Understanding the politics of Germany's position vis-à-vis Nord Stream 2 reveals much not just about European energy politics but about the status of European political solidarity writ large. This chapter speaks to this larger phenomenon by analyzing the politics of Nord Stream 2.

2 Tracing the Roots of Nord Stream 2

2.1 The Origins

Gas relations between the Soviet Union and the Federal Republic of Germany date back to the early 1970s.[3] They originally grew out of a desire by the incoming Social Democratic Chancellor, Willy Brandt, to improve relations with the Soviet bloc as part of an effort that came to be known as *Ostpolitik*. This sort of concrete cooperation in economic matters was perceived as a key instrument of détente and 'change through rapprochement' (*Wandel durch Annäherung*).[4] During this first phase of the relationship, "gas trade was developed and supported politically to have positive spillover effects."[5] The sale of Soviet gas to Germany quickly took off, especially in the wake of the 1973 and 1979 oil shocks, which prompted Bonn and other Western capitals to diversify their energy imports.[6]

In the 1990s, German–Russian gas relations ostensibly turned into a commercially motivated business relationship conducted mostly by private actors, although this was in reality still very much backed by the respective governments. The new gas relationship was formalized in 1994 with the adoption of the European Energy Charter Treaty. This Treaty, signed by more than 50 European countries, was created to integrate the post-Soviet energy sector with that of a newly liberated Eastern Europe and the EU.[7] These developments led to a major expansion of gas transport infrastructure toward and within Germany.

Germany subsequently turned its approach toward Russia into a new version of *Ostpolitik,* as evidenced by a plethora of treaties and proclamations which came about in the first few years of the new millennium. During the first two terms of Vladimir Putin's presidency, Berlin acknowledged Moscow's role as a key strategic partner and pursued a policy of 'rapprochement through interdependence' (*Annäherung durch Verflechtung*).[8] It was in this period, the early- and mid-2000s, that the Nord Stream project was initiated. Starting in 2005, the construction of the project now referred to as Nord Stream 1 took off. Gerhard Schröder, the German Chancellor who stepped down in that same year, had been a particularly outspoken supporter of the pipeline, even providing a government loan guarantee shortly before he left office.[9] The pipeline, which was inaugurated in 2011, connects Russia and Germany through the Baltic Sea. Currently, the Federal Republic receives around 50% of its gas from Gazprom, a state-owned Russian company with a near-monopoly on exports. Most of this is imported via Nord Stream 1.[10]

The 2000s also saw increased interest from third parties in the German–Russian gas relationship. This can be attributed in large part to the expansion and further integration of the EU. The 2004 enlargement mainly included Eastern European countries, many of which were more sensitive to the issue than the preexisting members. The Baltic states and Poland in particular opposed Nord Stream 1, on the basis that the new pipeline would circumvent and isolate them from the rest of Europe. Poland's then-foreign minister, Radosław Sikorski, somewhat hyperbolically compared it to the 1939 Molotov–Ribbentrop pact.[11]

This sentiment was further aggravated by the Ukrainian–Russian gas crises of 2006 and 2009. In brief, in the years following the 2004 pro-Western Orange Revolution in Kyiv, Moscow was no longer willing to continue supplying natural gas to Ukraine at prices well below what it was charging other customers, and Gazprom also insisted on the repayment of accumulated debt. The dispute led to several brief supply interruptions, which, due to the critical transit role enjoyed by the Ukrainian gas pipeline network, also affected a number of EU countries.[12] This episode naturally generated concern with regards to the reliability of the Ukrainian transit pathway and revived fears that Russia might use its energy supply for geopolitical purposes.[13] As mentioned above, it was also in the aftermath of the Orange Revolution that the construction of Nord Stream 1 finally commenced. Looking back, its completion did indeed reduce the proportion of Russian gas exports to Europe that were routed through Ukraine in favor of the more direct route through the Baltic Sea.[14] Ukrainian transit volumes dropped from around 100 billion cubic meters (bcm) in 2011, the year Nord Stream 1 became operational, to less than 60 bcm in 2014, before subsequently recovering somewhat to nearly 80 bcm in 2016. Between 2017 and 2019, transit volumes fluctuated around 90 bcm, but as I will show further below, this is unlikely to last.[15]

Finally, Brussels has become a progressively more important factor. The European Commission initiated its own EU–Russia energy dialogue in 2000 and later transformed the European gas market, for instance by launching the Third Energy Package in 2009. This legislation sought to increase competition and improve the functioning of the EU electricity and natural gas markets.[16] One crucial aspect has been 'unbundling,' whereby energy supply and generation are separated from transmission networks – naturally a major challenge to a vertically integrated company like Gazprom.

2.2 *A Contested Pipeline Project Emerges*

Nord Stream 2 was officially announced in June 2015. Its construction was complicated by a host of legal objections, new EU legislation, and the lack of clarity regarding US sanctions against key Russian actors. It now connects Ust-Luga in the Russian Federation with Greifswald, Germany, through an underwater route of approximately 1,200 km. The new pipeline would double the current Nord Stream capacity from 55 bcm p.a. to 110 bcm p.a. The project is operated by Nord Stream AG, a private company fully owned by Gazprom. The financing agreement between Gazprom and five European energy companies for the €9.5 billion project was confirmed in April 2017, with construction finally commencing in May 2018. The five European partners which are in equal parts financing 50% (or around €4.75 billion) of the new pipeline are Engie (France), OMV (Austria), Shell (UK/Netherlands), Uniper, and Wintershall Dea (both German firms).[17] The first two of these companies are in part state-owned.[18]

Even before Nord Stream 2 was officially announced, there were widespread concerns in the EU over expanding its gas relationship with Russia. These concerns became particularly acute in the context of the 2014 Ukraine crisis, when Russia illegally annexed Crimea and invaded the Donbass region. This resulted in an increasing securitization of natural gas issues in Europe, a development which was also partially responsible for the creation of the EU Energy Union. The Energy Union was designed to diversify the EU's gas supplies, curb dependency on Russia, and secure reliable gas provision.[19] Even within Germany itself, 2014 was a turning point with regards to how relations with Russia were perceived. During the previous two decades, the assumption in Berlin had been that more intensive engagement with Moscow, coupled with stronger economic ties, would slowly but surely help transform Russia's domestic situation and foreign outlook. However, even the fivefold increase in German exports to Russia between 2000 and 2011 had "promoted neither the rule of law nor a better investment climate," nor did it prevent Putin from upending the post-Cold War European security order.[20]

Critics asserted that the completion of Nord Stream 2 would likely cause financial and strategic damage to the CEE states and Ukraine. These states would allegedly find their negotiating position vis-à-vis Gazprom greatly weakened, since the gas giant would have the option of partially diverting its supply. Moreover, they would also face the loss of transit fees if more gas were rerouted directly through Germany, which would be particularly damaging for Ukraine.[21] At the height of the 2014 crisis, both the Kremlin and Gazprom called for a complete end to the gas transit through Ukraine, indicating that this is not necessarily a fanciful consideration.[22] In the past few years, Kyiv derived around $2 billion from transit fees every year, which amounts to roughly 2% of Ukraine's national gross domestic product (GDP) and more than 4% of its budget.[23] In addition to these financial consequences, there are also strategic security concerns. Freudenstein and Lilkov, for instance, assert that the construction of the new pipeline would "dangerously weaken the EU's strategic goals in Eastern Europe, disrupt the European Energy Security Strategy and damage member state unity."[24] Indeed, in 2016, the heads of state or government of the Czech Republic, Croatia, Estonia, Hungary, Latvia, Lithuania, Poland, Romania, and Slovakia sent a warning to the European Commission that the new pipeline would have "destabilising geopolitical consequences" and negative repercussions for the region's energy security.[25] The additional 55 bcm capacity of Nord Stream 2 would enable Gazprom to deliver the majority of its gas directly to Germany, circumventing the existing pipeline infrastructure geared toward Eastern Europe to some extent, which, according to Zachmann, would allow Russia to "turn off the gas tap for these countries, without breaking its commitments to Western European countries."[26]

Regarding Germany, the worry by policymakers and observers across the transatlantic community is that the Kremlin would use to its advantage the fact that Nord Stream 2 purportedly increases Germany's dependence on Russian gas. As President Trump erroneously proclaimed in 2018, "Germany is totally controlled by Russia, because they are getting 60 to 70% of their energy from Russia and a new pipeline."[27] A similar, although perhaps more nuanced, view is shared by many analysts. According to Collins,

> policymakers' visceral aversion to the potential short-term losses caused by a gas supply cutoff or a politically driven price increase could – particularly if dependence on Russian gas increases – expose them to manipulation, undermine their resolve to stand up to Russian revanchism in and near Europe, and, ultimately, divide and weaken the EU and NATO.[28]

The United States imposed sanctions on actors involved in the Nord Stream 2 construction in December of 2019. The pipeline had until then been slated to be completed in 2020, but this timetable was made redundant by the sanctions.[29] The Swiss group Allseas, the main contractor that had been laying the pipeline, suspended its operations immediately. Nevertheless, Gazprom has announced that it will complete the pipeline by 2021 at the latest, without foreign help if necessary.[30] Russian president Vladimir Putin himself commented on 11 January 2020 that Russia would "certainly be able to complete [the pipeline on its own] without inviting foreign partners. The timeframe is the only question."[31]

In the summer of 2020, the project came under increased scrutiny in Germany itself. The poisoning of the prominent Russian opposition activist Alexei Navalny has led to widespread calls to impose further sanctions on Russia, particularly if Moscow refuses to support an independent inquiry into the matter. Politicians from both within the German coalition government and across the opposition have explicitly proposed making the completion of Nord Stream 2 dependent on Russian compliance.[32]

In December 2020, the construction of Nord Stream 2 resumed after having been halted for an entire year. In light of the deterrent effect US sanctions had on private Western firms, Gazprom has ended up relying on a Russian-owned vessel to complete the final stretches of the pipeline. The first of two pipeline strings reached technical completion in June 2021 and was expected to be commissioned later in the same year.[33]

2 Why Germany Supports Nord Stream 2

2.1 It's the Economy, Stupid...?

Natural gas is the second most important energy source in the German economy, accounting for around 23% of primary energy consumption. It is also the only conventional energy source to have increased its market share over the last two decades. Germany is the world's third-largest natural gas importer after China and Japan, receiving over 100 bcm per year from beyond its borders. Imports have increased steadily due to a variety of factors. The *Energiewende*, the government-mandated transition away from nuclear plants in the wake of the Fukushima nuclear disaster in 2011, has created a need for other sources of electricity generation that coal and renewables could fill only partially. Gas prices have also fallen precipitously over the last decade, from a high of more than $10 p/btu to less than $6, meaning that although imports have receded in value terms, volumes have in fact increased. [34]

More than 90% of German gas demand is imported via pipeline, with nearly half originating in Russia, making Germany Moscow's largest client market.[35] At 35% of the total consumption, the German industry is among the major consumers of natural gas, particularly in energy-intensive sectors like metallurgy and chemicals. With 37%, however, the largest share is consumed by private households, where natural gas makes up around 50% of fuel for heating systems.[36] Although the gas in this case is supplied by private providers, the state has a legal mandate that requires it to secure provision to private households in the case of emergencies, further underlining the stake the government has in ensuring energy supply.[37]

The fact that natural gas plays such a critical role in the German economy is generally used to argue for investments in gas transport infrastructure, but this fact does not *ipso facto* mean that Nord Stream 2 is a necessary or appropriate project. A precise investment calculation for the new pipeline is very difficult due to uncertain and lacking framework data, but both business and macroeconomic analyses indicate that the pipeline project is far from economically viable. A Norwegian research group demonstrated that it is quite challenging to make a business case for Nord Stream 2, which in all likelihood will not be a profitable venture for Gazprom.[38] They argued that the construction of the pipeline will do very little to increase sales of Russian natural gas, either in Germany or in the EU, given the current market environment and spare capacity in the existing pipeline networks. Moreover, these low additional revenues are offset by very high costs. As a result, it is unlikely that the construction of Nord Stream 2 could be profitable, meaning that the project would essentially be cross-subsidized by Gazprom's other activities.[39]

Furthermore, an analysis by the Russian state-owned investment bank Sberbank concluded that Nord Stream 2 would destroy value instead of creating it. The estimated cost of approximately $17 billion, which includes the supply pipeline in Russia itself, is contrasted with the approximately $700 million that will be saved annually by eschewing transit through Ukraine. Based on the bank's underlying models, this would put the project's present value at around negative $6 billion.[40] The main author of this report was let go only a few days after its publication.[41] These rather negative assessments beget the question why anyone would invest in the project. For private companies, the rationale might partially be linked to the fact that they are only financial investors and Gazprom remains the sole shareholder of the Nord Stream 2 AG.[42] As long as the pipeline is completed, the loans provided by the European corporations are likely to be repaid, meaning their downside risk is limited. It is also crucial to underline the state-backed nature of Gazprom and, by extension, the gas pipeline. It is unlikely that the Kremlin would let the Nord Stream 2 AG default and allow a project as prestigious and strategically important as Nord Stream 2 to fail.

While the absence of a business case for Nord Stream 2 indicates that there is at least some geopolitical rationale from Russia's perspective, it does not tell us what Berlin's motives are. To answer this question, we need to know more about the economic picture on the German side. One crucial issue in this regard is the way in which the gas demand and import picture in the EU and Germany will develop throughout the 2020s. Projections of future demand are inherently precarious and rely on a number of uncertain assumptions, such as the development of gas prices, the levels of economic growth, and the impact of yet-to-be-implemented climate policies. It is therefore perhaps no surprise that they differ substantially from source to source. The European Commission itself anticipates EU gas demand remaining at its current levels of roughly 450 bcm p.a. through the 2020s.[43] The methodology used for the Commission's reference scenario has been heavily criticized, both by independent academics and the EU's own Court of Auditors, for systematically and consistently underestimating the role of renewable sources of energy, and thus overestimating demand for natural gas.[44] The proponents of Nord Stream 2 argue that gas import demand in Germany and across Europe is likely to increase, necessitating additional delivery capacity. Gazprom itself predicts European demand (including that of Switzerland and Ukraine) to fluctuate around 500 bcm p.a. until 2050, but for production to drop precipitously. The company thus projects European import demand to increase by 120 bcm p.a. over the next two decades.[45] It goes without saying that the Russian gas giant has every incentive to bolster the case for new pipeline capacity, and its projections need to be considered with that in mind. The International Energy Agency has projected the EU's gas demand to drop to around 380 bcm p.a. by 2040.[46]

All of these sources are in agreement, however, about the fact that EU domestic production will decrease substantially. Thus, even if overall gas demand in the Union were to remain stable throughout the coming decades, this would probably result in a considerable increase of imports. This is because, with Brexit, one of the largest producers has left the Union, and output in the remaining gas powerhouse, the Netherlands, is expected to fall substantially in the coming years. Due to the technical and financial risks associated with large-scale imports of LNG, Eser et al. estimate that much of this shortfall will likely need to be covered with increased pipeline imports from Norway and Russia.[47] It should also be noted that most of these projections precede the COVID-19 pandemic, whose impact on demand could be substantial in the short to medium term. They also do not take into account the significant gas deposits that have been explored in the Eastern Mediterranean in recent years, but, considering the geopolitical and commercial uncertainties that surround the exploitation of these sources, such an approach might be sensible.[48]

On the other hand, larger import volumes alone do not inevitably necessitate increased pipeline capacity. There are three major pipelines connecting Russia to the EU at the moment. These are the Ukrainian 'Brotherhood' network, the Yamal pipeline passing through Poland, and Nord Stream 1. Currently, neither Nord Stream 1 nor the pipeline system through Ukraine is operating near full capacity, the latter only receiving around 50% of possible throughput. Exports through the Ukrainian network could be increased by around 70 bcm p.a., significantly more than the extra capacity that Nord Stream 2 would add, calling into question the necessity of the project.[49]

For Germany, certain limited benefits might arise. Nord Stream 2 would potentially turn the country into a European gas trading hub, reselling significant amounts of the gas it receives from Russia to Eastern European markets. This would likely increase liquidity on its wholesale gas markets, stimulate competition, and solidify futures and spot markets, with the probable consequence of marginally lower gas prices across North Western Europe.[50] The possible price reduction for Germany itself would partially result from the fact that the new pipeline would not traverse the territory of any third states, thus obviating any outlays for transit payments.

The potential savings are, however, rather inconsequential. Even an ambitious price reduction of 10–20%, as outlined by Van Scherpenberg[51], would reduce the burden on German consumers by roughly $2–3 billion dollars annually.[52] It is extremely unlikely that these sums alone justify the domestic and international backlash the project has engendered, not least considering the continuously escalating US sanctions. There is of course also the fact that the German companies involved are heavily lobbying in favor of the new pipeline, on a state, federal, and European level.[53] Since this activity is mostly happening behind closed doors, however, its impact is difficult to assess.[54]

2.2 Politics Matter

In Germany itself, the political discussion with regard to Nord Stream 2 has become increasingly fraught. Politicians from nearly all parties have voiced their disapproval of the project, citing similar concerns as the country's international partners. The public, on the other hand, has consistently approved of the project, although the reasons for that are not easily discernible. The federal government, and in particular the Social Democratic Party, refuses to distance itself from the contentious pipeline, claiming that it is a purely economic project.

Although there used to be a consensus on the desirability of improved (energy) relations with Russia, this has changed throughout the last decade, starting with the gas disputes between Moscow and Kyiv in 2009. In the aftermath of the 2014 Ukraine crisis, critical voices have become more noticeable. Parliamentarians from all political parties have repeatedly railed against Nord Stream 2, questioning the reliability of Gazprom as a supplier and highlighting the potential political instrumentalization of the German–Russian gas relationship.[55] In 2016, the Christian Democrat Norbert Röttgen, chairman of the Bundestag's Committee on Foreign Affairs, and Reinhard Bütikofer, spokesperson of the European Green Party, came out in force against the project.[56] They accused the Federal Government of willfully disregarding Polish, Baltic, and Ukrainian security interests and castigated Chancellor Merkel for claiming that Nord Stream 2 was solely a commercial venture, devoid of politics. In a 2018 op-ed in the *Frankfurter Allgemeine Zeitung*, Röttgen, Bütikofer, the Bavarian Manfred Weber, leader of the largest faction in the European Parliament, and members of all major German political parties, except for the Social Democratic Party of Germany (SPD) and the far-right, pro-Russian Alternative for Germany (AfD), further outlined their opposition. They contended that the German proponents of Nord Stream 2 demonstrate a lack of solidarity with their European partners by jeopardizing their financial and security interests. In particular, they castigated the SPD for allegedly taking a position on Nord Stream 2 that is in strong contrast to the usual Social Democratic appeals to European solidarity and unity.[57]

The political discussion about the Nord Stream 2 pipeline project became more salient in 2020. This is linked to the fact that the project was nearing completion, and that the Kremlin's behavior has led to increasing resistance in parts of the political spectrum in Germany. First and foremost, this relates to the poisoning of Alexei Navalny on August 20, 2020. Two days after the assassination attempt, the Russian opposition politician was flown out to Berlin for treatment, which meant that the German government felt compelled to speak out on the issue, as did many of the highest-ranking politicians.[58]

Röttgen has repeated his criticism of the project and stated in an interview that "the only language that Putin understands is the language of natural gas."[59] Similarly, Christian Lindner, leader of the Free Democrats, erstwhile coalition partner of the Christian Democrats, opined that "[a] regime that organizes assassinations by poison is not a partner for large cooperative projects – including pipeline projects."[60] Katrin Göring-Eckardt, the leader of the Bundestag parliamentary group of the Green Party, has said that "Nord Stream 2 is not something that we can go ahead with together with Russia."[61]

In September 2020, the Greens even tabled a motion in parliament in which they demanded that the German Bundestag should "call on the Federal Government that the German government immediately distance itself from the Nord Stream 2 pipeline and prevent completion by means of suitable measures."[62] One day later, the AfD also tabled a motion regarding the pipeline, this one calling on the government to "to commit unequivocally to the realization of Nord Stream 2 and to support the rapid completion of Nord Stream 2 with all available resources at national, European and international level."[63] In a sign of the contentiousness of the issue, neither motion had any chance of success in the Bundestag.[64]

Another question is how the German public views the Nord Stream 2 project. Here, the picture is also fairly nuanced, but, overall, quite supportive. A survey published in January of 2019 showed that 73% of Germans supported the completion of the pipeline, with only 16% opposing it. This survey was conducted only a few months after Trump's incendiary comments about the project, and just at the time when Richard Grenell, the widely disliked US ambassador in Berlin, raised the specter of sanctions, which might have influenced responses. More than 75% of respondents perceived this behavior to be blackmail, and over 90% agreed with the claim that Trump's main interest lay in selling US liquified natural gas (LNG) to Germany.[65]

In September 2020, meaning after the Navalny poisoning, 38% of Germans were in favor of canceling the pipeline, but 60% still backed its completion. The strongest approval was unsurprisingly found among supporters of the AfD (73%), the Left (59%) (the pro-Russian successor to the former East German ruling party), and the SPD (58%). Only among supporters of the Green Party did a plurality (44%) oppose the pipeline, and it can be assumed that this is at least in part due to an instinctive hostility toward infrastructure that might prolong and expand the use of fossil fuels in the German economy.[66] One can thus certainly not speak of overwhelming popular pressure to cancel the pipeline project.

Next, we consider the federal government's position, which initially was to claim that Nord Stream 2 is a purely commercial project. It is important to note that Germany has been ruled by a coalition of the two largest parties since 2013, the center-left SPD and the center-right CDU/CSU. Support for Nord Stream 2 has primarily come from the former, which is the junior partner in the coalition. A number of the SPD's senior leaders have endorsed the project, most prominently the former Chancellor Gerhard Schröder, who also backed Nord Stream 1 during his tenure and provided it with a government loan guarantee. A few weeks after leaving office, he joined the Board of Directors of the Nord Stream AG, raising questions about conflicts of interest.[67] Employing former SPD bigwigs to represent Russian interests toward the West is a strategy that is often used by Russian energy firms. More profoundly, the SPD seems to perceive the construction and completion of Nord Stream 2 as indispensable to its continued desire for strategic cooperation with Russia, a legacy of Willy Brandt's *Ostpolitik* and the 'rapprochement through interdependence' of the 2000s. Part of the old guard of the SPD thus sees the bilateral gas trade as a strong signal of continued cooperation which gives the Russian government a meaningful stake in maintaining close relations with Germany.[68]

Within the government itself, "[t]he political framing of German-Russian relations by the two SPD-led ministries – the Ministry of Economic Affairs and Energy as well as the Foreign Office – relied on the traditional dual strategy of containment/cooperation and deterrence/dialogue."[69] President Frank-Walter Steinmeier is one of the main exponents of Social Democracy in Germany. During his tenure as foreign minister, he was the architect of the aforementioned 'rapprochement through interdependence' and even as president he has voiced his support for the pipeline.[70] When SPD Minister for Economic Affairs and Vice-Chancellor Sigmar Gabriel defended the project on a trip to Moscow in 2015, rejecting any 'external interference,' he was quickly accused of 'Schröderisation.'[71] Gabriel and other proponents of Nord Stream 2 have also repeatedly pointed toward Russia's historical reliability as a natural gas supplier, noting, among other things, that Moscow did not interrupt oil and gas deliveries to Western Europe during the darkest days of the Cold War, in the wake of the Soviet Union's collapse, or at the height of the Ukraine crisis.[72]

Chancellor Merkel herself had initially also insisted that the issues surrounding Nord Stream 2 were solely commercial in nature, before eventually acknowledging the inherent geopolitical aspects. On 10 April 2018, the long-standing leader stated that she had

> made very clear that a Nord Stream 2 project is not possible without clarity on the future transit role of Ukraine [...] so you can see that it is not just an economic issue, but there are also political considerations.[73]

She additionally claimed to have told Putin that "it cannot be that through Nord Stream 2, Ukraine has no further importance regarding the transit of gas."[74] The latter issue became particularly salient in 2019, since the prior gas transit agreement between Russia and Ukraine was about to expire. The German chancellor personally encouraged Putin and Ukrainian president Volodymyr Zelensky to conclude a follow-up deal. In part due to the German mediation efforts and the involvement of the EU, the two sides at last found a compromise solution on 30 December 2019. The new deal, signed by Gazprom and Naftogaz of Ukraine, contractually obliged the Russian energy giant to ship at least 65 bcm through the Ukrainian network in 2020, with further obligations to send a minimum of 40 bcm per annum until 2024.[75] Chancellor Merkel explicitly linked this development to her government's continued support for Nord Stream 2 at a joint press conference with President Putin in January 2020:

> Of course we also talked about the Nord Stream project. It has been legitimized by means of the new European law. We need to carry it through. It is gratifying that a positive five-year agreement has been reached regarding gas transit via Ukraine. [...] Germany and other European countries will benefit from Nord Stream.[76]

Shortly after confirming the importance of the Ukraine aspect, however, Merkel returned to her government's standard claim with regards to the nature of Nord Stream 2: "We will continue to support this project as we did in the past. But, let me reiterate, this is essentially an economic project."[77]

The partial success of the Russia–Ukraine agreement helps explain why the German government has stood firm on Nord Stream 2, with the Chancellor saying that the issue should be 'decoupled' from the Navalny poisoning.[78] In September 2020, the Social Democrat Vice-Chancellor and Finance Minister Olaf Scholz similarly voiced his continuing support for Nord Stream 2. He also repeated the claim that "Nord Stream 2 is a private energy project, which involves a great number of firms. [...] It's not a German state project, and that's what it's all about."[79] With regards to the Navalny poisoning, the German government eventually decided to push for sanctions at the EU level. Berlin refused, however, to target the pipeline project, and Brussels eventually settled for asset freezes and travel bans affecting six Russian individuals presumed to have been involved in or responsible for the assassination attempt.[80]

In a sense, the oft-repeated mantra that Nord Stream 2 is a commercial project is of course true, as it is not being financed or constructed by the German government or via its state-backed firms. A crucial question is thus whether Berlin would even be able to halt the project, should it want to. Most experts seem to agree that this would be possible, but, seeing as Nord Stream 2 has so far been granted all necessary permits and licenses, any government intervention would bring with it a host of problems. The German government is loath to undermine the legal framework for big energy investments. Considering its lack of national energy champions, such as for instance the French Engie or the Italian Eni, the German government is entirely reliant on (often foreign) private firms and cannot afford to imperil the reliability of its regulatory framework without good reason, for fear of jeopardizing future private investments.[81] Moreover, taking legal action to halt the project at this advanced stage could potentially mean the federal government would be liable for the lost investment. Another option would be to concede to imposing sanctions at the EU level, which in all likelihood would negate any claims for damages.[82] In light of reports that the German government allegedly offered to invest more than 1 billion euros into the construction of LNG terminals in return for the United States holding back on sanctions, it would seem, however, that Berlin is not ready to simply let Nord Stream 2 fall by the wayside.[83]

The question of why Germany continues to support the construction of Nord Stream 2 is not easily answered. As we have seen in the previous section, the economic benefits it would draw from the new pipeline are marginal at best and hardly justify the substantial geopolitical and domestic consequences the project is engendering. This makes it difficult to believe that the rationale for backing the pipeline is purely economic, as the German government insists. The fact that the approval of different political parties and their supporters have voiced in favor of the project is correlated with their current and historical attitudes regarding Russia further highlights the partially political nature of Nord Stream 2.

3 Implications of Nord Stream 2 for German and European Energy Security

Contrary to what most detractors claim, a detailed analysis of the energy and security implications of Nord Stream 2 reveals that it is not likely to significantly harm European strategic interests. Russia has historically used its 'energy weapon' by exploiting its control over Gazprom and other oil and gas firms with only limited success. Regarding the European energy market going forward, the interdependence created by gas pipelines renders a large-scale politically motivated supply interruption implausible, especially considering the developments in the commercial and regulatory environment, which have served to reduce Gazprom's leverage. Moreover, even if such a cut-off were to occur at some point after the completion of Nord Stream 2, the deleterious consequences would be limited. Only Eastern Europe would be significantly affected by such a cut-off, and even these negative repercussions could be mitigated by continued investment in the pan-European gas market as well as into alternative sources of energy supply.

3.1 Russia's Energy Weapon

As previously mentioned, a major concern voiced by the United States and several EU Member States is that Russia could use Nord Stream 2 to increase its influence in CEE states and Germany. The underlying rationale here is that the Kremlin could utilize its 'energy weapon' to advance its geopolitical interests, including against Germany itself. In this context, the term energy weapon denotes an "energy supplier state us[ing] its resources as a political tool to either punish or coerce (or sometimes a combination of both) its customers."[84] Even though Russian oil sales to the EU and its Member States dwarf those of gas in value (they are nearly twice as high), [85] the overwhelming scrutiny of the current energy relationship between Germany and Russia is directed toward natural gas rather than crude oil. Manipulating the latter is generally a less effective tactic; oil is a highly fungible product that is traded on efficient and globalized markets, such that substitute supplies could be purchased and transported with relative ease, should exports from Russia be interrupted. The natural gas market, on the other hand, "has been regional and pipeline-dependent and thereby inflexible."[86] This, in turn, gives suppliers significant leeway, since customers find it difficult to procure alternatives within a short timeframe and at a reasonable cost.

Naturally, this would only present a political issue if Moscow controlled the export of Russian gas via Gazprom, as several Western analysts allege.[87] Indeed, Stelzer professes that "to view Gazprom or any Russian energy company as anything other than instruments of Russian foreign policy is to be naïve in the extreme."[88] Here, critics draw attention to the fact that, although Gazprom is a public enterprise, its majority shareholder is the Russian state. The company itself has on many occasions rejected the allegations that it could be used as an instrument of the government, asserting that it is solely driven by commercial motivations. The Kremlin, however, has in various instances linked the exploitation of its energy resources to its foreign policy objectives.[89] Putin himself claimed in 2006 that "we intend to retain state control over the gas transport system and over Gazprom. [...] And the European Commission should not have any illusions: in the gas sector they will have to deal with the state."[90] Moreover, in the specific case of Nord Stream 2, the connection between the Kremlin and the pipeline project is even more pronounced, seeing as Matthias Warnig, a former Stasi officer and close confidant of Putin himself, is currently CEO of the Nord Stream AG. Countless analysts have documented the large number of supply disruptions to countries in Russia's 'near abroad' since 1991, concluding that many of them were at least partially related to Moscow's geopolitical designs.[91]

Gazprom's actions are thus often in part politically motivated, but this does not mean that there are no commercial rationales. Oftentimes, the economic and strategic cases overlap. Generally, "Russia seeks to expand its political influence abroad and maximize profits from its energy sales."[92] In terms of economic objectives, Gazprom seeks to reduce exposure to transit countries that could perceivably hold Russian energy sales hostage and use this as a tool in pricing negotiations. It also wants to establish ownership and control over energy infrastructure, for instance through debt-for-asset swaps. Naturally, these aims also align with the strategic objectives formulated in the Kremlin, since they increase the scope for politically motivated coercion. Stegen has shown that, historically, there has been an inverse correlation between the degree of pro-Western orientation of a government and the price of Russian gas.[93]

One of the most relevant examples can be seen in the on-and-off dispute with Ukraine. There, Russia's political and economic aims were fully compatible after the Orange Revolution in 2004, when a pro-Western government took over in Kyiv. Since they no longer wished to support Ukraine politically or "with gas subsidies, Russia's political leadership and Gazprom's managers were in agreement that the time was right to raise prices."[94] Gazprom proved much more willing to extend subsidies and compromise on pricing disputes when the pro-Russian government of Viktor Yanukovych was in power.[95]

A further point that needs to be considered with regard to Moscow's 'energy weapon' is whether the Kremlin has developed an aptitude to wield it successfully. Answering this will provide an indication of how useful this tool actually is and to what extent any steps in this direction should alarm the Member States of the EU. Russia has expended significant economic and political capital to secure energy transmission infrastructure, construct new routes, and set up avenues to influence countries in Europe and Asia, but has it attained its goals? As Stegen puts it, the key variable in the "*successful* implementation of the energy weapon is the targeted state's response: it must modify its behavior on account of the threats or actual disruptions [of the relevant energy supply]."[96] In many cases, this is difficult to evaluate, since the threat of punitive measures or the allure of subsidies might lead governments to adopt certain policies without this being made overt in any way, or indeed, without the subsequent occurrence of the anticipated consequence. There are nevertheless a few illuminating examples. During the early 1990s, Moscow found itself in a dispute with the Baltic states over the presence of Russian troops in these countries. The Kremlin threatened (and eventually carried out) a price hike in its supply of energy, but none of the countries concerned complied with Russia's demands (partially because US financial assistance and the near-implosion of the Yeltsin government helped mitigate this problem). In the 2000s, the Kremlin used a few conspicuously timed pipeline explosions to increase the pressure on Georgia to sell its transit assets to Russia, but without success. Indeed, in both these cases, the overt attempts to exercise influence led to a backlash that would go on to poison the relationship between the targeted states and Russia for years.[97]

On the other hand, there have also been occasions when Moscow has been more successful, such as during the Russian–Ukrainian negotiations over the Black Sea Fleet, both in the 1990s and in 2010. In the latter instance, Dmitry Medvedev, then president of Russia, even admitted that gas prices had played a role in securing the extension of the Black Sea Fleet's presence in the Crimean port of Sevastopol.[98]

This examination of the history of Moscow's attempts to use its energy weapon is only cursory and cannot be taken as definite evidence in favor, or otherwise, of its efficacy. It does, however, illustrate certain key principles. Most importantly, it underlines the fact that the possibility to interrupt supplies or at least credibly threaten to do so is not in and of itself sufficient to achieve the Kremlin's political aims, since accomplishing these goals is predicated on the targeted states adjusting their behavior.

3.2 Interdependence and Leverage

As noted above, energy interdependence extends both ways. Just as the EU relies on Russia for 40% of its gas imports, Moscow derives more than 40% of its budget from oil and gas revenues (although the vast majority of that comes from oil rather than gas sales). The Kremlin would thus be unlikely to risk its credibility as a reliable supplier. As Vantansever explains, Gazprom remains largely locked into the European market due to its "failure to diversify its pipeline exports to Asia and its late entry into the international LNG market."[99] Pipelines take decades to build and usually operate for decades more, meaning that the gas traveling through it becomes somewhat of a 'relationship commodity'.[100] This mutual dependence is unlikely to be reduced soon, notwithstanding the recent completion of the Power of Siberia pipeline through which Gazprom serves China.[101]

The transformations of the EU regulatory environment and the global gas market have further constrained Russia's leverage over its European clients, including Germany. The abovementioned 'Third Energy Package,' which the EU adopted in 2009, introduced the 'unbundling' of assets, in order to ensure that the production of resources would be owned and operated separately from the distribution network. This forced Gazprom to divest itself of its shares in several European gas companies.[102] Moreover, in the wake of several antitrust cases, the EU has prohibited the use of destination clauses and other territorial restrictions for the sale of gas.[103] This means that European customers are now largely free to resell gas across their borders, reducing "Gazprom's leverage with its importers and the feasibility of a gas blockade."[104] Russia is also eager to maintain its market share in the face of increasing competition from Algerian, American, and Qatari LNG, being keenly aware that any indications of unreliability would spur further investment into LNG transport and re-gasification infrastructure.[105]

As we have seen above, it is by no means clear that the volume of imported Russian gas into the EU will be significantly altered as a consequence of the new pipeline. Such a development would in fact mostly be determined by price signals. While we can expect gas imports to increase, it would appear that sufficient spare pipeline capacity already exists, and thus Nord Stream 2 as such will mostly affect the point of entry into the EU rather than the overall volumes. This might, for instance, result in lower volumes being shipped through Ukraine or Poland, but the overall financial and security impacts would be limited. As previously mentioned, Gazprom and Naftogaz have come to an agreement that covers the period up until 2024. Nothing stops Gazprom from diverting its natural gas through a newly completed Nord Stream 2, but the ship-or-pay provisions in the contract ensure that Ukraine will nevertheless have to be compensated. The newly agreed transit fees are mostly in line with those of the prior agreement.[106] In fact, Eser et al. have demonstrated that the impact of Nord Stream 2 alone will not lead to cripplingly low transit volumes through Ukraine even in the period following the new gas deal. They show that, in aggregate, transit volumes will fall by less than 20% (even though it should be noted that this does not take into account the effect of further pipelines such as Turkstream).[107] Interestingly, and in line with other analysts, they have found that the Yamal pipeline will probably be the one to suffer the most severe volume decrease from the completion of Nord Stream 2. Since the Polish government is trying to diversify away from Russian gas and has for years only collected minimal transit fees (at times less than $10 million annually), the actual financial impact of this is minor.[108]

3.3 Turning Off the Tap

In the unlikely event that supply interruptions were to occur, this would disproportionately affect Eastern European countries. The 'reverse-flow' capabilities needed to transfer gas in a West–East direction are still not as extensive as would be desirable. In the past, this meant that certain EU Member States, especially the Baltics, were virtually isolated islands in terms of natural gas, unable to fully cover consumption without relying on Russia. Even though this has since changed, storage capacity is still unevenly spread across the Member States and several CEE states would face some hardship from a potential Russian cut-off.[109] Although this does not directly affect Germany, it explains some of the criticism Eastern European countries have leveled at Berlin.

A 2014 scenario study by the German Institute for Economic Research has yielded mixed, but fairly positive, results regarding the estimated impacts of a total interruption of Russian gas deliveries.[110] In this scenario, several countries would have cut their consumption due to price increases. In Central and Western Europe, natural gas consumption would have fallen slightly by around 10% due to rising prices. For Germany itself, this would have implied a price rise of around 20%.[111] Although painful, this would hardly have a crippling effect on the German economy and thus would not engender the sort of dependence certain observers envision. As expected, the most severe restrictions were to be found in Russia's immediate neighborhood, particularly the Baltic States and Finland, where, according to the scenario, natural gas consumption was shown to fall sharply by around 70%. This was followed by Hungary, Croatia, Romania, and Bulgaria with a reduction of around 30%.[112]

If this is the situation as it presented itself in 2014, we need to take into account the changes that have occurred in the meantime and place them into the context of a completed Nord Stream 2 pipeline. Since, as pointed out above, Nord Stream 2 would primarily alter the entry point for Russian gas into Europe, does this imply that a partial Russian cut-off, i.e., rerouting all gas away from Ukraine, would become a more viable strategy? In part, the answer is yes, but a cut-off would still constitute a perilous play by Moscow. The new pipeline would indeed increase its ability to stop gas from flowing through Ukraine, but only at substantial cost to its own market share. Eser et al have found that in case of a partial cut-off focused on Ukraine, only 40% of the disrupted volumes would be rerouted through Poland and the Nord Stream pipelines. The remainder of the impacted demand would be substituted with gas from other sources, since the higher transit costs would lead to increased downstream prices for Russian gas. The shortfall would mostly be covered with elevated imports from Norway and with storage extraction.[113] Most EU Member States have significant storage capacity, collectively nearly equaling total Russian imports in any given year.[114] Moreover, if one accounts for increased imports of LNG and the progress that is being made toward infrastructure diversification, the situation is also improving across Eastern Europe. This further diminishes any potential added negotiation leverage that might arise for Gazprom from Nord Stream 2.

The last few years have seen substantial investment into reverse-flow capabilities across Eastern Europe, resulting in a more integrated pan-European gas market.[115] By the same token, there has also been significant development of LNG infrastructure and energy transmission networks. The EU has undertaken considerable investments that, among other things, have contributed to the completion of major infrastructure projects connecting the Baltic States and other such 'energy islands' to the European energy market. There have, for instance, been efforts to connect the Baltic's electricity infrastructure with that of Finland and Sweden. A further major success came in the form of the Klaipeda Floating Storage Regasification Unit, a floating Lithuanian LNG terminal that started operating in December 2014. This terminated the country's total dependence on Russian gas and diversified the whole region's supply.[116] A similar facility was recently constructed on the Croatian Island of Krk.[117]

These infrastructure investments, in combination with the abovementioned changes in the regulatory and market environment, constitute substantial progress toward the creation of a more unified, interconnected, and resilient gas market in Europe. Although Central and Eastern Europe will be disproportionately affected by Nord Stream 2, the pipeline's overall impact and deleterious consequences will be limited. They could further be mitigated by continued investment in the pan-European gas market and alternative sources of supply.

4 Conclusion

An analysis of the German rationale for supporting Nord Stream 2 shows that the project's limited economic benefits are unlikely to be the main reason for Berlin's backing. Examining the underlying commercial realities, it emerges that in spite of the fact that gas import demand in Germany and across the EU is likely to rise in the coming decades, the current pipeline infrastructure appears to be sufficient to meet this increase. The reasons why Germany supports the pipeline project are in fact mostly political rather than economic. It is in particular the SPD, a party with close ties to Moscow, that has vigorously defended Nord Stream 2 in the face of domestic and international opposition, at least in part due to the legacies of *Ostpolitik* and a desire to maintain strong relations with Russia.

Furthermore, worries about energy insecurity deriving from Moscow's geopolitical interference are overstated. Due to significant investment in LNG infrastructure, reverse-flow and gas storage capabilities, as well as a changing regulatory environment, the probability and potential impact of a politically motivated gas cut-off are currently manageable; Nord Stream 2 would not significantly alter this situation. It is clear that even though the new pipeline project is hardly necessary and might give rise to limited negative consequences in Central and Eastern Europe, these can and should be mitigated by continued integration of the European gas market in conjunction with further investment in LNG infrastructure and gas storage capacity. In this sense, Nord Stream 2 might even present an opportunity for the EU to become more united and resilient in the face of external shocks.

The 2015 Energy Union has certainly helped in addressing some of the shortfalls which the EU was and is still confronting, especially on issues of interconnectedness and energy efficiency. Despite this progress, the Nord Stream 2 saga reveals that some of the loftier aims pursued by the Energy Union still face significant hurdles. In its communication of the Energy Union package, coming a few months before the official announcement of Nord Stream 2, the Commission had outlined a vision according to which "Member States see that they depend on each other to deliver secure energy to their citizens, based on true solidarity and trust, and of an Energy Union that speaks with one voice in global affairs."[118] In light of the cacophony of voices and scathing indictments emanating from European capitals with regard to Nord Stream 2, it seems obvious that the EU has yet to live up to these ambitions.

These issues, of course, also have broader implications for European integration and foreign policy. It does, for instance, appear safe to assume that Berlin's seeming disregard for their energy security does not instill confidence in its Eastern neighbors when it comes to the matter of how Russian military aggression should be handled. If Germany can ostensibly not be relied on to act in the wider European interest with regards to natural gas, could it plausibly be expected to live up to its commitments and rush to the defense of Poland or the Baltics in the event of a large-scale conflict with Moscow? The Nord Stream 2 controversy thus raises a number of important questions, such as the extent of solidarity EU Member States can expect from one another, the manner in which common positions on difficult issues can be established, and how third parties such as Ukraine and Russia should be dealt with.

Notes

1 Angela Stent, *Putin's World: Russia against the West and with the Rest.* (New York: Twelve, 2019).
2 Which include Bulgaria, Croatia, the Czech Republic, Estonia, Hungary, Lithuania, Latvia, Poland, Romania, Slovenia, and Slovakia.
3 For the sake of conciseness and relevancy, this analysis will not consider the exchanges between the Soviet Union and its East German client state.
4 Aurelia Bros, Tatiana Mitrova, and Kirsten Westphal, *German-Russian Gas Relations: A Special Relationship in Troubled Waters* (Berlin: Stiftung Wissenschaft Und Politik, 2017). https://www.swp-berlin.org/en/publication/german-russian-gas-relations/.
5 Ibid., p. 6.
6 Ibid.
7 "Energy Charter Treaty," *International Energy Charter*, accessed September 10, 2020, https://www.energycharter.org/process/energy-charter-treaty-1994/energy-charter-treaty/.

8 Stent, *Putin's World.*
9 Rafał Bajczuk, "Dependence Management. The Background of the German Gas Policy," *OSW Centre for Eastern Studies,* July 6, 2016, https://www. osw.waw.pl/en/publikacje/osw-report/2016-07-06/dependence-management-background-german-gas-policy.
10 BP, "BP Statistical Review of World Energy", 2019, https://www.bp.com/content/dam/bp/business-sites/en/global/corporate/pdfs/energy-economics/statistical-review/bp-stats-review-2019-full-report.pdf.; Andrew Moravcsik, "Power of Connection: Why the Russia–Europe Gas Trade is Strangely Untouched by Politics," *Nature* 576 (December 2019): 30–31. www.nature.com, doi:10.1038/d41586-019-03694-y.
11 Henry Foy, "Eastern Europe to Confront Berlin over New Russian Gas Pipeline," *Financial Times,* November 29, 2015, https://www.ft.com/content/eb1ebca8-9514-11e5-ac15-0f7f7945adba.
12 "TIMELINE: Gas Crises between Russia and Ukraine," *Reuters,* January 11, 2009, https://www.reuters.com/article/us-russia-ukraine-gas-timeline-sb-idUSTRE50A1A720090111.
13 Bros et al., *German-Russian Gas Relations.*
14 Ibid.
15 "2019 Results: Gas Transit via Ukrainian GTS in 2019 Was 89.6 Bcm," *Naftogaz,* 2020, http://www.naftogaz.com/www/3/nakweben.nsf/0/CA66A758D9FDDBFBC2258507003F06B3.
16 "Third Energy Package," *European Commission,* accessed May 21, 2019, https://ec.europa.eu/energy/topics/markets-and-consumers/market-legislation/third-energy-package_en.
17 Réne Höltschi,"Brauchen Deutschland Und Europa Nord Stream 2 Überhaupt?" *Neue Zürcher Zeitung,* September 8, 2020, https://www.nzz.ch/wirtschaft/nawalny-und-nord-stream-2-braucht-es-die-pipeline-ueberhaupt-ld.1575334.
18 "Structure de l'actionnariat," *Engie.com,* accessed September 10, 2020, https://www.engie.com/actionnaires/action-engie/structure-de-lactionnariat.; "Shareholder Structure," *OMV.com,* accessed September 10, 2020, https://www.omv.com/en/investor-relations/omv-share/shareholder-structure.
19 Bros et al., *German-Russian Gas Relations.*
20 Stent, *Putin's World.*
21 Although Ukraine is not an EU member, it figures prominently in the debate. The EU and its Member States have expended meaningful resources and political capital on bolstering Kyiv's position vis-à-vis Moscow; depriving it of the economic benefits it derives from its vast gas infrastructure would run counter to these policies.
22 Bros et al., *German-Russian Gas Relations.*
23 Dimitar Lilkov and Roland Freudenstein, "European Energy Security IN FOCUS: The Case Against Nord Stream 2," *European Energy Security, Martens Centre,* 2018, https://www.martenscentre.eu/publication/european-energy-security-in-focus-the-case-against-nord-stream-2/.
24 Ibid.
25 Andrew Rettman, "Eastern EU Leaders to Warn Juncker on Nord Stream II," *EUobserver,* 2016, https://euobserver.com/foreign/132726.
26 George Zachmann, "Nord Stream 2 Means Gains for Germany but Pain for Europe," *Bruegel,* 2017, https://bruegel.org/2017/06/nord-stream-2-means-gains-for-germany-but-pain-for-europe/.
27 Mason, "Trump lashes Germany over gas pipeline deal"; the actual figures are discussed further below.

28 Gabriel Collins, "Russia's Use of the 'Energy Weapon' in Europe," *Baker Institute for Public Policy*, 2017, electronic brief, https://www.bakerinstitute.org/media/files/files/ac785a2b/BI-Brief-071817-CES_Russia1.pdf.
29 Lilkov and Freudenstein, "European Energy Security."
30 Nastassia Astrasheuskaya, "Russia to Go It Alone on Construction of Nord Stream 2 Pipeline," *Financial Times*, January 28, 2020, https://www.ft.com/content/a0f1b83c-41b4-11ea-bdb5-169ba7be433d.
31 Simon Pirani, Jack Sharples, Katja Yafimava, and Vitaly Yermakov, "Implications of the Russia-Ukraine Gas Transit Deal for Alternative Pipeline Routes and the Ukrainian and European Markets," *Oxford Institute for Energy Studies* (blog), 2020, https://www.oxfordenergy.org/publications/implications-of-the-russia-ukraine-gas-transit-deal-for-alternative-pipeline-routes-and-the-ukrainian-and-european-markets/.
32 Martin Arnold, "Berlin Hints at Nord Stream 2 U-Turn if Moscow Fails to Assist in Navalny Probe," *Financial Times,* September 6, 2020, https://www.ft.com/content/bd6dd6e5-ecdc-48b2-8145-ab72865cb2dd.
33 Stewart Elliot, "Commissioning Work to Fill First Nord Stream 2 Gas String to Begin June 11: Operator," *S&P Global*, June 10, 2021, https://www.spglobal.com/platts/en/market-insights/latest-news/natural-gas/061021-commissioning-work-to-fill-first-nord-stream-2-gas-string-to-begin-june-11-operator.
34 Bajczuk, "Dependence Management."
35 Ibid.
36 AG Energiebilanzen, "Bilanzen 1990-2017."
37 Bros et al., *German-Russian Gas Relations.*
38 Finn Roar Aune, Rolf Golombek, Arild Moe, Knut Einar Rosendahl, and Hilde Hallre Le Tissier, "The Future of Russian Gas Exports," *Economics of Energy & Environmental Policy* 6, no. 2 (2017). https://econpapers.repec.org/article/aeneeepjl/eeep6-2-rosendahl.htm.
39 Claudia Kemfert, Anne Neumann, Leonard Göke, Franziska Holz, and Christian von Hirschenhausen. "DIW Berlin: Erdgasversorgung: Weitere Ostsee-Pipeline ist überflüssig." *DIW Berlin*, 2018. https://doi.org/10.18723/diw_wb:2018-27-1; This does not mean that it was necessarily a bad investment for the European energy companies that were involved. Since they contributed loans rather than equity, they stand a very good chance of recovering their investments in the case of completion. (Henry Foy and Derek Brower, "EU Gas Groups Exposed as Pipeline Politics Threaten Nord Stream 2," *Financial Times,* September 14, 2020, https://www.ft.com/content/2c713b40-ae7f-47a7-b050-e91ca0879c8f.)
40 Alex Fak and Anna Kotelnikova, "Russian Oil and Gas: Tickling Giants," *Sberbank*, 2018. https://globalstocks.ru/wp-content/uploads/2018/05/Sberbank-CIB-OG_Tickling-Giants.pdf.
41 "Russisches Geldhaus: Sberbank entlässt Analysten nach kritischem Bericht über Gazprom," *Wirtschaftswoche*, accessed November 27, 2020, https://www.wiwo.de/russisches-geldhaus-sberbank-entlaesst-analysten-nach-kritischem-bericht-ueber-gazprom/22598714.html.
42 "Nord Stream 2 AG and European Energy Companies Sign Financing Agreements," *Engie.com*, 2017, https://www.engie.com/en/journalists/press-releases/nord-stream-2.
43 "EU Reference Scenario 2016 | Energy," *European Commission*, 2016, https://ec.europa.eu/energy/data-analysis/energy-modelling/eu-reference-scenario-2016_en.
44 Kemfert et al. "DIW Berlin: Erdgasversorgung."
45 "Gas Market Outlook: A New Pipeline for Europe's Energy Future," *Nord-Stream 2*, 2017, https://www.nord-stream2.com/media/documents/pdf/en/2018/07/brochure-gas-market-outlook-en.pdf.

46 S&P Global Platts, "IEA Cuts 2040 EU Gas Demand Forecast by Further 22 Bcm," *S&P Global Platts*, November 13, 2019, https://www. spglobal.com/platts/en/market-insights/latest-news/natural-gas/111319-iea-cuts-2040-eu-gas-demand-forecast-by-further-22-bcm.
47 Eser et al., "Impact of Nord Stream 2 and LNG on Gas Trade and Security of Supply in the European Gas Network of 2030." *Applied Energy* 238 (March 2019): 816–30. doi:10.1016/j.apenergy.2019.01.068.
48 Simone Tagliapietra, "Eastern Mediterranean Gas: What Prospects for the New Decade?," *Bruegel*, February 5, 2020, https://www.bruegel.org/2020/02/eastern-mediterranean-gas-what-prospects-for-the-new-decade/.
49 Lilkov and Freudenstein. "European Energy Security."
50 Bros et al., *German-Russian Gas Relations*.
51 Van Scherpenberg, "Nord Stream 2 und die Energiesouveränität Europas."
52 This calculation naturally depends on the imported volumes and price levels in any given year. In 2016, Germany's natural gas import bill was around $20 billion. Of the imported gas, around two thirds were actually consumed domestically, whereas most of the remaining gas was reexported. (Bajczuk, "Dependence Management"; "TABLE-Germany's 2016 Gas Imports down 3 Pct, Costs down 27 Pct," *Reuters*, February 20, 2017, https://www.reuters.com/article/germany-gas-imports-idUKL8N1G548F.)
53 Konrad Popławski, "German Energy Companies Lobby for Nord Stream 2," *OSW Centre for Eastern Studies*, September 21, 2016. https://www.osw.waw.pl/en/publikacje/analyses/2016-09-21/german-energy-companies-lobby-nord-stream-2.
54 Another explanation that has been proposed is the increased security of supply that the new pipeline would allegedly introduce. As mentioned previously, the political and financial tensions between Russia and Ukraine have led to (very brief) partial interruptions in gas flow across the Ukrainian pipeline system. The current geopolitical issues plaguing the relationship between Moscow and Kyiv, i.e., the illegal annexation of Crimea and the war in Eastern Ukraine, have led to trepidations that such events might recur. Some observers insist that the construction of Nord Stream 2 will make it harder for Ukraine to embroil Berlin in its squabbles with the Kremlin and thus add to Germany's energy security. While this argument has some superficial merit, it is not convincing. It disregards the reality that, far from wanting to extricate itself from the Ukraine–Russia conflict, Berlin has repeatedly inserted itself into the dispute, be it by imposing sanctions on Moscow, by playing a leading role in the negotiations in the Normandy format, or by insisting that gas flows through Ukraine persist even after the completion of Nord Stream 2. Moreover, as we will see below, even a complete disruption of transit through Ukraine would not have significant effects on prices in Germany. This hypothesis is thus not dealt with any further.
55 Bros et al., *German-Russian Gas Relations*; Handelsblatt, "Ostseepipeline: Widerstand gegen Nord Stream II bei Union, Grünen und FDP," *Handelsblatt*, February 20, 2018, https://www.handelsblatt.com/politik/deutschland/ostseepipeline-widerstand-gegen-nord-stream-ii-bei-union-gruenen-und-fdp/20983054.html.
56 Wehner Markus and Reinhard Veser, "Nord Stream 2: Widerstand Gegen Putins Pipeline Wächst," *Frankfurter Allgemeine,* 2016, https://www.faz.net/aktuell/politik/inland/nord-stream-2-widerstand-gegen-putins-pipeline-waechst-14507991.html.
57 Reinhard Bütikofer, "Fremde Federn: Nord Stream 2 schadet Europa – Gastbeitrag in der F.A.Z," *Reinhard Bütikofer* (blog), accessed November 28, 2020. https://reinhardbuetikofer.eu/2018/02/20/fremde-federn-nord-stream-2-schadet-europa-gastbeitrag-in-der-f-a-z.

58 "Alexei Navalny: Russian Activist Discharged from Berlin Hospital," *BBC News*, September 23, 2020, https://www.bbc.com/news/world-europe-54262279.

59 Chazan, "Merkel Faces Calls to Scrap Nord Stream 2."

60 Aussenpolitik, "Der versuchte Giftmord muss politische Konsequenzen haben," *Freie Demokraten - FDP*, accessed November 28, 2020, https://www.fdp.de/_der-versuchte-giftmord-muss-politische-konsequenzen-haben.

61 "Grüne fordern Aus für Nord Stream 2," *Der Spiegel*, 2020. https://www.spiegel.de/politik/deutschland/nawalny-gruene-fordern-ende-von-nord-stream-2-a-cedd2b9f-cf38-40a1-9aa0-b530f9d994c9.

62 "Grüne für Stopp, AfD für Weiterbau der Gaspipeline Nord Stream 2," *Deutscher Bundestag*, 2020,https://www.bundestag.de/dokumente/textarchiv/2020/kw38-de-nord-stream-2-792670.

63 Ibid.

64 Chazan, "Merkel Faces Calls to Scrap Nord Stream 2."

65 "Mehrheit der Deutschen für Bau von Nordstream 2," *Neue Presse*, 2019, https://www.neuepresse.de/Nachrichten/Politik/Deutschland-Welt/forsa-Umfrage-Mehrheit-der-Deutschen-fuer-Bau-von-Nordstream-2. For the sake of transparency, it should be noted that the head of the opinion polling company that had conducted the survey, Manfred Güllner, is a close friend of none other than Gerhard Schröder. ("Umfragen: SPD Wirft Meinungsforschern Meinungsmache Vor - Politik - Tagesspiegel," *Der Tagesspiegel*, 2008, https://www.tagesspiegel.de/politik/umfragen-spd-wirft-meinungsforschern-meinungsmache-vor/1197446.html.)

66 "RTL/ntv-Trendbarometer / Forsa-Aktuell: CDU/CSU, SPD und AfD in der fünften Woche unverändert - Mehrheit der Deutschen für Fertigstellung von Nord Stream II - 95 Prozent gegen Flüssiggas aus USA," *PressePortal*, 2020, https://www.presseportal.de/pm/72183/4704690.

67 Bajczuk, "Dependence Management"; "Nord Stream 2 - Pipe Production in the Europipe Pipe Mill," *Nord Stream 2 AG*, 2016, https://www.nord-stream2.com/media-info/images/pipe-production-in-the-europipe-pipe-mill-141/.; Rosneft, "Board of Directors," 2020. https://www.rosneft.com/governance/board/.

68 Lilkov and Freudenstein, "European Energy Security."

69 Bros et al., *German-Russian Gas Relations*, 40.

70 Markus Wehner, "Bundespräsident Frank-Walter Steinmeier Besucht Russland." *Frankfurter Allgemeine Zeitung*, 2017, https://www.faz.net/aktuell/politik/bundespraesident-frank-walter-steinmeier-besucht-russland-15261770.html.; "Steinmeier Calls Nord Stream 2 a Private Initiative," Ukrinform, 2018, https://www.ukrinform.net/rubric-economy/2475010-steinmeier-calls-nord-stream-2-a-private-initiative.html.

71 Julia Smirnova, "Sigmar Gabriel Gibt Beim Treffen Mit Wladimir Putin Den Schröder," *Welt*, October 29th, 2015, https://www.welt.de/politik/ausland/article148156440/Gabriel-spielt-in-Moskau-den-Gerhard-Schroeder.html.

72 Bajczuk, "Dependence Management."

73 Schmitt, "The Neue Ostpolitik Approach."

74 "Merkel Says Nord Stream 2 Not Possible without Clarity for Ukraine." *Reuters*, April 11, 2018, https://www.reuters.com/article/us-germany-ukraine-idUSKBN1HH1KW.

75 Simon Pirani and Jack Sharples, "The Russia-Ukraine Gas Transit Deal: Opening a New Chapter," *Oxford Institute for Energy Studies* (blog), 2020, https://www.oxfordenergy.org/publications/the-russia-ukraine-gas-transit-deal-opening-a-new-chapter/

76 "News Conference Following Russian-German Talks," President of Russia, accessed December 28, 2020, http://en.kremlin.ru/events/president/news/62565.

77 Ibid.
78 Chazan, "Merkel Faces Calls to Scrap Nord Stream 2."
79 "Kein Staatliches Projekt: Für Scholz Kommt Ein Baustopp von Nord Stream 2 Nicht Infrage," *Die Welt*, September 23, 2020, https://www.welt.de/politik/deutschland/article216346884/Kein-staatliches-Projekt-Fuer-Scholz-kommt-ein-Baustopp-von-Nord-Stream-2-nicht-infrage.html.
80 Laurenz Gehrke, "EU Sanctions Senior Russians over Navalny Poisoning," *POLITICO*, October 15, 2020. https://www.politico.eu/article/eu-agrees-to-sanction-six-russians-over-alexei-navalny-poisoning/.
81 Chazan, "Merkel Faces Calls to Scrap Nord Stream 2."
82 Christian Rath, "Nord Stream 2: Sanktionen ohne Entschädigung," *Legal Tribune Online*, 2020, https://www.lto.de/recht/kanzleien-unternehmen/k/nordstream-2-sanktionen-russland-alexej-nawalny-investitionsschutz-entschaedigung/.
83 "Nord Stream 2: Bundesregierung bietet eine Milliarde Euro zur Rettung der Pipeline," *Die Zeit*, September 16, 2020, https://www.zeit.de/politik/ausland/2020-09/nord-stream-2-ostsee-pipeline-finanzierung-olaf-scholz.
84 Smith Stegen, "Deconstructing the 'Energy Weapon.'"
85 "EU Imports of Energy Products - Recent Developments," *European Commission*, 2020, https://ec.europa.eu/eurostat/statistics-explained/index.php?title=EU_imports_of_energy_products_-_recent_developments.
86 Elena Kropatcheva, "He Who Has the Pipeline Calls the Tune? Russia's Energy Power against the Background of the Shale 'Revolutions'" *Energy Policy* 66 (2014): 1–10.
87 Smith Stegen, "Deconstructing the 'Energy Weapon'."
88 Irwin Stelzer, "Energy Policy: Abandon Hope All Ye Who Enter Here," *Hudson Institute*, 2008, http://www.npolicy.org/article.php?aid=354&tid=5.
89 Smith Stegen, "Deconstructing the 'Energy Weapon'."
90 Lilkov and Freudenstein, "European Energy Security," p. 3; Anna-Sophie Maass, *EU-Russia Relations, 1999-2015: From Courtship to Confrontation.* (Routledge, 2016).
91 Robert W. Orttung and Indra Overland, "A Limited Toolbox: Explaining the Constraints on Russia's Foreign Energy Policy," *Journal of Eurasian Studies* 2, no. 1 (January 2011): 74–85. doi:10.1016/j.euras.2010.10.006.
92 Ibid., p.75
93 Smith Stegen, "Deconstructing the 'Energy Weapon'."
94 Orttung and Overland, "A Limited Toolbox", p. 75.
95 Smith Stegen, "Deconstructing the 'Energy Weapon'."
96 Ibid p. 6510, emphasis in original.
97 Smith Stegen, "Deconstructing the 'Energy Weapon'."
98 Ibid.
99 Vantansever, "The Future of EU-Russian Energy Relations."
100 Moravcsik, "Power of Connection."
101 The Power of Siberia currently has a capacity of only 38 bcm and in any case does not tap the same natural gas deposits as the Western-leaning pipeline infrastructure. (George Zachmann, "The European Union-Russia-China Energy Triangle," *Bruegel*, 2019. https://bruegel.org/2019/12/the-european-union-russia-china-energy-triangle/).
102 Grigas, "Is Russia's Energy Weapon Still Potent?"
103 Paul Greening, "Revisiting LNG Resale Restrictions – Implications of Recent EU Decisions," *Akin Gump Strauss Hauer & Feld LLP*, accessed December 9, 2019, https://www.akingump.com/en/experience/industries/energy/speaking-energy/revisiting-lng-resale-restrictions-implications-of-recent-eu.html.

104   Grigas, "Is Russia's Energy Weapon Still Potent?"
105   Ibid.
106   Pirani and Sharples. "The Russia-Ukraine Gas Transit Deal."
107   Eser et al., "Impact of Nord Stream 2."
108   Pirani and Sharples, "The Russia-Ukraine Gas Transit Deal."
109   Engerer et al., "Europäische Erdgasversorgung trotz politischer Krisen sicher."
110   Engerer et al., "Europäische Erdgasversorgung trotz politischer Krisen sicher.";
      A Bruegel study has resulted in similar conclusions. (George Zachmann,
      "InteractiveChart: HowEuropeCanReplaceRussianGas," *Bruegel* (blog), https://
      bruegel.org/2014/03/interactive-chart-how-europe-can-replace-russian-gas/.)
111   Engerer et al., "Europäische Erdgasversorgung trotz politischer Krisen sicher."
112   Ibid.
113   Eser et al., "Impact of Nord Stream 2."
114   Engerer et al., "Europäische Erdgasversorgung trotz politischer Krisen sicher."
115   Silvia Favasuli, "How Reverse Flows Are Changing European Gas," *Interfax
      Global Energy,* May 5, 2017, https://interfaxenergy.com/article/25776/how-
      reverse-flows-are-changing-european-gas.
116   Grigas, "Is Russia's Energy Weapon Still Potent?"
117   Collins, "Russia's Use of the 'Energy Weapon' in Europe"; Krasimira
      Marinova, "First Croatian LNG Terminal Officially Inaugurated in Krk
      Island," *Innovation and Networks Executive Agency of the European Commission,*
      January 29, 2021, https://ec.europa.eu/inea/en/news-events/newsroom/first-
      croatian-lng-terminal-officially-inaugurated-krk-island.
118   "Energy Union Package: A Framework Strategy for a Resilient Energy Union
      with a Forward-Looking Climate Change Policy," *European Commission,* 2015,
      https://eur-lex.europa.eu/resource.html?uri=cellar:1bd46c90-bdd4-11e4-bbe1-0
      1aa75ed71a1.0001.03/DOC_1&format=PDF.

Bibliography

"Alexei Navalny: Russian Activist Discharged from Berlin Hospital." *BBC News,*
    September 23, 2020. https://www.bbc.com/news/world-europe-54262279.
Arnold, Martin. "Berlin Hints at Nord Stream 2 U-Turn if Moscow Fails to Assist
    in Navalny Probe." *Financial Times,* September 6, 2020. https://www.ft.com/
    content/bd6dd6e5-ecdc-48b2-8145-ab72865cb2dd.
Astrasheuskaya, Nastassia. "Russia to Go It Alone on Construction of Nord Stream
    2 Pipeline." *Financial Times,* January 28, 2020. https://www.ft.com/content/
    a0f1b83c-41b4-11ea-bdb5-169ba7be433d.
Aussenpolitik. "Der versuchte Giftmord muss politische Konsequenzen haben."
    Freie Demokraten – FDP, accessed November 28, 2020. https://www.fdp.
    de/_der-versuchte-giftmord-muss-politische-konsequenzen-haben.
Bajczuk, Rafał. "Dependence Management. The Background of the German
    Gas Policy." *OSW Centre for Eastern Studies,* July 6, 2016. https://www.
    osw.waw.pl/en/publikacje/osw-report/2016-07-06/dependence-management-
    background-german-gas-policy.
"Bilanzen 1990 bis 2019," AG Energiebilanzen, 1990-2017. https://ag-energiebilanzen.
    de/daten-und-fakten/bilanzen-1990-bis-2019/.
"Board of Directors," *Rosneft,* 2020. https://www.rosneft.com/governance/board/.
BP. "BP Statistical Review of World Energy." 2019. https://www.bp.com/content/
    dam/bp/business-sites/en/global/corporate/pdfs/energy-economics/statistical-
    review/bp-stats-review-2019-full-report.pdf.

Bros, Aurelia, Tatiana Mitrova, and Kirsten Westphal. *German–Russian Gas Relations: A Special Relationship in Troubled Waters.* Berlin: Stiftung Wissenschaft Und Politik, 2017. https://www.swp-berlin.org/en/publication/german-russian-gas-relations/.

Bütikofer, Reinhard. "Fremde Federn: Nord Stream 2 schadet Europa – Gastbeitrag in der F.A.Z." *Reinhard Bütikofer* (blog), accessed November 28, 2020. https://reinhardbuetikofer.eu/2018/02/20/fremde-federn-nord-stream-2-schadet-europa-gastbeitrag-in-der-f-a-z/.

Chazan, Guy. "Merkel Faces Calls to Scrap Nord Stream 2 after Navalny Poisoning." *Financial Times*, 3 September 2020. https://www.ft.com/content/81e7d355-e478-49fc-ba75-49f43cbfc74f.

Collins, Gabriel. "Russia's Use of the 'Energy Weapon' in Europe." *Baker Institute for Public Policy*, 2017. https://www.bakerinstitute.org/media/files/files/ac785a2b/BI-Brief-071817-CES_Russia1.pdf.

Elliot, Stewart. "Commissioning Work to Fill First Nord Stream 2 Gas String to Begin June 11: Operator." *S&P Global*, June 10, 2021. https://www.spglobal.com/platts/en/market-insights/latest-news/natural-gas/061021-commissioning-work-to-fill-first-nord-stream-2-gas-string-to-begin-june-11-operator.

"Energy Charter Treaty." *International Energy Charter*, accessed September 10, 2020. https://www.energycharter.org/process/energy-charter-treaty-1994/energy-charter-treaty/.

"Energy Union Package: A Framework Strategy for a Resilient Energy Union with a Forward-Looking Climate Change Policy." *European Commission*, 2015. https://eur-lex.europa.eu/resource.html?uri=cellar:1bd46c90-bdd4-11e4-bbe1-01aa75ed71a1.0001.03/DOC_1&format=PDF.

Eser, Patrick, Ndaona Chokani, and Reza S. Abhari. "Impact of Nord Stream 2 and LNG on Gas Trade and Security of Supply in the European Gas Network of 2030." *Applied Energy* 238 (March 2019): 816–30. doi:10.1016/j.apenergy.2019.01.068.

"EU Imports of Energy Products - Recent Developments." *European Commission*, 2020. https://ec.europa.eu/eurostat/statistics-explained/index.php?title=EU_imports_of_energy_products_-_recent_developments.

"EU Reference Scenario 2016 | Energy." *European Commission*, 2016. https://ec.europa.eu/energy/data-analysis/energy-modelling/eu-reference-scenario-2016_en.

Favasuli, Silvia. "How Reverse Flows Are Changing European Gas." *Interfax Global Energy*, May 5, 2017. https://interfaxenergy.com/article/25776/how-reverse-flows-are-changing-european-gas.

Fak, Alex, and Anna Kotelnikova. "Russian Oil and Gas: Tickling Giants." *Sberbank*, 2018. https://globalstocks.ru/wp-content/uploads/2018/05/Sberbank-CIB-OG_Tickling-Giants.pdf.

Foy, Henry. "Eastern Europe to Confront Berlin Over New Russian Gas Pipeline." *Financial Times*, November 29, 2015. https://www.ft.com/content/eb1ebca8-9514-11e5-ac15-0f7f7945adba.

Foy, Henry and Derek Brower. "EU Gas Groups Exposed as Pipeline Politics Threaten Nord Stream 2." *Financial Times,* September 14, 2020. https://www.ft.com/content/2c713b40-ae7f-47a7-b050-e91ca0879c8f.

"Gas Market Outlook: A New Pipeline for Europe's Energy Future." *NordStream 2*, 2017. https://www.nord-stream2.com/media/documents/pdf/en/2018/07/brochure-gas-market-outlook-en.pdf.

Gehrke, Laurenz. "EU Sanctions Senior Russians Over Navalny Poisoning." *POLITICO*, October 15, 2020. https://www.politico.eu/article/eu-agrees-to-sanction-six-russians-over-alexei-navalny-poisoning/.

Greening, Paul. "Revisiting LNG Resale Restrictions – Implications of Recent EU Decisions." *Akin Gump Strauss Hauer & Feld LLP*, accessed December 9, 2019. https://www.akingump.com/en/experience/industries/energy/speaking-energy/revisiting-lng-resale-restrictions-implications-of-recent-eu.html.

Grigas, Agnia. *Hybrid CoE Strategic Analysis 2: Is Russia's Energy Weapon Still Potent in the Era of Integrated Energy Markets?* Helsinki: Hybrid CoE, November 2017.

"Grüne fordern Aus für Nord Stream 2." *Der Spiegel,* 2020. https://www.spiegel.de/politik/deutschland/nawalny-gruene-fordern-ende-von-nord-stream-2-a-cedd2b9f-cf38–40a1–9aa0-b530f9d994c9.

"Grüne für Stopp, AfD für Weiterbau der Gaspipeline Nord Stream 2." *Deutscher Bundestag,* 2020. https://www.bundestag.de/dokumente/textarchiv/2020/kw38-de-nord-stream-2-792670.

Handelsblatt, "Ostseepipeline: Widerstand gegen Nord Stream II bei Union, Grünen und FDP," *Handelsblatt*, February 20, 2018, https://www.handelsblatt.com/politik/deutschland/ostseepipeline-widerstand-gegen-nord-stream-ii-bei-union-gruenen-und-fdp/20983054.html.

Höltschi, Réne. "Brauchen Deutschland Und Europa Nord Stream 2 Überhaupt?" *Neue Zürcher Zeitung,* September 8, 2020. https://www.nzz.ch/wirtschaft/nawalny-und-nord-stream-2-braucht-es-die-pipeline-ueberhaupt-ld.1575334.

"Kein Staatliches Projekt: Für Scholz Kommt Ein Baustopp von Nord Stream 2 Nicht Infrage." *Die Welt,* September 23, 2020. https://www.welt.de/politik/deutschland/article216346884/Kein-staatliches-Projekt-Fuer-Scholz-kommt-ein-Baustopp-von-Nord-Stream-2-nicht-infrage.html.

Kemfert, Claudia, Anne Neumann, Leonard Göke, Franziska Holz, and Christian von Hirschenhausen. "DIW Berlin: Erdgasversorgung: Weitere Ostsee-Pipeline ist überflüssig." *DIW Berlin,* 2018. https://doi.org/10.18723/diw_wb:2018-27-1.

Kropatcheva, Elena. "He Who Has the Pipeline Calls the Tune? Russia's Energy Power Against the Background of the Shale 'Revolutions.'" *Energy Policy* 66 (2014): 1–10.

Lilkov, Dimitar, and Roland Freudenstein. "European Energy Security IN FOCUS: The Case Against Nord Stream 2." *European Energy Security, Martens Centre,* 2018. https://www.martenscentre.eu/publication/european-energy-security-in-focus-the-case-against-nord-stream-2/.

Maass, Anna-Sophie. *EU-Russia Relations, 1999–2015: From Courtship to Confrontation.* Routledge, 2016.

Marinova, Krasimira. "First Croatian LNG Terminal Officially Inaugurated in Krk Island." *Innovation and Networks Executive Agency of the European Commission,* January 29, 2021. https://ec.europa.eu/inea/en/news-events/newsroom/first-croatian-lng-terminal-officially-inaugurated-krk-island.

Markus, Wehner. "Bundespräsident Frank-Walter Steinmeier Besucht Russland." *Frankfurter Allgemeine Zeitung,* 2017. https://www.faz.net/aktuell/politik/bundespraesident-frank-walter-steinmeier-besucht-russland-15261770.html.

Markus, Wehner, and Reinhard Veser. "Nord Stream 2: Widerstand Gegen Putins Pipeline Wächst." *Frankfurter Allgemeine,* 2016. https://www.faz.net/aktuell/politik/inland/nord-stream-2-widerstand-gegen-putins-pipeline-waechst-14507991.html.

Mason, Jeff. "Trump Lashes Germany Over Gas Pipeline Deal, Calls it Russia's 'Captive'," *Reuters*, 11 July 2018. https://www.reuters.com/article/us-nato-summit-pipeline-idUSKBN1K10VI.

"Mehrheit der Deutschen für Bau von Nordstream 2." *Neue Presse*, 2019. https://www.neuepresse.de/Nachrichten/Politik/Deutschland-Welt/forsa-Umfrage-Mehrheit-der-Deutschen-fuer-Bau-von-Nordstream-2.

"MerkelSaysNordStream2NotPossibleWithoutClarityforUkraine." *Reuters*, April 11, 2018. https://www.reuters.com/article/us-germany-ukraine-idUSKBN1HH1KW.

Moravcsik, Andrew. "Power of Connection: Why the Russia–Europe Gas Trade is Strangely Untouched by Politics." *Nature* 576 (2019): 30–31. www.nature.com, doi:10.1038/d41586-019-03694-y.

"News Conference Following Russian-German Talks." President of Russia, accessed December 28, 2020. http://en.kremlin.ru/events/president/news/62565.

"Nord Stream 2: Bundesregierung bietet eine Milliarde Euro zur Rettung der Pipeline." *Die Zeit*, September 16, 2020. https://www.zeit.de/politik/ausland/2020-09/nord-stream-2-ostsee-pipeline-finanzierung-olaf-scholz.

"Nord Stream 2 AG and European Energy Companies Sign Financing Agreements." *Engie.com*, 2017. https://www.engie.com/en/journalists/press-releases/nord-stream-2.

"Nord Stream 2-Pipe Production in the Europipe Pipe Mill." *Nord Stream 2 AG*, 2016. https://www.nord-stream2.com/media-info/images/pipe-production-in-the-europipe-pipe-mill-141/.

Orttung, Robert W., and Indra Overland. "A Limited Toolbox: Explaining the Constraints on Russia's Foreign Energy Policy." *Journal of Eurasian Studies* 2, no. 1 (January 2011): 74–85. doi:10.1016/j.euras.2010.10.006.

Pirani, Simon, Jack Sharples, Katja Yafimava, and Vitaly Yermakov. "Implications of the Russia-Ukraine Gas Transit Deal for Alternative Pipeline Routes and the Ukrainian and European Markets." *Oxford Institute for Energy Studies* (blog), 2020. https://www.oxfordenergy.org/publications/implications-of-the-russia-ukraine-gas-transit-deal-for-alternative-pipeline-routes-and-the-ukrainian-and-european-markets/.

Pirani, Simon, and Jack Sharples. "The Russia-Ukraine Gas Transit Deal." *The Oxford Institute for Energy Studies* (blog), https://www.oxfordenergy.org/publications/russia-poland-gas-relationship-risks-and-uncertainties-of-the-ever-after/.

Popławski, Konrad. "German Energy Companies Lobby for Nord Stream 2." *OSW Centre for Eastern Studies*, September 21, 2016. https://www.osw.waw.pl/en/publikacje/analyses/2016-09-21/german-energy-companies-lobby-nord-stream-2.

Rath, Christian. "Nord Stream 2: Sanktionen ohne Entschädigung." *Legal Tribune Online*, 2020. https://www.lto.de/recht/kanzleien-unternehmen/k/nordstream-2-sanktionen-russland-alexej-nawalny-investitionsschutz-entschae-digung/.

Rettman, Andrew. "Eastern EU Leaders to Warn Juncker on Nord Stream II." *EUobserver*, 2016. https://euobserver.com/foreign/132726.

Roar Aune, Finn, Rolf Golombek, Arild Moe, Knut Einar Rosendahl, and Hilde Hallre Le Tissier. "The Future of Russian Gas Exports." *Economics of Energy & Environmental Policy* 6, no. 2 (2017). https://econpapers.repec.org/article/aeneeepjl/eeep6-2-rosendahl.htm.

"RTL/ntv-Trendbarometer / Forsa-Aktuell: CDU/CSU, SPD und AfD in der fünften Woche unverändert - Mehrheit der Deutschen für Fertigstellung von

Nord Stream II -95 Prozent gegen Flüssiggas aus USA." *PressePortal* (blog), 2020. https://www.presseportal.de/pm/72183/4704690.

"Russisches Geldhaus: Sberbank entlässt Analysten nach kritischem Bericht über Gazprom." *Wirtschaftswoche*, accessed November 27, 2020. https://www.wiwo. de/russisches-geldhaus-sberbank-entlaesst-analysten-nach-kritischem-bericht-ueber-gazprom/22598714.html.

"Shareholder Structure." *OMV.com*, accessed September 10, 2020. https://www. omv.com/en/investor-relations/omv-share/shareholder-structure.

Smirnova, Julia. "Sigmar Gabriel Gibt Beim Treffen Mit Wladimir Putin Den Schröder." *Welt,* October 29, 2015. https://www.welt.de/politik/ausland/ article148156440/Gabriel-spielt-in-Moskau-den-Gerhard-Schroeder.html.

S&P Global Platts. "IEA Cuts 2040 EU Gas Demand Forecast by Further 22 Bcm." *S&P Global Platts*, November 13, 2019. https://www.spglobal.com/platts/en/ market-insights/latest-news/natural-gas/111319-iea-cuts-2040-eu-gas-demand-forecast-by-further-22-bcm.

"Steinmeier Calls Nord Stream 2 a Private Initiative." *Ukrinform*, 2018. https:// www.ukrinform.net/rubric-economy/2475010-steinmeier-calls-nord-stream-2-a-private-initiative.html.

Stelzer, Irwin. "Energy Policy: Abandon Hope All Ye Who Enter Here." *Hudson Institute*, 2008. http://www.npolicy.org/article.php?aid=354&tid=5.

Stent, Angela. *Putin's World: Russia Against the West and with the Rest*. New York: Twelve, 2019.

"Structure de l'actionnariat." *Engie.com*, accessed September 10, 2020. https://www. engie.com/actionnaires/action-engie/structure-de-lactionnariat.

"TABLE-Germany's 2016 Gas Imports down 3 Pct, Costs down 27 Pct." *Reuters*, February 20, 2017. https://www.reuters.com/article/germany-gas-imports-idUKL8N1G548F.

Tagliapietra, Simone. "Eastern Mediterranean Gas: What Prospects for the New Decade?" *Bruegel*, February 5, 2020. https://www.bruegel.org/2020/02/ eastern-mediterranean-gas-what-prospects-for-the-new-decade/.

"TIMELINE: Gas Crises Between Russia and Ukraine." *Reuters*, January 11, 2009. https://www.reuters.com/article/us-russia-ukraine-gas-timeline-sb-idUSTRE 50A1A720090111.

"Third Energy Package." *European Commission*, accessed May 21, 2019. https:// ec.europa.eu/energy/topics/markets-and-consumers/market-legislation/ third-energy-package_en.

"Umfragen: SPD Wirft Meinungsforschern Meinungsmache Vor - Politik – Tagesspiegel." *Der Tagesspiegel,* 2008. https://www.tagesspiegel.de/politik/ umfragen-spd-wirft-meinungsforschern-meinungsmache-vor/1197446.html.

Van Scherpenberg, Jens. "Nord Stream 2 und die Energiesouveränität Europas." *GWP – Gesellschaft. Wirtschaft. Politik* 1 (2019): 41–48.

Vatansever, Adnan. "The Future of EU-Russian Energy Relations." In David Koranyi (ed.), *A Eurasian Energy Primer: A Transatlantic Perspective*. Washington, DC: Atlantic Council, 2013, 37–50.

Zachmann, George. "Interactive Chart: How Europe Can Replace Russian Gas." *Bruegel* (blog), 2014. https://bruegel.org/2014/03/interactive-chart-how-europe-can-replace-russian-gas/.)

Zachmann, George. "Nord Stream 2 Means Gains for Germany but Pain for Europe." *Bruegel*, 2017. https://bruegel.org/2017/06/nord-stream-2-means-gains-for-germany-but-pain-for-europe/.

Zachmann, George. "The European Union-Russia-China Energy Triangle." *Bruegel*, 2019. https://bruegel.org/2019/12/the-european-union-russia-china-energy-triangle/.

"2019 Results: Gas Transit via Ukrainian GTS in 2019 Was 89.6 Bcm." *Naftogaz*, 2020. http://www.naftogaz.com/www/3/nakweben.nsf/0/CA66A758D9FDDBFBC2258507003F06B3.

7 Will 27 Become One? The Linkage between Europe's Domestic and Foreign Politics and the Prospect of a Single EU Seat at the United Nations Security Council

Faïz El Mamoune

1 Introduction

> *And if we are serious about the European project, then the EU should also speak with one voice in the UN Security Council. Here is my proposal: In the medium term, France's seat on the Security Council could be converted into a seat for the EU.*

This proposal was made by Olaf Scholz, German Vice-Chancellor and Minister of Finance, during his speech on the future of Europe at Humboldt University in November 2018. He deplored that European integration has been reduced to the creation of a Single Market which is why, as he explained, "populists and eurosceptics are gaining traction, despite continued majority support for the European Union." Olaf Scholz's statement did not fail to provoke strong reactions throughout Europe. If this proposal was very well received in Germany – evidenced by Angela Merkel's remark that this seat should have the ability of "bringing together European voices in the United Nations Security Council" – it did not find the same resonance in France. Indeed, in a rare surge of solidarity, the entire French political class firmly rejected Scholz's idea.[1] While both the extreme left and right denounced the proposal as an attack on French sovereignty, Minister of Europe and Foreign Affairs Jean-Yves Le Drian outright concluded that the German proposal was 'stupid.'[2] Then-French Ambassador to the United Nations (UN), Nicolas Delattre, attempted to close the discussion by invoking the legal constraints of France's replacement by the European Union (EU) in the UN Security Council (UNSC).[3]

The tension around this subject reappeared following President Macron and Chancellor Merkel's signing of the Aachen Treaty in January 2019,[4] an event which the French opposition used to criticize the government for its apparent willingness to share the French seat at the UNSC with Germany. In reality, as journalist Jacques Pezet indicates by quoting historian Hélène Miard-Delacroix, this Treaty is part of a long tradition of Franco-German cooperation, initiated by the 1963 Élysée Treaty.[5]

DOI: 10.4324/9781003182344-8

Turmoil around the idea of a permanent European seat reflects a deep opposition between two visions: a German vision favorable to the Europeanization of foreign policy and a French vision, which favors a traditional approach centered around a pivotal role for nation-states. The Europeanization of the Member States' presence at the United Nations is far from being a new idea. Some nonpermanent Member States at the Security Council, such as Italy and Portugal, have previously considered making their seats an '*EU laboratory.*'[6] However, a Europeanization of the UNSC never really materialized since nonpermanent members generally take the opportunity to defend their national interests, as Germany did in its vote on resolution 1973 (2011) authorizing armed action in Libya.[7] Likewise, France never shared its permanent seat with other European countries, even though in 2019 it set up, for the first time, a twin presidency with Germany at the UNSC.

Thus, the proposal of a general European seat replacing the French seat at the UNSC is a long-lasting issue with great implications for EU foreign policy. Academics have mainly studied this topic from a legal angle, [8] rather than from a political perspective. This chapter, however, queries political questions arising out of the idea of a European seat in the UNSC: *Is such an EU seat in the UN Security Council desirable? Does Brexit accelerate the need to move toward an EU seat in order to better serve European interests in foreign policy?*

At first glance, the categorical French refusal to abandon its seat may appear to be a form of selfishness or the will to preserve one of the last manifestations of France's power in the international arena. This is a fair criticism, especially given that French politicians are likely opposed to a common seat so they can better prioritize national interests on the international stage; some may even push back against a unified seat for electoral reasons. This chapter is not a plea in favor of a French-led diplomacy, but rather intends to provide a *realist* analysis of the implications of the German proposal for the functioning of the EU's internal cohesion and effectiveness of its foreign policy. Despite considerable progress, the EU as a regional organization has not yet succeeded in equipping itself with the tools that would allow it to secure a prominent place in a new multilateral order between China, the United States, or even the emerging powers. Given this current failure, maintaining the status quo with a strong French delegation at the service of the EU actually benefits the interests of all Member States and Europeans. Indeed, France has often been one of the few countries to recognize the current limits of the EU and has campaigned strongly for an independent and strategically powerful Europe. This can be traced back to De Gaulle, who explained that "While waiting for the sky to clear up, France pursues by its own means what a European and independent policy can and must be."[9] From this perspective, nothing could be more counterproductive than establishing a permanent European seat in the early 2020s. The current situation allows, on the contrary, the EU to continue

190   *Faïz El Mamoune*

to influence global affairs through the intermediary of a Member State and to participate in important decisions made by the United Nations. This affords the EU time to build the political capital and infrastructure necessary to pursue a permanent seat at a later time.

An immediate creation of a common EU seat in the UNSC is not only difficult but undesirable, as it constitutes 'triple trouble' for the interests of the European Union. This triple trouble could lead to:

1   The dysfunction and imbalance of the Franco-German engine essential to European construction;
2   The weakening of the EU's role at the UN and therefore on the international stage;
3   The strengthening of internal divergences within the EU, which could lead to a lack of coherence and credibility on geostrategic issues.

2 The EU in UN Politics: Between Rising Influence and Structural Challenges

International organizations have existed for centuries,[10] but the novelty of the United Nations in the aftermath of the Second World War lies in "the decisive shift in mainstream thinking away from the former bread-and-butter study of international organization and law towards global governance."[11] The element of global governance is essential for understanding the conditions under which the UN was constructed and above all the relationship between the UN and regional organizations like the EU.

2.1 The UNSC: Multilateralist or Cold War Hangover?

The Charter of the United Nations states the organization's objective of settling international disputes through the Security Council. The Security Council is the central organ in the maintenance of peace and security in the world. In accordance with the objectives and principles of the Charter, it is "the only international body which can legalize and legitimize, in the vast majority of cases, the use of force in an inter or intra-state conflict."[12] It is made up of five permanent members who enjoy the right of veto, namely the United States, China, France, Great Britain, and Russia, plus ten nonpermanent members who are elected for a period of two years by the General Assembly.[13]

The geographic representation of nonpermanent members has evolved over time. The United Nations General Assembly fixed the following pattern since 1963:

-   Five from African and Asian States;
-   One from **Eastern European States**;

- Two from Latin American States;
- Two from **Western European and other States**.

Reform advocates often point to this seat distribution system, highlighting its high degree of imbalance between global regions. It is also used by Europeans in favor of a common EU seat, who argue that change is necessary to erase the appearance of a division between Eastern and Western Europe, a division that traces its roots to the Cold War-era division of Europe.

The Security Council's operation has been criticized, especially during the Cold War, because of the abuse of veto power on matters falling within the circle of influence of the five permanent members.[14] Indeed, the decisions of the Security Council are based on the unanimity of the permanent members.[15] This privilege is based on a collective security regime built on the joint responsibility of the permanent members and it is from this composition that the Security Council draws its strength and effectiveness.[16] Moreover, this unanimity prevents the possibilities of confrontations between the great powers and, therefore, spares the world from a hypothetical generalized war. As Berlia underlines "(...) It is the powers likely to start the conflict who are responsible for maintaining the peace. Their disagreement, in one case as in another, compromises everything; their agreement at least ensures the maintenance of peace."[17]

The Security Council is the central cog of the United Nations. The Charter of the United Nations empowers this body to sanction any aggressive action that undermines international order.[18] By associating law and force, through Chapter VII, it offers a legal basis and a set of sanctions ranging from economic measures to military action.[19] While the Security Council has been given the primary responsibility for peacekeeping, its action is limited to developing standards that the UN itself cannot implement.[20] The execution of the acts it adopts necessarily goes through third parties. Sometimes perceived as an international legislator because of the extent of its normative power, the Security Council intervenes only at the stage of the development of standards whose execution is carried out through the members of the United Nations which apply them.[21]

Since the collapse of the Soviet bloc, the United Nations has promoted multilateralism as the best way to face challenges the magnitude of which are matched only by their complexity.[22] In an increasingly multipolar world, this has meant expanding UN dialogues such that states are no longer the sole interlocutors with the organization.[23] For example, the impetus with which the Secretary-General of the United Nations set out, in 1992, to strengthen ties between the United Nations and regional organizations, devoting an entire chapter to their cooperation in the Agenda for Peace, reflects an awareness of this need.[24]

2.2 The United Nations: A Privileged and Obvious Partner in the Global Strategy for the European Union's Foreign Policy

In this multilateral approach, the European Union, keen to develop its potential in terms of external action, has a particular role to play. With the development of its Common Security and Defence Policy (CSDP), the European Union has been forced to engage in increasingly close relations with the United Nations.[25] The acts of the Security Council become the organic link between two entities that were not intended to meet. The resolutions have over time become a key part of the relationship between the two organizations, even though the European Union is not a member of the United Nations.[26] This consideration has major implications for the international legal dimension of the European Union and constitutes an element likely to enrich the reflection on a potential permanent European seat at the Security Council of the UN. Understanding the stakes of such a problem first requires an analysis of the elements that have contributed to the development of the European Union's external action.

In many respects, it should be unlikely that the EU and the UN would interact in any formal way. The UN has been since its founding an interstate organization designed to act in the service and at the disposal of nation states.[27] The EU is not a nation state, nor does it claim such a status. Indeed, the departure of the United Kingdom from the Union [28] only serves to further emphasize the challenge to a cohesive European Union. This is the first time that a Member State has decided to leave the regional organization since its formation and is part of a wider trend of rising skepticism and rejection of the EU among Member States.

> One reason for creating the European Community (was) to enable Europe to play its full part in world affairs. ... It (is) vital for the Community to be able to speak with one voice and to act as one in **economic relations** with the rest of the world.

It is in these terms that Walter Hallstein, the first President of the Commission of the European Economic Community, spoke about the future of Europe in 1962. If trade relations seem to be at the heart of the European Economic Community's external action, the latter did not at the time have a *stricto sensu* external policy.[29] This is a prerogative that will, over the years, be reinforced through provisions in European treaties. It was not until the establishment of European Political Cooperation (EPC) in 1970 that the idea of going beyond the economic framework germinated.[30] The rapprochement of states inevitably called for a strengthening of their relations in a wider field, as it appeared abnormal that States which had established very strong links between themselves in the economic field could, outside the fields established by the Treaty, be able to behave in a strictly individualistic manner and totally ignore the notion of solidarity.[31]

The informal initiative of the EPC led the way to the Single Act of 1986 and its Article 30.[32] The hesitations of certain Member States in the face of the assertion of a common foreign policy, accompanied by legal instruments more suited to this ambition, were truly overcome with the creation of the CSDP and the adoption of the Treaty on European Union in 1992.[33] Largely driven by Germany and France, the CSDP was meant thus to give concrete form to the wishes expressed in the Davignon report, drafted 20 years earlier, in order to pursue a specific policy rather than produce endless declarations.[34]

As an economic and commercial power, the European Union is fully committed to the multilateralist path traced by the United Nations, using its normative and institutional instruments obtained over time.[35] The establishment of a common foreign and security policy for EU members, first with the signing of the Maastricht Treaty in 1992, is marked by the breadth of its field of action which now "covers all areas of foreign policy and all questions relating to the Union's security, including the progressive framing of a common defence policy that might lead to a common defence."[36]

Such a provision opens the way to new perspectives for the EU on the international scene. It increases the credibility of its external action. However, the EU's ambition is limited by lightly restrictive means of action. While unanimity governs the CSDP, it is above all down to the European Council to set the broad guidelines and to decide on common strategies, positions, or actions.[37]

The prerogatives of a common foreign policy for the EU were further strengthened by the Treaty of Amsterdam in 1997.[38] The Treaty established common strategies for areas in which the Member States have common interests and served to specify their objectives and their duration.[39] It is on this basis that the Council adopts its positions. The real progress on this point was based on the fact that the Member States were required to comply with the common actions adopted by the European Council.[40]

Therefore, it seems that each modification of the Treaties is followed by an extension of the external competences of the European Community. This tendency has manifested itself above all in the field of cooperation with third parties.[41] This development is mainly due to the signing of the last major treaty on European construction, namely the Treaty of Lisbon.[42] Aspiring to make the EU a more coherent and influential international actor, the Treaty of Lisbon introduced a set of structural innovations affecting the Union's external representation, including the bestowment of a legal personality to the EU.[43] More precisely, the Treaty of Lisbon enabled the EU to simultaneously acquire a Presidency of the European Council and a High Representative of the Union for Foreign Affairs and Security Policy, who is now appointed.[44] This last appointment is crucial for the foreign policy of the EU within the UN.

Indeed, before the Lisbon Treaty, the presidency of the EU was responsible for informing other EU members about UN activities and organizing

internal coordination meetings over UN affairs.[45] The workload of the presidency was colossal, given that "there were over 1,000 meetings in New York
per year."[46] But what that meant above all was the presidency had been the
leading agent on behalf of the EU in CSDP matters. In other words, they
had great decision-making power over the priorities addressed that were
influenced by their own interests and perspectives.[47] The Treaty of Lisbon
has established a more stable representation system, allowing the EU to
gain more strength overall as an external agent.[48]

It should be noted, however, that even before the signing of the Lisbon
Treaty, EU members of the UNSC had to abide by the provisions of former
Article 19 of the Treaty on the European Union. These provisions had
vested in all EU members of the Security Council, permanent and nonpermanent, "the responsibility to liaise with each other and to keep the other
EU members fully informed on Security Council issues." In this sense, the
two permanent members – France and the United Kingdom – were under
obligation to "ensure the defense of the positions and the interests of the
Union." The same Article 19 also stipulated that this obligation should
be without "prejudice to their responsibilities under the provisions of the
United Nations Charter." Thus, EU members of the UNSC were obli-
gated to represent pan-European interests within the Council prior to the
Treaty of Lisbon. What was novel about the new Treaty requirements was
the creation of two new offices, the High Representative and the European
External Action Service (EEAS), that have allowed the European Union to
act more like a sovereign state than ever before. Like the High Representative, the EEAS was created following the Treaty of Lisbon to assist the High
Representative in fulfilling their mandate.[49] EEAS personnel supplement
the structures of EU Delegations in third countries and international organizations.[50] It is in this perspective that the Treaty of Lisbon is unique in the
European representation at the UN and the UNSC.

By deploying its foreign policy, the EU is committed to seek partnerships
with other international actors. This is true first and foremost at the United
Nations, which "providing it undergoes appropriate reform, remains the
most suitable framework to face the challenges posed by globalization."[51]
Indeed, the first articulation of the EU's foreign policy and security doctrine in 2003, which prepared the future evolution of the Union, required it
to embrace *'effective multilateralism.'* This has further increased the significance of the United Nations to the EU's international presence.[52] As Anne
Hamonic underlines, several common points unite the two organizations:
the desire to promote international peace and security but also, and more
certainly, the difficulties in implementing their ambitious plans.[53] This par-
allelism of forms and of efforts constitutes a natural link that ensures the
convergence of common interests.[54] As the common foreign and security
policy of the European Union becomes a daily reality, the activities of its
members in the UNSC increasingly take into account the EU dimension in
international security questions.[55]

The UN–EU relationship is a complex one where rules of law collide with political issues.[56] The CSDP has become the vector of the European Union's external action, whose influence outside its borders requires close collaboration with the world organization.[57]

As early as 1974, the European Community was granted observer status, in addition to its membership in most of the specialized agencies of the United Nations (Resolution 3208 of the United Nations General Assembly). Today, the European Union is represented in many conferences conducted under the aegis of the United Nations as a full member. Institutional cooperation between the two organizations is not neglected, as periodic meetings between representatives of the EU and the UN Secretary-General demonstrate.[58] The Union does not hide the importance of forging privileged links with the world organization, which partly explains its presence alongside the UN in a very wide range of activities.[59] The EU and the UN are thus combining their efforts in the areas of development cooperation, the fight against terrorism and cross-border crime, and sustainable development.

Despite the importance of the relationship between the two organizations, the European Union remains, for the time being, excluded from the collective security process, at least from the arena where decision-making takes place. Since 2011, the EU has secured an 'enhanced' observer status at the United Nations General Assembly (UNGA).[60] Thus, the EU can be invited to participate in the General Debate but it can also intervene and exercise the right of reply concerning EU positions.[61] This enhanced observer status allows the EU to present proposals or amendments as agreed by all Member States.[62] This change was likely the trigger that initiated the first calls for formal EU coordination in the future.

Although calls for the establishment of a permanent European seat within the UNSC have become more pressing in recent years, in particular due to Brexit, they are far from recent. In fact, they date back to the end of the 2000s, which corresponds with the establishment of the CSDP as well as the obtaining of the status of '*enhanced*' observer for the EU at the UN.[63] It seems, therefore, that it is part of a more general desire of the EU to assert itself as a leading player on the international scene.

To date, all proposals made by EU representatives in the UN must first be approved by all EU Member States.[64] The new status acquired in 2011 permits the Union to be inscribed on the list of speakers among representatives of major groups, meaning that EU representatives now can rank among the first speakers in UN discussions.[65] Nevertheless, the power of the EU within the UN remains limited since it cannot vote on or challenge UN resolutions and decisions, nor can it raise a point of order or put forward candidates in the UNGA.

Given the current role that the EU holds in the UN, it must be asked what the EU's motivations for obtaining a single seat on the UNSC are, beyond the normative and political power it would imply.

The new Belgian Ambassador to the United Nations, Marc Pecsteen de Buytswerve, provided a useful argument in an interview conducted in 2020. He first reminded us that in accordance with the provisions of the Lisbon Treaty, EU members have until now respected their commitment and have actively worked to coordinate the positions of EU members at the UN. He deplored, however, that such a prerogative was not or little applied within the framework of UNSC. But, for the Ambassador, the establishment of a permanent EU seat within the UNSC is mainly supported by the fact that regional representation had less chance for corruption and the pursuit of individual interests.

It seems that on many occasions the permanent members, including Europeans, have shown selfishness in their decision-making. The ambassador rejected such a possibility within the framework of a regional organization like the EU, which does not define its own interests at the expense of the views of others. Thus, for the Belgian ambassador, a permanent EU seat would not just strengthen the weight of the EU on the international scene, thereby making it an important global player, but it would also be part of a logical continuation toward a political construction of the EU that would above all return credibility to the UNSC, which has been considered obsolete or not representative of the realities of today. In other words, a reform of the composition of the UNSC would not just benefit both the EU and the UN but would, more broadly, strengthen the doctrine of multilateralism.

2.3 The Legal Constraint of an EU Permanent Seat at the UNSC

There is no doubt that a single EU seat in the UNSC is part of a medium-term strategy to strengthen the presence of Europe on the world stage. The departure of the United Kingdom from the European Union greatly increases France's responsibility toward its European partners to circulate information, as well as to express European concerns to other members of the Security Council. This element cannot be taken lightly. Nevertheless, from a legal point of view, the proposal presents a number of difficulties.

According to the UN Charter, only states can be members, and according to the EU Treaty, the common foreign policy cannot affect Members States' membership on the UNSC.[66] A variety of proposals have been made to circumvent this difficulty, all of which require imaginative suggestions for legal acrobatics. In strictly legal terms, there is indeed no ground for debate. Even the experts who have delved into the issue recognize the difficulty of the task. However, several alternative formulas are often considered to bypass the legal constraints and establish a permanent European seat on the UNSC.[67]

The first option would be to rely on the idea of the representativeness of regional groups within the UNSC.[68] Under the current United Nations Charter, it would appear that only states belonging to regional groupings may become Security Council nonpermanent members. Reference should be made to Article 23, para 1, and to the GA Resolution 1991-XVIII, which clearly stipulates regional groups for the SC electoral process.[69] But, for many, this resolution does not seem to coordinate with current realities. Indeed, dividing Europe between the West and the East no longer makes sense in the context of the EU. Merging these two subcategories into one then pre-prepares the path for a single representation of the EU at the UNSC.

The other option which appears the most obvious, and which is legally possible but politically difficult to achieve, is to set up an amending protocol allowing regional representation within the SC.[70] This would mean a Charter amendment. The protocol would have to be ratified by all UN members, a result difficult to achieve, especially if we take into account the latest developments within the UN in regards to the EU.[71] Indeed, before obtaining its observer status at the UN, the EU had requested the same representation rights – except voting rights – as full members. This proposal was rejected by a coalition of countries ranging from Australia to the Caribbean Community, which precisely demanded the same rights for other regional blocs.[72] This amendment presents, however, a number of advantages since it would not mend or abolish the veto right which would eventually enable the support of the permanent countries within the UNSC.

Finally, the UN could also take into account the specific nature of the EU, a one-of-a-kind organization in the world.[73] The United Nations could thus establish that the EU, because it has a certain number of competencies similar to a State, has the authority to implement UN resolutions and in particular those of the UNSC, in a number of fields.[74]

The prospect of granting a permanent seat on the UNSC to the European representation does not present only legal limits. It also raises political questions, and in particular on the nature and the balance of Franco-German relations. These relations were from the start at the heart of European construction and initiated many breakthroughs that have been beneficial for all European countries. Even though it has been subject to many crises and increasingly challenged by new players (new Eastern European members, for example), no better alternatives have emerged to replace the Franco-German *engine*.

3 European Construction at Risk? The Dysfunction and Imbalance of the Franco-German Engine as a Direct Consequence of a Permanent EU Seat at the UNSC

Franco-German relations are characterized by a density of exchanges and by an institutional network of governmental cooperation that is unique in the world.[75] This cooperation is underpinned by a standard of consultation and consensus-building on important international issues, especially in the field of European politics. This solid institutional base and the determination of the two countries to overcome their centuries-old conflict by inserting their bilateral relationship into a European framework have enabled them to become the cornerstone of European construction.[76] This comes with a dual function: that of initiating projects to deepen the integration or extension of its fields of action, and that of finding at the bilateral level compromise formulas acceptable by all member countries. Of course, this *'engine'* role in European construction has sometimes been a myth, but it has often turned out to be a *functional myth* for both countries and the European Union as a whole.[77]

The many cooperation initiatives between France and Germany have not prevented misunderstandings.[78] The two states have not always been able to hide and overcome their differences in political conception. In other words, the Franco-German engine evokes the political reality of Franco-German relations within the European project, but it also expresses more subjective geopolitical perceptions related to the history and projects of the two nations as well as their role at European and world levels.[79]

Underlying the notion of the Franco-German couple is a complex web of historically charged power relations.[80] The issue of the Franco-German relationship was first linked to internal power issues, that is to say, the balance of power between Germany and France. The desire for rapprochement between Germany and France stems from the historic rivalry between the two countries.[81] Bilateral rapprochement and the European integration project, in which Franco-German balance was sought, was the path chosen for its peaceful resolution. Indeed, the balance within the so-called couple has been based, particularly over the last few decades, on the principle that France's diplomatic-military power serves as a counterpoint to German economic superiority.[82] In order to understand how this balance was established and why it remains essential, a review of Franco-German relations over the last 50 years is necessary.

3.1 The Geopolitics of a Long-Standing Relationship

The contemporary dynamic between the two countries largely derives from the strategic conceptions of the first Franco-German couple: de Gaulle and Adenauer.[83] The two statesmen originated the contemporary Franco-German couple and its particular orientation vis-à-vis the European project.[84] This new stage in the rapprochement between Germany and France, on the model of a Europe of nations, offered an alternative and more strategic vision to the Franco-German reconciliation initiated by Robert Schuman and Konrad Adenauer under the leadership of Jean Monnet.[85] The Élysée treaty negotiated by de Gaulle and Adenauer, signed in 1963, aimed to bring together French and German visions on all strategic questions, in order to support each other mutually to gain geopolitical autonomy in the context of the Cold War.[86]

General de Gaulle's geopolitical visions of France and Adenauer's Germany did not completely coincide: the Gaullists wanted a close Franco-German relationship to balance both the Union of Soviet Socialist Republics and the USA.[87] They had a Eurocentric vision of the European project, while the Germans were more Atlanticists and wanted to link Europe with the USA.[88] They viewed Europe as an integrated subset of the Euro-Atlantic area. More generally, France and Germany, due to their respective histories, retained a different strategic culture.[89] On the one hand, Germany's approach is still affected by the aftermath of the Second World War.[90] The country remains extremely wary of any armed operation. Since reunification, it has tried to maintain a strategic culture based on multilateralism, supporting both the North Atlantic Treaty Organization (NATO) and European defense policies.[91] The German army must respect the limits imposed by a political order marked by a culture of distrust in the use of force, slowing down the number of foreign operations that the country can carry out.[92] The international ambition of the German state is almost nonexistent. Germany's priority remains in Europe.[93] Berlin cultivates the belief in peace ensured by the very existence of a European Community and shows little interest in its foreign policy. In a neo-realist approach, Germany primarily defends its own interests by developing strategic alliances.[94] Its foreign policy is thus based on two main principles: Western roots and a culture of restraint.[95] The construction of Europe was made with the German conviction that its role in the world should be limited to the economic, commercial, and, to a lesser extent, diplomatic fields.[96] The Germans have now achieved their goals since their surrender in 1945: German unification on equal terms with other states and the stabilization of their eastern flank.[97] This situation pushes the Germans to seek the *status quo*. Their objective today is to preserve this achievement which places them in a favorable geopolitical situation unprecedented since the creation of the first Reich under Bismarck.[98]

Germany's economic success and supremacy were particularly evident in the aftermath of reunification. The country emerged as an example to follow, with others keen to replicate its economic model.[99] Indeed, Germany benefits from multiple historical links with the East even if they are marked by terrible tragedies; is endowed with strong industrial resources; and represents the crucial goal of European construction of the twenty-first century, namely the insertion of the *other Europe* into international economic circuits.[100] Germany was able to establish such economic domination, in particular through the turn taken by European construction in the 1990s. At the end of the Second World War, Germany "had none of the trappings of great power status."[101] By the 1970s, it had become the undisputed economic locomotive of the European economy, such that economic interdependence turned to its advantage, notably in its bilateral relations with other European partners.[102]

For France, since the Napoleonic wars at the end of the nineteenth century, Germany has been the nation of reference.[103] Each victory or success of this country represents, for France, a moment of truth, highlighting its own shortcomings. The division of Germany from 1945 to 1990 partially masked this inferiority complex, but the fact remains that, throughout these decades, France, in the economic and monetary fields, endeavored to match Germany's economic performance with little success.[104] The unification of 1990 forced France to question the meaning and future of European construction, as well as the price to pay for Germany to remain, by its side, the engine of this process.[105] This examination of conscience was made, in particular, by the establishment of the single currency which was part of a French attempt to reestablish an equal relationship with Germany from a monetary point of view.[106] This episode proceeded to further widen the economic gap between the two countries.

Unlike Germany, however, France has always embraced the idea of playing a specific role in the international scene, and it is this diplomatic and military expertise that France brings to the engine of Europeanization.[107] France is the archetype of the sovereign state, established long before the Westphalian treaties of 1648.[108] This remains very important today: even if France is committed to European construction, the country doesn't want to merge into a federal state and intends to preserve diplomatic and military autonomy. France thinks of itself as a powerful and independent actor on the world stage.[109] Gaullism in its principles is somehow persistent in France's foreign policy.[110] The country has cultivated an obsession with its status, its rank, a form of *'greatness,'* in particular resulting from its colonial past.[111]

When European construction did accelerate, the European Economic Community, the ancestor of the EU, provided France with an additional instrument, strengthening its external action and broadening its influence.[112] At the same time, France retained all the attributes of its former glory: a permanent seat at the United Nations Security Council, an independent nuclear deterrent, and special links with sub-Saharan Africa and the Maghreb.

France's arguments for justifying its diplomatic superpower are effective. With more than 160 embassies around the world, its diplomatic network is the third most extensive, after that of the United States (168) and China (164) but far ahead of Germany (145) and the United Kingdom (148). France also justifies the strength of its political power on the international scene by its presence on almost all the continents of the world.[113] Thanks to its overseas departments scattered throughout the world, France has the second-largest exclusive economic zone in the world.[114] French remains the official language not only of most international institutions, from the UN to NATO, the International Criminal Court to the International Monetary Fund, but also of nearly 30 countries around the world.[115]

One of the key elements of French diplomacy, and which constitutes an essential element for our reflection, is *European construction*.[116] France seeks to establish the European project as one of peace, of reconciliation with the former brother-enemy Germany, of economic and social prosperity, and also of the emergence of a *'powerful Europe'* capable of multiplying French power.[117] It seems important to underline this French specificity since it reinforces our central argument that France is, in reality, a very good messenger of European construction. Its diplomatic action is not only meant to defend national interests but seeks to promote the European agenda on the international scene.[118] In this sense, Europeans would have every interest in trusting France as a permanent member of the UNSC to speak on their behalf.

3.2 The Franco-German Couple: A Marriage of Convenience That Must Be Preserved

Recent French efforts to strengthen its diplomatic and military domination were mainly initiated to counteract the shift in the center of gravity toward Germany and the East, notably in the early 2000s when several countries of the former Soviet bloc joined the Union.[119] France then accepted a deepening of the eurozone in exchange for increased European cooperation in defense matters.[120] This is how it became the second pillar of the Maastricht Treaty in 1992 and took the name of CSDP. Thus, since the end of the Second World War and until at least German reunification, Franco-German collaboration "has been based upon a delicate and shifting equilibrium between the two countries, according to which German economic supremacy was counterbalanced by French political influence."[121] Germany has often been presented as an economic giant but a political pygmy.[122] For its part, French policymakers have continued to feed the vestiges of France's status as a great power in order to strengthen its diplomatic and military power.[123] The events which led to German reunification and their aftermath undoubtedly have questioned the cohesion of the Franco-German relationship.[124] Nonetheless, as McCarthy shows, Germany and France are *doomed to partnership*.[125]

Even though the Franco-German balance is therefore not, strictly speaking, an institution, it's not just a simple transcription of facts either. This is a necessary balance which holds a lot of symbolism at several levels, from the national level of both countries to the European level and beyond the borders of Europe.

For the French, it is a question of linking Germany to the European project in an irremediable way, because the project is still, for some, the mark of French ascendancy in the aftermath of the Second World War.[126] Conversely, the European project is proof of the Western anchorage of the Germans and a means of increasing their influence without worrying about their partners.[127]

More broadly, the European project offered the possibility for Germany to recreate a positive identity in opposition to a dark collective memory. For its part, France has been able to maintain its role of great power.[128] In short, in addition to being at the initiative of the most significant advances in European construction, the Franco-German couple found in the latter more advantages than constraints that this same integration of the Union could underline.[129]

At the European level, the particular responsibility of the two countries toward the European project underlines the difference between the couple who arrogate to themselves a particular role. The Franco-German couple has, in fact, been built around European construction.[130] It has provided the two countries with a multilateral framework for the development of their relations.[131]

At the global level, the role of the model of peace between the two former rivals is a brand image intended to promote the model of European integration and strengthen its legitimacy vis-à-vis other global players.[132] The construction of the Franco-German couple is based on a break in the history of representations, including that of hereditary enemies.[133] The three Franco-German wars (1870, 1914–1918, 1939–1945) have given way to increased cooperation between the two belligerents since the 1950s.[134]

There is currently no credible alternative to this Franco-German axis. From a purely structuralist point of view, their geographical positions have allowed the Franco-German relationship to be placed at the top of the pyramid of power in the European project.[135] The Franco-German couple, in addition to their image of unity, has until today held an irreplaceably pivotal role between Northern and Southern Europe due to their economic, demographic, and political weight.[136] More abstractly, the couple represents a bridge between other European cultures: the Mediterranean basin and Central Europe, Latin, Germanic, and Slavic Europe. It was therefore the initial Franco-German differences that opened up to European compromises.[137] The Franco-German relationship functioned as a centripetal force when they agreed to oppose centrifugal forces in the European Union.

The Franco-German couple appears inevitably as the foundation of European integration. The events which have marked the construction of Europe bear witness to this observation. Indeed, the EU has never functioned so well as when the Franco-German couple was confined to its prerogatives and each party honored its part of the deal. The example of the relations between President Pompidou (1969–1974) and Chancellor Brandt (1969–1972) is a convincing example.[138] While the German Chancellor favored initiatives which were based on principles of social democracy, in particular in the sphere of social policy and upon integrationist principles in European policy (notably including the direct election of the European Parliament), Georges Pompidou subscribed clearly to the conservative line of his predecessor De Gaulle.[139] President Pompidou then turned his back on greater economic convergence with Germany to promote domestic growth. The differences in style between the two heads of state put the relationship under strain.[140] However, their individual awareness of the importance of the Franco-German relationship for the rest of Europe enabled them to initiate the most important European policy initiatives.

Conversely, differences in the role of each within the Franco-German couple have drastically slowed down European construction. Thus, the arrival in power of François Mitterrand provoked, at the outset, a cooling of relations between the two countries. President Mitterrand wanted a new rebalancing in European alliances and wanted to abandon the exclusivity of France's relations with Germany in favor of other countries such as Italy, Spain, and the United Kingdom.[141] Economically, Mitterrand's government rejected the German social-economic model. Mitterrand specifically rejected the implicit linkage of the Barre plan between convergence with German economic performance and internal economic modernization.[142] Instead, he favored a Keynesian approach in the early 1980s to reduce unemployment before taking the turn of austerity. The lack of coordination with European partners and in particular Germany did not allow it to impose its European-wide economic relaunch – in the form of the Chandernagor memorandum – which was blocked by an alliance between Thatcher and Schmidt.[143]

This concrete example shows the centrality of the Franco-German couple in any initiative in favor of European construction and the importance of the fragile balance which it implies: Germany as an economic power and France as a military and diplomatic power.[144] More recently, the differences between Germany and France on the issue of the eurozone, migrants, or even external relations with Russia, for example, have contributed to the accumulation of crises in the EU.[145] None of them could be resolved definitively, but are subject to precarious and temporary compromises due to growing disagreements.

As mentioned previously, the fall of the Berlin Wall and the enlargement of the European Union, through their geopolitical repercussions, had an impact on the foundations of the Franco-German relationship.[146] The political affirmation of a unified and economically dynamic Germany, with the loss of French influence, may have fueled fears about the fragile balance of the Franco-German couple. Many are, in fact, the experts who announced the divorce of the couple.[147] Without minimizing the past and present differences between the two countries or the challenges that await them in the context of increasing crises, the Franco-German relationship remains indeed essential to strengthening European construction.[148] In reality, the Franco-German couple became even more valued after reunification. In effect, this made it possible to contain Germany while safeguarding French influence.[149] Any threat to the Franco-German balance has been and continues to be fought with determination.[150] Even though experts argue that the balance has shifted in favor of Germany due to the shift of the center of gravity toward Central and Eastern Europe, this has not prevented the general maintenance of a privileged relationship between the two countries.[151] There may be less place for symbolism in the balance of power between Germany and France but it remains the cornerstone of European integration.[152]

It suffices to look at two recent events in European construction to understand why the Franco-German relationship is the one that keeps the EU on track and why there is no better alternative to date. In 2015, the Greek public debt crisis prompted clashes between France and Germany.[153]

On the one hand, France called to support Greece at any cost and feared an implosion of the eurozone while Greek citizens voted against the latest draft bailout in a referendum.[154] For its part, Germany warned against any unconditional debt write-off.[155] This opposition between the two European giants prevented a rapid and effective resolution of the conflict and weakened the cohesion of the whole eurozone.[156] Conversely, more recently, when it was a question of helping Italy hit hard by the COVID-19 crisis, France and Germany managed to put their differences aside.[157] They thus jointly defended a massive recovery plan which was accepted by all member countries.[158] Despite the initial and lively opposition of the Frugal 4 (Netherlands, Austria, Sweden, Denmark), the Franco-German engine has convinced and has shown once again that even if the Member States are organizing against it, it remains difficult to replace. The construction and maintenance of European integration consistently flounders without the support of the Franco-German couple.

More specifically, France, parallel to its loss of influence on the international scene since the end of the Cold War, has come to recognize the need to operate more through multilateral structures.[159] For its part, Germany has also in certain respects adopted a more independent foreign policy. The result of these opposing movements has been a convergence in favor of a greater European security and defense identity, still led by France.[160] From an economic point of view, France has been able to show its spirit of initiative, in particular by being the force behind the Economic Monetary Union, even if Germany has always been able to retain its advantage in this field.[161]

From the 2000s, Franco-German equilibrium can be best described as *one of asymmetrical interdependence.*[162] In other words, the Franco-German relationship has managed to adapt itself to challenging circumstances and has withstood the test of time. Its internal equilibrium has shifted, and yet it has become somehow convergent as the economic and security issues of post-Cold War Europe become apparent.[163] Thus, it is no coincidence that Berlin's efforts, in the case of the UNSC permanent seat but also on various defense-related issues, aim to diminish or even eliminate France's relative advantages in order to change this *rapport de force.*[164] The Europeanization of French trump cards would, in fact, tip the balance in Germany's favor and would undoubtedly participate in the return of a hegemonic power within the European scene.[165]

This might seem to Berlin as a worthy goal; on several occasions, German leaders have brushed aside these allegations by reaffirming Germany's profoundly European and democratic character as well as its attachment to multilateralism as a principle.[166] What is certain is that such a transformation would not be in the best interest of the EU as a whole. On the contrary, it would simultaneously lead to the weakening of the EU's role at the UN and therefore on the international stage, and the strengthening of internal divergences within the EU which could result in a lack of coherence and credibility on geostrategic issues for the Union.

4 The Boomerang Effect of an EU Permanent Seat at the UNSC: A Weaker EU on the International Scene and Exacerbation of Internal Differences

4.1 The Interconnected Threads of the Interaction between Domestic and Foreign Politics in Europe. The EU's Internal and International Identity at Stake.

The objective of strengthening the EU's position at the UN and in its bodies is part of a logical and pragmatic approach. Indeed, the EU is a regional organization that wants to be the message-bearer in favor of multilateralism and the UN appears as an ideal forum for this fight.[167] Likewise, many of the EU's key foreign policy goals require a certain level of engagement with the UN system.[168] And for many Member States, it has become evident that in a changing international environment with the ascendancy of new countries in international politics, the relevance of the EU at the UN could mean a better way to collectively raise their international clout.[169] But behind this goal, which is entirely desirable for European interests, lie deep internal differences between the Member States which affect not only the credibility and the effectiveness of the bloc's foreign policy but also its stability and the model that the EU seeks to promote.

Historically speaking, there is often a positive correlation between the degree of the EU's external effectiveness and its internal cohesiveness.[170] The more the EU expresses itself with a single voice without the Member States protesting, the more the bloc is able to ensure its sustainability and achieve its objectives on the international scene. This correlation was particularly observed during European negotiations with weaker actors since *cohesiveness shows resolve and strength*.[171] But it is also applicable to stronger players, especially the United States and China. For example, in the recent solar panels trade dispute between the EU and China, low internal cohesiveness between Member States weakened the Union's position vis-à-vis its Chinese counterpart.[172] When the European Commission threatened to impose tariffs on solar panels, the Chinese government turned its back on the Commission and preferred to negotiate directly with Germany, which, with the support of a dozen other countries, sided with China. This attitude not only undermined the authority of the Commission but also rekindled the internal tensions of the bloc between the partisans of a rapprochement with China and the countries defending a firm position.[173] The bloc's lack of cohesion on international issues is exploited by the competitors of the European Union who see it as a way of weakening the EU in negotiations.

This is the same logic that underpinned the Belt and Road Initiative (BRI), China's intercontinental economic program. When Italy decided in 2019 to approve BRI-linked agreements, Giuseppe Conte's government was accused of threatening European unity.[174] For Italy, it was mainly a question of asserting its national independence from the EU and some dominant states, especially Germany.[175] Italy's government coalition also saw an opportunity to reopen certain EU issues where it feels it has been strongly disadvantaged by a Berlin-dominated union.[176] Topics of tension included migration, budget rules, and potentially monetary policy – a prospect that the EU did not want to see the light of day because it could literally break the bloc apart.[177] All the more so since the EU does not have the effective mechanisms to settle disputes between Member States, which may push them to resort to external actors, including China, Russia, and the United States, to challenge the status quo.[178] These examples show the interconnectivity between a low degree of internal cohesiveness and the EU's effectiveness when negotiating with a powerful actor and especially how internal cohesiveness is necessary for the EU to be externally effective.

One can find these same problems with the presence of the EU within the institutions of the UN, which makes us doubt the feasibility of a permanent European seat. Indeed, while Germany strives for a permanent seat in the SC, "Italy (...) prefers to support an increase in non-permanent members with the possibility of immediate re-election or a category of non-permanent members with a longer mandate."[179] Behind this opposition, Italy does not want to be the only great European power that does not benefit from a permanent seat at the UNSC.[180] This divergence of positions between Germany and Italy highlights once again one of the major weaknesses of possible allocation of a permanent seat to the EU, namely the inability of the Union to formulate a common position on major foreign policy issues.[181] Even if Italy and Germany agree on a European seat, in the long run, major contradictions persist in such a recommendation in light of their initial oppositions: who will be at the head of the European delegation to the UNSC?

Furthermore, the supposed improvements of the Treaty of Lisbon have not really borne fruit.[182] The international upheavals of the last 20 years have shown that European states have not been able to present common foreign policy positions, in part because military activities continue to fall under national competences.[183] Military intervention remains optional and national troop contributions to bloc-sanctioned interventions remain voluntary.[184] The absence of a provision requiring military unanimity does not allow the EU to present a common position on the war in Syria or against the increasing specter of Russia. European countries are not able to be on the same page either because they do not share the same objective and analysis, or because they do not all agree to defend their common position in case of divergence with the United States.[185] Granting the EU a permanent seat on the UNSC would therefore not only face strong opposition from other candidates but above all would participate in strengthening already existing internal divergences within the EU.

Another element put forward to oppose such a reform consists in taking a stand against an argument often used by defenders of a European seat, namely the persuasive force that a single European voice would have in the UNSC. In fact, it would participate more in the weakening of the EU's role at the UN and therefore on the international stage. It is important to remember that the objective here is not to wholly discredit the idea of having a permanent European seat at the UNSC. Indeed, I am convinced that in the long term it can be a desirable and logical goal for the EU and all Member States. The goal is, above all, to highlight that the realities of European construction on the international scene are not at present up to the ambition of such a project. Important structural limits persist, such as a lack of cohesion in the bloc. They must be overcome before a permanent European seat in the UNSC can be considered, while other temporary alternatives can be favored in the meantime to strengthen the European presence on the international scene.

4.2 One Voice Does Not Equal a Choir

In an interview, Belgian Ambassador to the UN Mr. Pecsteen de Buytswerve talked about the importance of the UNSC as the UN's main decision-making body. He then proposed two reforms to this essential body. First, and foremost, the veto power should be reformed so that it could no longer be abused by individual permanent members. The Belgian Ambassador suggested incorporating limitations like requiring vetoes from two permanent members in order for it to be valid, or for several elected members to have a joint veto power. Second, Mr. Pecsteen de Buytswerve emphasized the need to have a coalition of countries to defend and block ideas. He was clearly in favor of regional representation in the UNSC. Indeed, taking the example of the Republic of South Africa wanting a permanent seat, the ambassador questioned the impact that such a candidacy would have on the African representative on the UNSC. For him, it is better to turn to a regional organization that has to be representative of the whole regional group like the African Union. Besides being less concerned with corruption and self-interest, regional organizations would represent the positions of multiple countries more effectively.

The arguments of the ambassador are not necessarily shared by all European policymakers. Christopher Patten, former European Commissioner for External Relations, affirmed that European countries were mistaken in wanting to have a permanent seat reserved for the EU in the Security Council. Indeed, instead of absolutely wanting to *speak with one voice*, their efforts should focus on having a multitude of seats – permanent and nonpermanent ones.[186] Patten justifies his argument by explaining that "we get more attention and better effect if we sing to the same song sheet."[187] Patten's argument holds up especially if we look again at the composition of the UNSC. Europe has at least four seats on the Security Council. For the period 2019–2020, the European countries represented in the UNSC included France, the United Kingdom, Germany, Belgium, and Estonia. One remark is that Europe is not limited to the EU and, according to the

Belgian Ambassador to the UN, European countries are very like-minded on about 99% of issues. Even with Brexit, the United Kingdom likely would still align with other European countries on potential changes in tactics (veto power) and negotiation. It is the remaining 1% consisting of differing views and sensibilities which could prevent the EU from having a clear and common position on geopolitical issues. It is thus easier to have several seats in the Security Council and to try to establish a consensus to counterbalance the positions of countries like Russia or China.[188]

It should also be recalled that European diplomacy has been forged in recent years, and in particular since the establishment of the Lisbon Treaty, on the basis of strengthening its relations with key partners.[189] With this in mind, the EU initiated discussions with Canada on a new free trade agreement.[190] However, the relationship between the two stakeholders is not only economic as Canada engages with the EU *on matters of wider global interest*.[191] Both are members of NATO and participants in foreign policy dialogues. The question of Afghanistan is considered, for example, essential to their cooperation, and Canada and the EU are trying to agree on their positions.[192] In the same logic, the EU is trying to develop a coherent foreign policy with its partners in Southeast Asia to become an effective interlocutor in the region.[193] Thus, European countries would gain more by first strengthening their cooperation with their international partners – like Canada, Japan, India, Africa – to have the most weight in the UN General Assembly but also in the UNSC, which could counterbalance the veto right of the permanent members.

4.3 The Real Issue: The Lack of Cooperation between EU Member States

Although with the ratification of the Lisbon Treaty in 2007 the EU hoped to become an actor with a coherent foreign policy on the international scene, [194] this objective is difficult to achieve today, particularly within the UN. What is detrimental to European diplomacy in international institutions is not its lack of representativeness but its inability to develop common positions. Despite the fact that EU Member States can often be incoherent at the UNGA, the EU remains the only regional organization that "can increase its level of voting cohesion in contested votes."[195] In the UNSC, EU performance is a mixed picture since "the EU Member States participate effectively but arguably not so efficiently in the shaping of UNSC activities."[196]

Therefore, why grant the EU such power, despite its status as a major economic and political actor, if it is not capable of presenting common positions on all subjects? The reform of the Security Council should go in the direction of simplifying procedures, not complicating them.[197] By comparing the EU to six other organizations – the African Union, Arab League, Association of Southeast Asian Nations (ASEAN), Caribbean Community

(CARICOM), Economic Community of West African States (ECOWAS), and Mercosur – it has been shown that "when a cohesive vote by the EU is unlikely to change the outcome of a resolution, the EU seems to put little effort in its coordination process."[198] In this case, Member States differ from the EU's majority position. More concretely, this means that if a nearly unanimous vote is expected, EU Member States are "more likely to follow their specific national interest, even if this is in contrast to the majority position of the EU."[199] There is a dichotomy between small and large EU countries in the way they vote.[200] For example, findings show that EU resolutions concerning conflicts in the Middle East often lead to a solid voting cohesion while resolutions on nuclear weapons and colonialism are met with a strong decrease in voting cohesion.[201] The EU shows a high level of voting cohesion on contested votes while internal divergences may be greater than in other regional organizations if there is overall a huge majority within the UNGA. Thus, the path taken by the EU for defending a common position within international organizations seems to be the right one, as it allows states to periodically 'go their own way' without impacting overall consensus.

The EU's problem of coherence is not limited only to the General Assembly. It also and above all concerns the UNSC. Indeed, if one takes into account the resources allocated to the UNSC by, for instance, France and the United Kingdom, we can conclude that in the majority of cases these resources have been invested in efforts to safeguard Member States' privileged positions.[202] Otherwise, resources have been mobilized to pursue national priorities, as in the case of Germany, or to undermine other EU partners' political aspirations, as in the case of Italy or Spain.[203] In this sense, the "EU performance record is very poor."[204] Even if improvements are to be noted which can "testify to the growing relevance of the EU for its Member States as a means to ascertain collectively their international clout in the context of a changing international environment," we are far from an ideal and effective cooperation.[205]

These actions continue to chip away at the coherence of EU foreign policy, which undermines the EU's claim to a permanent seat. Moreover, even though the differences between EU Member States within the framework of the UNSC resolutions may be considered marginal by some, the EU is not even capable of proposing a common position on a reform of the UNSC.[206] By causal effect, "the Member States' different status in the UN system and their diverging political aspirations predispose against such a uniform approach."[207] The establishment of a permanent European seat at the UNSC undoubtedly occupies an essential place in the debates for reform, but this idea is not shared by all the Member States. This makes it difficult to set up in the short- to medium-term and should, on the contrary, encourage us for the moment to pay more attention to the mechanisms that have been set in place with the Lisbon Treaty.[208] A self-evaluation would then lead to adjustments, which in turn would allow better cohesion and a collective EU presence in the UNSC.

5 Conclusion

Requests to reform the UNSC accelerated in the aftermath of the Cold War in order to reflect new international developments. However, little actual progress has been achieved thus far. The blockage of reforms is explained, in large part, not only by the multiplicity of national interests involved but also by the need to keep a balance between representation, legitimacy, and efficiency, in compliance with the rules laid down by the UN Charter.

These reflections and debates around the UNSC coincided with the beginning of the establishment of a proper EU foreign policy. Indeed, it was during this period that the Union began to equip itself with the tools, notably with the Maastricht Treaty, to make its voice heard on the international scene. Quickly, the UN, one of whose main objectives is the promotion of multilateralism, appeared as an essential ally and an ideal platform for Europeans. The United Nations Security Council also appears to be an object of envy for the EU, both for the power it confers – undoubtedly the only effective body of the UN – and for its members. Indeed, it is the only body in which the three other great powers sit – the United States, China, and Russia. To obtain a seat for the EU would mean that it is on an equal footing with them and that it has become an indisputable player in global affairs.

However, between the European construction which was marked by several failures during the 2000s and the deep internal differences between the Member States, the European Union has not managed to present a common front on all geopolitical issues. These weaknesses have been used by its adversaries, in particular, to challenge the EU's legitimacy to have a permanent seat at the UNSC. Even worse, the Europeans until now do not seem to agree on the most appropriate reform to improve the representativeness of the EU within the UN institutions. While there has long been a question of supporting the German candidacy for a permanent seat, this proposal has been received with reluctance by Member States like Italy, which pushes more for an EU seat. In the end, Germany expressed itself in favor of such a seat only if France abandoned its own. Disorders still persist within the EU over such a proposal.

Beyond the impossibility for the EU to acquire a permanent European seat due to the legal limits of the UN Charter, I argue that this proposal, although interesting and ambitious on paper, is not desirable at present. Instead of serving the interests of the EU, it would, in reality, contribute to the dysfunction and imbalance of the Franco-German engine essential to the European construction, the weakening of the EU's role at the UN and therefore on the international scene, and the strengthening of internal divergences within the EU which could end up leading to a lack of coherence and credibility on geostrategic issues for the Union. In other words, the EU would not have an interest in pursuing such an objective for the moment because of the major political problems that this could create or reinforce.

If we agree that the proposal to have a European seat at the United Nations Security Council is neither feasible nor desirable at this moment, it would be reasonable to ask about possible alternatives to strengthen the European Union's presence at the UN, including in the Security Council.

One of the possible avenues is, of course, to maintain the status quo. The current situation has more advantages than the proposal. Indeed, it is important to remember that the European Treaties already commit Member States to defend common EU positions inside the Security Council. There cannot be unity without trust. Thus, it seems essential that Member States maintain their support for France in its ability to best defend European interests at the United Nations Security Council.

One could rightly wonder why other European states should trust France to best represent their interests in the UN. Several arguments point in this direction. First, European cooperation is a central axis of modern French diplomacy. France is aware that the EU is the best way to defend the interests and security of its citizens while strengthening the assertion of European sovereignty in the world. In short, France presents itself as the best possible spokesperson for the EU. This is a win-win game since, on the one hand, the EU sees its interests defended and represented on the international scene thanks to one of its founding Member States and, on the other, France knows that it needs the multiplying power of Europe to keep playing a major role on the international scene.

Second, despite a few rare exceptions, France has so far respected its European commitments established through various treaties and continues to consult its partners before each UNSC meeting to coordinate their responses. The French government has also been the investigator of several initiatives on the European presence at the UNSC. One can think in particular of the dual presidency in 2019 and 2020 with Germany – a first in the history of the UN and which once again underlines France's absolute commitment to the EU. In other words, France's record speaks for itself and should be convincing for skeptical Europeans.

Finally, it is important to remember that France does not per se oppose reform of the UNSC. On the contrary, the country is rather favorable to it and militates actively for the integration of Germany within this institution as a permanent member. France is in favor of a reform that makes sense and could materialize quickly, without major legal constraints, which is not the case when it comes to an EU permanent seat at the UNSC. Indeed, the possibility of a permanent German seat on the UNSC is a sound one, as it would open the way to more European representativeness and would benefit the interests of the EU even more.

In fact, this idea could be a real first step in strengthening the European presence at the UNSC. If it proves to be a success, this provision could be extended, for example, to the other Member States of the European Union. Thus, such proposals would allow Europe to win more seats in the Council and therefore better influence negotiations and decisions while dealing with the United States, Russia, or China.

But it is important to remember that the United Nations and especially the United Nations Security Council are places of high power politics. Alliances remain essential in order to tackle the challenges of the twenty-first century, from global warming to cybersecurity to the fight against terrorism. Europe, even if it finds itself in numerical superiority in these institutions, cannot do all the work alone. In order to have a strong Europe inside the United Nations that is able to carry important messages on the international scene, it is necessary for the EU to continue to develop its relations with countries that share the same values. In this sense, strengthening transatlantic relations or working closely with countries like Japan and India should be the European Union's priority at the UN, rather than the unrealistic pursuit of a single EU seat in the UNSC.

Notes

1 Jacques Pezet, "Que prévoit vraiment le traité d'Aix-la-Chapelle?" *Libération*, January 18, 2019.
2 "Donner le siège de la France à l'ONU à l'Europe? «Stupide» (Le Drian)", *Le Figaro*, March 29, 2019.
3 Pezet, "Que prévoit vraiment le traité d'Aix-la-Chapelle?"
4 Ibid.
5 Charles de Gaulle and Konrad Adenauer signed the Élysée Treaty in 1963. At the time, this founding text made it possible to set a pattern of meetings and exchanges between France and Germany of symbolic and functional nature. The signing of the Treaty of Aachen then made it possible to update this cooperation in order to better meet the challenges, no longer of the post-war era, but of the twenty-first century.
6 Anne Hamonic, *Les relations entre l'Union européenne et l'ONU dans le domaine de la gestion des crises* (Bruxelles: Bruylant, 2018).
7 Ibid.
8 The main legal obstacle would be that membership is principally reserved for nation states, with the subsequent exclusion of regional organizations. In addition, the permanent members of the Security Council are determined by the UN Charter, and amending it would be politically inconceivable. Spyrous Bavoukos and Dimitrios Bourantonis, *The EU in UN Politics. Actors, Processes and Performances* (London: Palgrave Macmillan, 2017).
9 Hajnalka Vincze, "One Voice, But Whose Voice? Should France Cede Its UN Security Council Seat to the EU?" *The Foreign Policy Research Institute*, March 20, 2019.
10 For instance, several countries came together, in the nineteenth century, to form the International Telegraph Union. At the time, this union had to reflect the requirements to adapt to technological innovations and market forces pushing for modernization of media. See Thomas G. Weiss, "The United Nations: Before, During and After 1945," *The Royal Institute of International Affairs* 91, no. 6 (2015): 1222.
11 Ibid, 1221.
12 Alexandra Novosseloff, "L'élargissement du Conseil de sécurité : enjeux et perspectives," *Relations Internationales* 128: , no. 4 (2006),): 3.

13 Spyros Blavoukos and Dimitrios Bourantonis, "The EU's Performance in the United Nations Security Council," *Journal of European Integration*, 33, no. 6 (2011): 731.
14 Gary Wilson, *The United Nations and Collective Security* (Routledge, 2014) 1st Edition, 29.
15 Ibid, 26.
16 Ibid, 5.
17 Pierre Desenaclens, *La Crise des Nations Unies* (Paris: Presses Universitaires de France, 1988), 53.
18 Wilson, *The United Nations,* 60.
19 Ibid, 23.
20 Wilson, *The United Nations,* 87.
21 Ibid, 87.
22 Joachim Krause and Natalino Ronzitti, *The EU, the UN and Collective Security. Making Multilateralism Effective* (Routledge, 2012), 136.
23 Ibid, 136.
24 Ghali Boutros, "An Agenda for Peace: Preventive Diplomacy, Peacemaking and Peacekeeping," in *Repertoire of the Practice of the Security Council* (United Nations, 1992), 765. https://www.un.org/en/sc/repertoire/89-92/Chapter%208/GENERAL%20ISSUES/Item%2029_Agenda%20for%20peace_.pdf.
25 Maximilian B. Rasch, *The European Union at the United Nations: The Functioning and Coherence of EU External Representation in a State-centric Environment* (Brill Academic Publishers, 2008), 2.
26 Ibid, 2.
27 Ibid, 1.
28 Nota bene: *Most of the research work from this chapter was conducted before the official withdrawal of the United Kingdom from the European Union and the signature EU–UK Trade and Cooperation Agreement (1 January 2021)*
29 Federiga Bindi and Irina Angelescu, *The Foreign Policy of the European Union: Assessing Europe's Role in the World* (Brookings Institution Press, 2012), Second Edition, 11.
30 Ibid, 16.
31 Ibid, 16.
32 Ibid, 22.
33 Ibid, 25.
34 Ibid, 25.
35 Jean-Marie Guéhenno, *The European Union and the United Nations: Partners in Effective Multilateralism* (Paris: The European Union Institute for Security Studies, 2005), 7.
36 Consolidated version of the Treaty on the Functioning of the European Union. 2012. *EUR-Lex. European Union Law.* https://eur-lex.europa.eu/legal-content/EN/TXT/?uri=CELEX%3A12012E%2FTXT.
37 Bindi and Angelescu, *The Foreign Policy of the European Union,* 25.
38 Xi Jin and Madeleine O. Hosli, "Pre-and Post-Lisbon: European Union Voting in the United Nations General Assembly", *West European Politics* 36, no. 6 (2013): 1277.
39 Ibid, 1277.
40 Ibid, 1277.
41 Bindi and Angelescu, *The Foreign Policy of the European Union,* 41.
42 Ibid, 41.
43 Jin and Hosli, "Pre-and Post-Lisbon: European Union Voting," 1274
44 Ibid, 1274.
45 Ibid, 1277.
46 Ibid, 1277.

47 Ibid, 1278.
48 Ibid, 1279.
49 Nicoletta Pirozzi and Natalino Ronzitti, *The European Union and the Reform of the UN Security Council: Toward a New Regionalism?* (Istituto Affari Internazionali, 2011), 16.
50 Ibid, 16.
51 Hamonic, *Les relations entre l'Union européenne*, 24.
52 Spyros Blavoukos and Dimitrios Bourantonis, *The EU in UN Politics: Actors, Processes and Performances.* (London: Palgrave Macmillan, 2017), 1.
53 Hamonic, *Les relations entre l'Union européenne*, 25.
54 Ibid, 25.
55 Ibid, 25.
56 Blavoukos and Bourantonis, *The EU in UN Politics*, 1.
57 Ibid, 1.
58 Ibid, 2.
59 Hamonic, *Les relations entre l'Union européenne*.
60 Jin and Hosli, "Pre-and Post-Lisbon: European Union Voting," 1277.
61 Ibid, 1277.
62 Ibid, 1278.
63 "There is a Seat on the UN Security Council for the European Union – The French Seat," Rick Denny, Global Policy Forum, December 22, 2010.
64 Jan Wouters and Matthieu Burnay, "The EU and Asia in the United Nations Security Council," *SSN* (2011), https://papers.ssrn.com/sol3/papers.cfm?abstract_id=2020332.
65 Wouters and Burnay, "The EU and Asia in the United Nations Security Council."
66 Pirozzi and Ronzitti, *The European Union and the Reform of the UN Security Council*, 8.
67 Ibid 10.
68 Ibid, 10.
69 Ibid, 10.
70 Pirozzi and Ronzitti, *The European Union and the Reform of the UN Security Council*, 1.
71 Ibid, 11.
72 Ibid, 12.
73 Ibid, 12.
74 Ibid, 12.
75 Carine Germond and Henning Türk, *A History of Franco-German Relations in Europe: From "Hereditary Enemies" to Partners* (Palgrave Macmillan, 2008), 1.
76 Ibid, 165.
77 Ibid, 263.
78 Alistair Cole, *Franco-German Relations (Political Dynamics of the European Union)*, (Routledge, 2001), 104.
79 Germond and Türk, *A History of Franco-German Relations in Europe*, 1.
80 Ulrich Krotz and Joachim Schild, *Shaping Europe: France, Germany, and Embedded Bilateralism from the Elysée Treaty to Twenty-First Century Politics* (Oxford: Oxford University Press, 2012).
81 Germond and Türk, *A History of Franco-German Relations in Europe*, 151.
82 Vincze, "One Voice, But Whose Voice?"
83 Germond and Türk, *A History of Franco-German Relations in Europe*, 151.
84 Ibid, 151.
85 Ibid, 151.
86 Krotz and Schild, *Shaping Europe*.
87 Germond and Türk, *A History of Franco-German Relations in Europe*, 151.
88 Ibid, 151.

89 Cole, *Franco-German Relations,* 165.
90 Helga Haftendorn, *Coming of Age: German Foreign Policy Since 1945* (Rowman & Littlefield Publishers, 2006).
91 Ibid.
92 Ibid.
93 Ibid.
94 Ibid.
95 Haftendorn, *Coming of Age.*
96 Ibid.
97 Ibid.
98 Ibid.
99 Ibid.
100 Ibid.
101 Cole, *Franco-German Relations,* 14.
102 Ibid, 14.
103 Germond and Türk, *A History of Franco-German Relations in Europe,* 13.
104 Ibid, 89.
105 Ibid, 235.
106 Ibid, 235.
107 Philip H. Gordon, *A Certain Idea of France* (Princeton: Princeton University Press, 1993).
108 Ibid.
109 Frédéric Bozo, *French Foreign Policy since 1945: An Introduction* (Berghahn Books, 2016).
110 Gordon, *A Certain Idea of France.*
111 Ibid.
112 Ibid.
113 Bozo, *French Foreign Policy since 1945,* 1.
114 Ibid.
115 Ibid.
116 Gordon, *A Certain Idea of France.*
117 Germond and Türk, *A History of Franco-German Relations in Europe,* 211.
118 Bozo, *French Foreign Policy since 1945,* 151.
119 Krotz and Schild, *Shaping Europe.*
120 Cole, *Franco-German Relations,* 165.
121 Ibid, 17.
122 Ibid, 17.
123 Ibid, 17.
124 Cole, *Franco-German Relations,* 18.
125 Ibid, 16.
126 Krotz and Schild, *Shaping Europe.*
127 Ibid.
128 Cole, *Franco-German Relations,* 4.
129 Ibid, 4.
130 Germond and Türk, *A History of Franco-German Relations in Europe,* 165.
131 Cole, *Franco-German Relations,* 4.
132 Krotz and Schild, *Shaping Europe.*
133 Germond and Türk, *A History of Franco-German Relations in Europe,* 113.
134 Ibid, 166
135 Krotz and Schild, *Shaping Europe.*
136 Ibid.
137 Germond and Türk, *A History of Franco-German Relations in Europe,* 166.
138 Cole, *Franco-German Relations,* 15.
139 Ibid, 15.

140 Ibid, 15.
141 Ibid, 16.
142 Cole, *Franco-German Relations*, 16.
143 Ibid, 16.
144 Ibid, 16.
145 Krotz and Schild, *Shaping Europe*.
146 Ibid.
147 Ibid.
148 Ibid.
149 Krotz and Schild, *Shaping Europe*.
150 Cole, *Franco-German Relations*, 20.
151 Ibid, 21.
152 Ibid, 21.
153 Marcus Waler, Inti Landaure, and Andrew Ackerman, "France Supports Greece in EU Debt Battle". *The Wall Street Journal*, February 1, 2015.
154 Ibid.
155 Ibid.
156 Ibid.
157 Antonio De Lecea, "EU deal is a win-win for all sides," *Atlantic Council* (blog), July 22, 2020, https://www.atlanticcouncil.org/blogs/new-atlanticist/eu-deal-is-a-win-win-for-all-sides/.
158 Ibid.
159 Cole, *Franco-German Relations*, 126.
160 Ibid, 126.
161 Ibid, 103.
162 Ibid, 152.
163 Ibid, 152.
164 Vincze, "One Voice, But Whose Voice?"
165 Vincze, "One Voice, But Whose Voice?"
166 Cole, *Franco-German Relations*, 21.
167 *The United Nations and the European Union: An Ever Stronger Partnership*, eds. Jan Wouters, Frank Hoffmeister, and Tom Ruys (T.M.C. Asser Press, 2006), 4.
168 Ibid, 4.
169 Blavoukos and Bourantonis, *The EU in UN Politics*, 738.
170 Eugénia Da Conceição-Heldt and Sophie Meunier, "Speaking with a Single Voice: Internal Cohesiveness and External Effectiveness of the EU in Global Governance," *Journal of European Public Policy* 21, no. 7 (2014): 971.
171 Ibid, 971.
172 Ibid, 972.
173 Ibid, 972.
174 Bruno Maçães, "China's Italian Advance Threatens EU Unity," *Nikkei Asia*, March 25, 2019, https://asia.nikkei.com/Opinion/China-s-Italian-advance-threatens-EU-unity.
175 Ibid.
176 Ibid.
177 Ibid.
178 Ibid.
179 Pirozzi and Ronzitti, *The European Union and the Reform of the UN Security Council*, 1.
180 Ibid, 1.
181 Ibid, 1.
182 Bindi and Angelescu, *The Foreign Policy of the European Union*, 1.

183 Ibid, 217.
184 Ibid, 217.
185 Ibid, 216.
186 Vincze, "One Voice, But Whose Voice?"
187 Ibid.
188 Marc De Buytswerve Pecsteen, "Discussion with the Belgian Representation at the United Nations," interview by Columbia University students in the Global Thought Program, 2019/2020.
189 Bindi and Angelescu, *The Foreign Policy of the European Union,* 215, 237, and 247.
190 Ibid, 237.
191 Ibid, 253.
192 Ibid, 253.
193 Ibid, 270.
194 Ibid, 270.
195 Nicolas Burmester and Michael Jankowski, "Reassessing the European Union in the United Nations General Assembly", *Journal of European Public Policy,* 21, no. 10 (2014): 1491.
196 Blavoukos and Bourantonis, *The EU in UN Politics,* 742.
197 Ibid.
198 Burmester and Jankowski, "Reassessing the European Union in the United Nations General Assembly", 1508.
199 Ibid, 1508.
200 Ibid, 1508.
201 Ibid, 1498.
202 Blavoukos and Bourantonis, *The EU in UN Politics,* 742.
203 Ibid, 742.
204 Ibid, 742.
205 Blavoukos and Bourantonis, *The EU in UN Politics,* 742.
206 Ibid, 738.
207 Ibid, 738.
208 Ibid, 739.

Bibliography

Bindi, Federiga and Irina Angelescu. *The Foreign Policy of the European Union: Assessing Europe's Role in the World.* Washington, DC: Brookings Institution Press, 2012.

Blavoukos, Spyros, and Dimitrios Bourantonis. "The EU's Performance in the United Nations Security Council." *Journal of European Integration* 33, no. 6 (2011): 731.

Blavoukos, Spyrous, and Dimitrios Bourantonis. *The EU in UN Politics. Actors, Processes and Performances.* London: Palgrave Macmillan, 2017.

Boutros, Ghali. "An Agenda for Peace: Preventive Diplomacy, Peacemaking and Peacekeeping." *Repertoire of the Practice of the Security Council.* United Nations, 1992. https://www.un.org/en/sc/repertoire/89-92/Chapter%208/GENERAL%20ISSUES/Item%2029_Agenda%20for%20peace_.pdf

Bozo, Frédéric. *French Foreign Policy Since 1945: An Introduction.* New York: Berghahn Books, 2016.

Burmester, Nicolas, and Michael Jankowski. "Reassessing the European Union in the United Nations General Assembly." *Journal of European Public Policy* 21, no. 10 (2014): 1491.

Cole, Alistair. *Franco-German Relations (Political Dynamics of the European Union)*. Abingdon and New York: Routledge, 2001.

Consolidated version of the Treaty on the Functioning of the European Union. 2012. *EUR-Lex. European Union Law.* https://eur-lex.europa.eu/legal-content/EN/TXT/?uri=CELEX%3A12012E%2FTXT

De Buytswerve Pecsteen, Marc. "Discussion with the Belgian Representation at the United Nations." Interview by Columbia University students in the Global Thought Program, 2019/2020.

Da Conceição-Heldt, Eugénia, and Sophie Meunier. "Speaking with a Single Voice: Internal Cohesiveness and External Effectiveness of the EU in Global Governance." *Journal of European Public Policy* 21, no. 7 (2014): 971.

De Lecea, Antonio. "EU Deal is a Win-Win for all Sides." *Atlantic Council* (blog), July 22, 2020. https://www.atlanticcouncil.org/blogs/new-atlanticist/eu-deal-is-a-win-win-for-all-sides/.

Desenaclens, Pierre. *La Crise des Nations Unies*. Paris: Presses Universitaires de France, 1988.

"Donner le siège de la France à l'ONU à l'Europe? «Stupide» (Le Drian)." *Le Figaro*, March 29, 2019.

Germond, Carine, and Henning Türk. *A History of Franco-German Relations in Europe: From "Hereditary Enemies" to Partners*. New York: Palgrave Macmillan, 2008.

Gordon, Philip H. *A Certain Idea of France*. Princeton: Princeton University Press, 1993.

Guéhenno, Jean-Marie. *The European Union and the United Nations: Partners in Effective Multilateralism*. Paris: The European Union Institute for Security Studies, 2005.

Haftendorn, Helga. *Coming of Age: German Foreign Policy Since 1945*. Lanham: Rowman & Littlefield Publishers, 2006.

Hamonic, Anne. *Les relations entre l'Union européenne et l'ONU dans le domaine de la gestion des crises*. Bruxelles: Bruylant, 2018.

Jin, Xi, and Madeleine O. Hosli. "Pre-and Post-Lisbon: European Union Voting in the United Nations General Assembly." *West European Politics* 36, no. 6 (2013): 1277.

Krause, Joachim, and Natalino Ronzitti. *The EU, the UN and Collective Security. Making Multilateralism Effective*. London: Routledge, 2012.

Krotz, Ulrich, and Joachim Schild. *Shaping Europe: France, Germany, and Embedded Bilateralism from the Elysée Treaty to Twenty-First Century Politics*. Oxford: Oxford University Press, 2012.

Maçães, Bruno. "China's Italian Advance Threatens EU Unity." *Nikkei Asia*, March 25, 2019. https://asia.nikkei.com/Opinion/China-s-Italian-advance-threatens-EU-unity.

Novosseloff, Alexandra. "L'élargissement du Conseil de sécurité: enjeux et perspectives." *Relations Internationales* 128, no. 4 (2006): 3.

Pezet, Jacques. "Que prévoit vraiment le traité d'Aix-la-Chapelle?" *Libération*, January 18, 2019.

Pirozzi, Nicoletta, and Natalino Ronzitti. *The European Union and the Reform of the UN Security Council: Toward a New Regionalism?* Rome: Istituto Affari Internazionali, 2011.

Rasch, Maximilian B. *The European Union at the United Nations: The Functioning and Coherence of EU External Representation in a State-Centric Environment.* Leiden: Brill Academic Publishers, 2008.

Vincze, Hajnalka. "One Voice, But Whose Voice? Should France Cede Its UN Security Council Seat to the EU?" *The Foreign Policy Research Institute*, March 20, 2019.

Waler, Marcus, Inti Landaure, and Andrew Ackerman. "France Supports Greece in EU Debt Battle." *The Wall Street Journal*, 1 February 2015, https://www.wsj.com/articles/french-finance-minister-says-greece-needs-new-contract-with-europe-1422820339.

Weiss, Thomas G. "The United Nations: Before, During and After 1945." *The Royal Institute of International Affairs* 91, no. 6 (2015): 1221–1235.

Wilson, Gary. *The United Nations and Collective Security.* London: Routledge, 2014.

Wouters, Jan, Frank Hoffmeister, and Tom Ruys (eds.). *The United Nations and the European Union: An Ever Stronger Partnership.* The Hague: T.M.C. Asser Press, 2006.

Wouters, Jan, and Matthieu Burnay. "The EU and Asia in the United Nations Security Council." *SSN*, 2011, https://papers.ssrn.com/sol3/papers.cfm?abstract_id=2020332

Index